REBEL

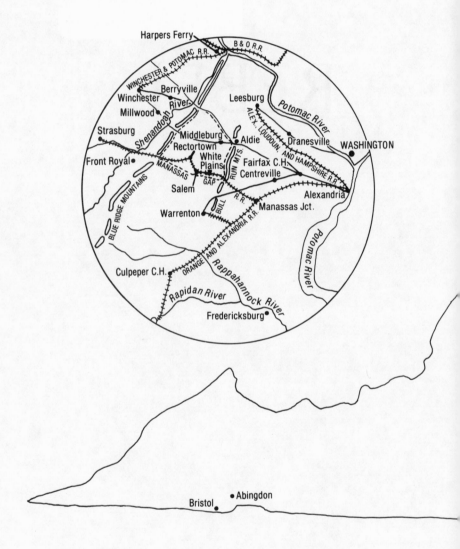

Harpers Ferry

B & O R.R.

WINCHESTER & POTOMAC R.R.

Berryville

Winchester

Millwood

Shenandoah River

Strasburg

Middleburg

Rectortown

Front Royal

White Plains

MANASSAS

GAP

Salem

Warrenton

Leesburg

Potomac River

ALEX. LOUDOUN, AND HAMPSHIRE R.R.

Aldie

Dranesville

WASHINGTON

Fairfax C.H.

Centreville

Alexandria

Manassas Jct.

BULL RUN MTS.

R.R.

BLUE RIDGE MOUNTAINS

Potomac River

Culpeper C.H.

ORANGE AND ALEXANDRIA R.R.

Rapidan River

Rappahannock River

Fredericksburg

Bristol

Abingdon

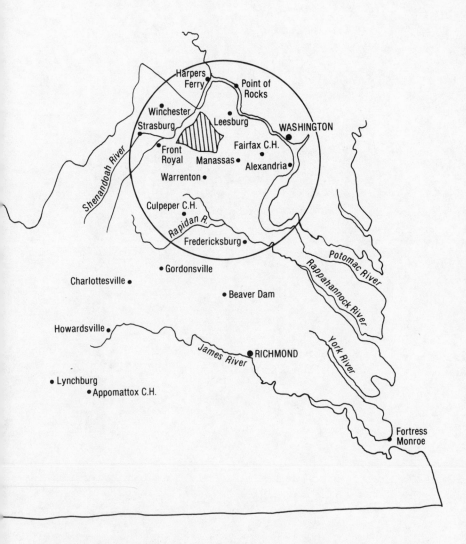

Virginia, with expanded view of northern section. Shaded area represents "Mosby's Confederacy." Only major northern Virginia roads are shown. Salem is present-day Marshall.

REBEL

THE LIFE AND TIMES
OF
JOHN
SINGLETON
MOSBY

KEVIN H. SIEPEL

St. Martin's Press
New York

Design by Kingsley Parker

Library of Congress Cataloging in Publication Data
Siepel, Kevin H.
    Rebel, the life and times of John Singleton Mosby.
    Includes index.
    1. Mosby, John Singleton, 1833–1916. 2. United
States—History—Civil War, 1861–1865—Underground move-
ments. 3. Guerrillas—Southern States—Biography.
4. Soldiers—Southern States—Biography. 5. Diplomats—
United States—Biography. I. Title.
E467.1.M87S56   1983   973.7'45'0924   83–9761
ISBN 0-312-66559-8
ISBN 0-312-01507-0 (pbk.)

To
Maria Carmen Garcia Pascual
and
In Memory of Peter

CONTENTS

ACKNOWLEDGMENTS

I wish to acknowledge my indebtedness first of all to my wife, Maria Carmen, for sharing my optimism about this project and for bearing with my determination in carrying it out. Without her understanding I could not have accomplished my goal. The staffs of two libraries were especially helpful: in the Fairfax County Public Library I wish to thank Harva Sheeler, Dorothea DeWilde, and Eric Grundset for easing me into my Civil War Research; in the Nebraska State Historical Society I offer thanks to L. G. DeLay and his associates, who sketched out the Nebraska fencing crisis for me. Ruth Van Ackeren was also helpful in this area. A particular word of thanks is due to Mosby biographer Virgil Carrington Jones for his gracious offers of assistance, and to Admiral Beverly Mosby Coleman and Pauline Coleman Blackwell—Colonel Mosby's grandchildren—both of whom took the time to invite me into their homes and chat about the subject of this biography. My brother, sister, parents, and others who either offered helpful criticism of the manuscript or simply lured my exuberant children from my desk already know that they have my sincere gratitude. Special thanks go to my sister for making copying facilities available; to the Buffalo and Erie County Public Library, Buffalo, New York, for making it possible to print a number of photos; and to Ellis Booker of St. Martin's Press, without whose assistance this book might not have seen the light of day.

My warmest thanks are reserved for anyone who spoke an encouraging word to me during this project, for they truly supplied the most treasured assistance of all.

I would like to thank the following for permission to quote from copyrighted or privately owned material: Alderman Library, Manuscripts Department, University of Virginia; Mrs. Pauline C. Blackwell; D. Tennant Bryan; Cabell Foundation, Inc.; Adm. Beverly M. Coleman; Margaret Burnley Geil; Hayes

Memorial Library, Fremont, Ohio; Huntington Library, San Marino, California; Robert H. Kean; Museum of the Confederacy, Richmond, Virginia; William R. Perkins Library, Manuscript Department, Duke University; Mrs. Virginia R. Ritchie; Earl Gregg Swem Library, College of William and Mary; University of California at Santa Barbara; University of North Carolina Press; Virginia Historical Society; and the Virginia State Library, Archives Branch.

Finally, although I am indebted to a number of persons for whatever virtues this book may possess, the responsibility for its shortcomings or outright errors remains, unfortunately, mine alone.

FOREWORD

The military feats of John Mosby and his raiders in support of the Southerners are well known by those who refer to what is more generally known as "The Civil War," as "The War Between the States." Although his particular achievements are less known by Northerners, his reputation for heroism, resourcefulness, and daring in action is still noted. Had he fought on the winning side, he would undoubtedly be remembered as a national hero.

This book is about his military achievements, but, almost incidentally, stands as evidence of his character. More interesting than reports of raider triumphs are the reports of his commentary on the war and military leaders—those in a position of political leadership. It is a credit to the wisdom of Southern commanders superior in rank to Mosby that they did not try to fit him into any orderly line of command, but rather used him as they did, or better, let him act as he did.

Mosby's military record brought him fame and notoriety, and this was to condition his life for the fifty years he lived after the end of the war. This is not because his own character and actions were strongly influenced by his war experiences, but rather because other persons in dealing with Mosby never could, or in some cases never wanted to, set the record aside.

One can speculate as to what Mosby's professional and, possibly, political record might have been without the intervention of the war. *Rebel* is not speculation: It is biography and history, principally of Mosby and the half century between the end of the war and Mosby's death in 1916.

It is the story of a rebel, sometimes with a cause, more often without, but with principles, and with persons either deserving and receiving his support or becoming the subjects of his attacks. Sometimes he seemed to be in revolt, even against himself, certainly against the restraints imposed upon him by profession, politics, and his superiors.

As he had been a severe critic of military commanders during the war, when he turned to politics in subsequent years he, too, was a severe critic of political leaders, including presidents. In the era of Reconstruction he supported Republicans for the presidency, most notably Grant and Hayes. Mosby was called a "turncoat" by some Southerners because of his support of Republicans.

He fought the battle of corruption, or rather against the corrupt, for he was quick to personalize almost every issue that drew his attention, as when he discovered dishonesty and illegal activities in the Foreign Service after he was appointed to a consular post in China in 1878. And again when he was sent to Colorado and Nebraska as an agent of the Interior Department to see to it that the 1885 Fence Law, a point of conflict between cattlemen and farmers, was obeyed.

His politics, like his military service, brought about no sweeping change. It affected immediate decisions and persons. American consuls were punished and consulates were reformed. Cattle barons removed their fences. The War in the Philippines was fought despite his opposition. His early offer to perform military service in the Spanish-American War was rejected by the Army.

The Mosby life story, while not typical, may not have been in its essential characteristics very different from that of other political figures who lived in the troubled and confused years of the Civil War, the period of Reconstruction, or the uncertain years of the last decades of the nineteenth and early twentieth century. There were persons like James Shields, an Illinois politician in the 1830s and '40s, a Democrat and an opponent of Abraham Lincoln, who had challenged Lincoln to a duel because of scurrilous letters attributed to Lincoln and appearing in the Sangamo *Journal*. The duel never came off, and Lincoln went on to the presidency. Shields became a justice of the Illinois Supreme Court, was a major in the Mexican War, a brigadier general in the Civil War, resigning his commission when not promoted by Lincoln. He was subsequently governor of the Oregon Territory and a U.S. Senator from Missouri as well as Minnesota. After his political years, he distinguished himself in a quarrel with the Catholic hierarchy.

In another time and without the military service, Mosby might well be compared to Senator Wayne Morse of Oregon. Morse was elected to the Senate as a Republican. Subsequently he declared himself to be an Independent, and then ran and was elected as a Democrat. Like Mosby, Morse was a moralist, imposing harsh judgment and punishment on culprits, when he could. Morse personalized issues. He was against the Vietnam war, but not just as a war, but as McNamara's war.

As Mosby held for individual responsibility, so did Morse. Both were, if not "loners," then separatists. Senator Morse had little time for "the club" approach to political matters, or for particular friendships that might involve political compromise. Yet he could hold, as friends, those with whom he disagreed and quarrelled, and he could be forgiving. Mosby might well have been a politician, much like Morse, in Morse's time, since in military action, Morse would have undoubtedly performed best outside customary lines of authority and organization.

In this book, Kevin Siepel has made four significant contributions. First, he has given a full character picture of Mosby the soldier, politician, literate man, and devoted, almost sentimental, family man. Second, he offers additional information relative to Mosby's military record, not just as to his own activities, but as to his judgment on men, military strategy, and tactics of the Civil War. Third, he has given us most interesting insights and knowledge of the politics of the half century following the war, especially Mosby's part in it, and his observations on it. And finally, he has provided a case study, not of a typical American politician, but of a recurring type: independent, progressive, unpredictable, those properly called "rebels."

—Eugene J. McCarthy

INTRODUCTION

Once asked if he believed in hell, John Mosby answered stonily that of course he did—that any Southerner who did not believe in it had obviously never tried to vote Republican and live in Virginia.

The anecdote gets to the essence of Mosby rather quickly. There was more to him than the glamorous figure remembered. The image of the galloping night rider, black ostrich plume bobbing above and scarlet-lined cape streaming behind, is real enough, but has tended to obscure the rest of the man. Witty, well-read, generous, sometimes tender, transcendently honest, he was also obstinate, cantankerous, and curt. An eloquent man, he nonetheless communicated best with a questioning eye and sardonic half-smile. Now that he basks in the same devotional glow brightening the memories of the Confederate demigods—of Lee, Stuart, Jackson—it is easy to forget that the South was a long time in coming to love this prickly little Virginian. It is easier still to forget that both before and after his Confederate days, John Mosby was an iron-clad American. His niche in the Southern pantheon, though well merited, is only a part of what he deserves.

In the North he was once considered a simple brigand, and Southern leaders for a time also suspected he was little more. He was, it was usually agreed, a hard man to know. One of the few human beings who have indeed marched to a "different drummer," he acted throughout his life with an almost religious indifference to public opinion. He was, in this sense, the truest of rebels.

Physically weak, he was drawn to strength. He gravitated to strong men without regard to party or section: to Lee, the South's Apollo (who once said that the only fault he found with Mosby was that he was always getting wounded); to Stuart, the Knight-Protector; to Grant, the Northern Conqueror; to Garfield, of Robust Promise; to Roosevelt, All-

American Achiever. He tended to respect his enemies, and cultivated the friendship of those he found worthy. He drew strength from great men of every persuasion, and stood ready to lend his own strength. His steady stream of ideas, seldom marred by muddiness or uncertainty, sometimes made men wince.

If there be a single vein, however, that surfaces with regularity in the corpus of Mosbiana left us, it is that of contrariness—not necessarily a refractoriness for its own sake, but a mind-set that frequently took on that appearance. He was an incurable "aginner," a man who could almost kick against the goad and whittle against the grain at the same time. As a sickly youth he refused to be part of his doctors' vision, which dictated that he soon die of consumption, and insisted upon surviving a torrent of sometimes danger-filled years, eventually to die in bed in his eighties. In a prewar secessionist population his was one of the lone voices for union, for moderation and caution. Trapped, after Lincoln's election, in a hothouse of sectional enthusiasm, he—purposely, one suspects—projected the image of a reluctant warrior, of one still unsold on the cause. Once he had bought the idea, however—or once, at least, he had realized his state was about to be invaded—he outsoldiered the rest by light years. When uniforms too ugly to be worn by unwashed mountain recruits were issued to his company, lawyer Mosby did not hesitate to put one on, and wore it with pride. When Jeb Stuart first needed a man for a foul-weather scouting expedition, an eager Adjutant Mosby volunteered. When weary men had thrown down their arms at war's end, Colonel Mosby the partisan leader vowed to fight on alone.

After the war his streak of contrariness became remarkable. He stood among a mere handful of Southern men who called for healing, who announced that the war was over and that the South had lost, who counseled cooperation with the North and oblivion of the past. Within a few years of the final cannonade he embraced the Conqueror in the White House, effectively turning his face from the path of separateness being embarked upon by the solid South. His message was one of reconciliation in a land that had seen and still harbored a large measure of hatred. He spoke out for union—union of sentiment over and above mere political unity. He preached that the uncooperative South had no worse enemy than itself.

He was treated as a leper by men and women who considered his memory too short. At length eased out of the country's sight for a variety of reasons, he hurried to kick open a vipers' nest in China and rushed into print again, now as a reformer. He was irrepressible. He leapt over superiors' heads and dashed around behind them, guerrilla-style. He dealt directly with presidents, kindling rage among lesser men. In later years, successively baffled by an inscrutable McKinley and put out of a job by Taft, he insisted on voting for them both. It was a matter of principle, and he was a principled man. In his old age he continued to flay sacred cows, one of these being college football. Amusing to others, his attack was a natural consequence of his strange, lifelong aversion to athletics and games.

His objectives were nearly always attained by the most irregular methods. He loved to dart in from the fringes, partisanlike, throw affairs at the center into confusion, and retire again to the edges to watch. His sudden forays were frequently timed well enough that he could stage-manage events by himself.

He was an electric man, one who usually polarized his environment. You were either for John Mosby or against him, and he was either for or against you. He had few lukewarm relationships.

He would have been beamingly happy at the modern upwelling of affection for him, and at remembrances of his birthday, but Virginians ought not to be offended that he might not have attended festivities held in his honor. He had no stomach for speeches or sentiment. "Ipecac," he used to grunt as he shuffled off. He was like that.

Whether one be attracted to this little man from the South or not, it must be conceded that he was as colorful a character as this nation has produced. Once one has met him, too, it becomes hard to imagine certain affairs without the special stamp of John Singleton Mosby.

WAR

Pvt. John S. Mosby in January 1863, at the outset of his partisan career. He is shown in the uniform he wore on the night of General Stoughton's capture, two months later. *Credit:* The Memoirs of Colonel John S. Mosby

1

SHIFTING SANDS

I never had any talent or taste for stump speaking . . . but
with my strong convictions I was a supporter of Douglas and
the Union.

—John S. Mosby, *Memoirs*

IT WAS APRIL. In Abingdon, Virginia, kitchen gardens
were bristling with new lettuce and spinach, doorsteps
were bright with daffodils, and the cheerful sounds of
courting birds rose upon warm breezes.

Despite the season's promise, however, this particular April
day in Abingdon was not a happy one. The "black nigger"
Republican in Washington, the "Illinois baboon," had been
on the job only six weeks and was already stirring a simmering pot. Solid evidence for this could be had in the town's
small telegraph office, where a stunning message was crackling in: 75,000 men were being called up to crush insurrection
in South Carolina. The words were scribbled by an open-
mouthed operator, and the scrap of paper passed to an
equally dumbstruck customer, who raced out at once into the
muddy street to spread the alarming news.

A slightly built, sandy-haired young man was the first to
cross his path, and was therefore the first to hear. This man,
after taking the trouble to verify the report from the operator
himself, hurried off at once to tug impatiently at the bell of a
mansion near the edge of town. A servant admitted him, then
left to announce to former United States Secretary of War
John Buchanan Floyd that a Mr. Mosby wished to see him.
Floyd, himself a recent casualty of Washington politics (but
more directly of his own stupidity), had fled the capital the
previous December, charged, among other things, with having shipped Federal arms to Southern arsenals.

The former cabinet officer stood now before the slouching
country lawyer as an ordinary citizen, astonished to hear that
the tyro President was looking for troops to send against

Southerners. Mosby did not know Floyd well, having met him just three months earlier, but he liked being around powerful men almost as much as he relished bearing a tidbit of news. He was happy he'd gotten to Floyd first today, and listened eagerly now as the older man spoke of a dark future and of a war that would be the bloodiest the world had ever seen.

Floyd dismissed his visitor with the admonition that, in spite of what might lie ahead, the new President would have to be resisted sharply.

Mosby was agitated when he left the house, knowing he must finally decide an issue he had been avoiding for some time. Floyd had fewer qualms: he quickly set about organizing the Virginia Highlands against the President. He urged Virginians not only to refuse to fight against their brothers to the south but to see that the fires of rebellion were spread as quickly as possible.

Floyd's summons to arms spread like a drum roll throughout the farms and mountains of southwest Virginia. In every corner of this outpost of democratic traditions, feelings long pent up were now let go, and while a few prescient men stood by to shake their heads, hundreds of others better schooled in the arts of riding and shooting than in foretelling the future began to gear for war.

Bristol is a town tucked into the toe of Virginia, where the state wiggles in between Tennessee and modern West Virginia to prod the side of Kentucky. Part of the town lies in Virginia and part in Tennessee. John Mosby had appeared here three years earlier—in the fall of 1858—and had tacked up a lawyer's shingle outside some rented rooms at the corner of Fourth and Cumberland streets. He had arrived with his wife, who, rumor had it, was from Kentucky, and it was easy to guess that nearness to his in-laws had had something to do with the young man's moving into these western parts. He had come from around Charlottesville, it was said.

Because the newcomer was a fairly close-mouthed type, no one was able to find out much more about him, and it is likely that his penetration of Bristol society took time. The couple undoubtedly knew some lean days, but eventually—since Mosby was the only lawyer in town—his new neighbors began to come with their deeds, their contracts, and their petty squabbles, and before long he and his young wife were making their way.

What his neighbors may not have known was that this was not the new attorney's first practice; he had spread his legal wings in Albemarle County three years before coming to Bristol. Shortly after his admission to the bar in September 1855—a turbulent youth largely forgotten—he had gone into a law office at Howardsville, about thirty miles south of Charlottesville, on the upper reaches of the James. Nothing is known of his successes or failures in these early days beyond what is told in a letter to his mother in June 1856. In this letter he informed her that he had just had "quite an important case" at a magistrate's court—"nearly sixty dollars in issue"—but, he said, he was weary of the "treadmill of life in Va."[1]

With studied casualness, he tacked on a postscript referring to a Miss Clarke, who had been staying at Howardsville and was about to be taken away by her father, a delegate to the upcoming Democratic National Convention at Cincinnati.

The Miss Clarke in question was Pauline Clarke, of Franklin, Kentucky. Her father, Beverly L. Clarke, was a man of accomplishment: attorney, state legislator, congressman, once candidate for governor, presidential elector, and soon to be U.S. Minister to Guatemala. The casualness of Mosby's postscript masked his true interest in Clarke's daughter, and before long he was courting her. By the end of the year he had visited her family in Kentucky, and evidently more tired than ever of the "treadmill of life in Va.," was looking into the possibility of settling further west.

In December 1856 he wrote to his sister Victoria, from Memphis:

> I am very much pleased with Memphis. I think it an excellent location for a lawyer. There is so great an amount of business that the courts sit all the year nearly. . . . I think I shall come back to Va. and spend a month or so—get my law books and settle here. The good lawyers here make ten, fifteen, and twenty thousand dollars a year. . . . I expect to start home on the Monday after Christmas day. . . . Very probably I will bring Pauline home with me.[2]

Pauline's Kentucky home was just five miles from Tennessee, and only forty miles from Nashville, the biggest city in those parts. One year after Mosby's trip west, on December 30, 1857, he married Pauline Clarke in a Nashville hotel. In keeping with the Clarke family's desires, the ceremony was performed according to the rites of the Roman Catholic Church; in keeping with the bride's social station, the wedding was attended by several dignitaries, among them a U.S. senator from Tennessee named Andrew Johnson.[3]

The couple took up residence with Mosby's parents until the following year, when they moved not to Memphis but to Bristol, southwest Virginia.

Mosby entered into his new role of young husband and provider against a steadily thickening national sky. Despite mid-century America's promise of wealth for all, the nation had taken an economic battering during the fifties: "recession" in 1854, bona fide depression in 1857. The fifties had also been a decade of convulsive political change. A new Republican party, welded, in Henry Adams's phrase, in "fierce heat," was raising itself up from the ashes and broken dreams of several others, ranging from Abolitionists through Free-Soilers to old-line Whigs. At the party's heart lay abolitionism pure and simple, which proved to be a more than sturdy core: the Republican party membership was fattening like a rolling snowball in March.

During the summer of 1858, one of its lesser-known spokesmen, a gawky beanpole of a man from Illinois who drew as much applause for his wit as quiet smirks for his appearance, expounded the subtleties of the Republican position in a series of debates that he hoped would win him a Senate seat from Illinois. His opponent was the urbane Democrat, the "Little Giant," Stephen A. Douglas. Although the lanky Springfield man's appearance was unappealing and his nasal voice a trial to endure, his tongue was agreeably earthy and his wit razor-keen. The Illinois debates were to prove significant, for the issues raised there by the salty-tongued Lincoln—although they actually cost him the senatorship—so fractured the Democratic party as to open his road to the presidency itself two years later.

The most unsettling fact of life in midcentury America, however, was not politics but slavery. While in 1850 only a third or less of white families in the South owned slaves, slavery was America's most scarlet sin. The South as an entity was a great slaver—on the eve of the war master of nearly 4 million souls—and throughout the 1850s it was this special outrage that did most to prime the charge.[4]

As the storm clouds gathered, Mosby stuck to business, both in his Bristol office and at monthly court days in Abingdon, a dozen miles to the northeast. His family prospered and grew: on May 10, 1859, his first child, May Virginia, was born, and the new parents were plunged into the thousand unfamiliar details of parenthood.

Five months after May Virginia's birth the first sharp blow of the coming conflict was struck: an abolitionist and longtime agitator named Brown seized the United States arsenal at Harpers Ferry, Virginia, and announced his intention of arming black men with the captured weapons. In response, President Buchanan ordered a detachment of marines under Col. Robert E. Lee of Virginia to terminate the affair, and Lee, aided by a young cavalry officer named Stuart, carried out his task with efficiency. After Brown was seized, he was tried and hanged—doing more by his death for the cause of abolition than he had ever done in his life.

The most dangerous man to the Southerner, however, was not to be the martyred Brown but the "baboon from the West," the lanky Illinoisan, who was, incredibly, making a bid for the Republican presidential nomination.

By early summer 1860 it was becoming clear that voters in November would be presented with a broad array of candidates and viewpoints, even among the Democrats themselves. The Democratic Convention, meeting in Charleston in April, had stumbled and fallen on the question of slavery. Southern extremists had insisted that neither Congress nor the territorial governments had the right to say whether a man could own slaves or not. Northern Democrats had taken a more moderate position: that the territorial legislatures should be able to set whatever policy they liked regarding slavery. The convention came unglued on this point, reconvened at Baltimore in June, and came apart again. This time no attempt was made to mend fence. The moderates selected Stephen A. Douglas of Illinois as their candidate, and ten days later the fire-eaters put up John C. Breckinridge of Kentucky. A third candidate, John Bell, of Tennessee, was hurriedly pushed forward by the "Constitutional Union Party" in an almost pathetic effort to heal the breach. Bell stood foursquare on the sacredness of the Union and Constitution, and left the issue of slavery almost undiscussed.

The last Unionist bond—a great party that spoke with authority in both North and South—was now broken.

In mid-May, between the first two Democratic conventions, the Republicans met at Chicago, and Lincoln was able to capitalize on the disarray of his better-known opponents. He would carry the election much as he had carried the nomination, with less than 40 percent of the popular vote.

J. Austin Sperry, editor of the secessionist *Bristol Courier,* had for some time been an observer of Mosby's political stance, and took special note during this campaign. "Mosby," he wrote,

> pursued the even tenor of his way until the memorable Presidential Campaign of 1860. So guarded had been his political utterances that but few of the villagers knew with which of the parties to class him, when he suddenly bloomed out as an elector on the Douglas ticket. This seemed to fix his status as a Union Democrat. I say seemed, for I am now inclined to think his politics was like his subsequent fighting—independent and irregular.[5]

Sperry recalled that during the "stirring times" following Lincoln's election that fall, he was accosted by Mosby and made the butt of a barrage of anti-secessionist remarks— Mosby even suggesting that he would cheerfully serve as hangman for such a "disunionist" as the *Bristol Courier's* editor.

"Do you know what secession means?" Mosby asked him. "It means bloody war, followed by feuds between the border states, which a century may not see the end of."

Sperry disagreed. "I see no reason why secession should not be peaceable," he said. "But in the event of the dreadful war you predict, which side will you take?"

"I shall fight for the Union, sir," answered Mosby, "—for the Union, of course, and you?"

To this Sperry replied acidly that he would fight for his "mother section" and run a bayonet through Mosby if they should ever meet in battle.

"Very well—we'll meet at Philippi," retorted the attorney with a touch of drama, and stalked away.

Sperry noted drily that by the following April Mosby had joined the ranks of the secessionists, while Mosby in later years observed that he himself had been at Philippi, but had not seen Sperry there. He did eventually give Sperry the reason for his change of heart. "Virginia is my mother, God bless her!" he told him. "I can't fight against my mother, can I?" [6]

While Lincoln waited to be sworn in, constructive political dialogue in the South was becoming lost in secessionist babble. But it was no longer a harmless rhetoric. In December, with a lame duck in the White House and an enemy of slavocracy waiting to take his place, South Carolina boldly announced withdrawal of its ratification of the U.S. Constitution, and its secession from the Union. By February 1, 1861, Mississippi, Florida, Alabama, Georgia, Louisiana, and Texas had followed her out, and three days later delegates were assembling at Montgomery, Alabama, to form a new country, adopt a new flag, and write a new Constitution.

Until March 4, Inauguration Day, the President-elect would be powerless to stem the rapid unraveling of the nation's fabric. It was whispered that Lincoln would never be inaugurated anyway, because he would not be permitted to reach Washington alive. In late February, though, he did arrive, having been spirited through a seethingly hostile Baltimore by night. On the day of his inaugural, army sharpshooters and lookouts lined the rooftops along Pennsylvania Avenue and the ceremony itself was carried out with maximum dispatch. The nervous Illinoisan was taking command of a nation which, all knew, was at war with itself, and only the shooting remained to be heard. It was not a joyous occasion.

Lincoln's first challenge materialized on the day following his inauguration, when he was handed a letter from Maj. Robert Anderson, commanding at Fort Sumter, South Carolina. The letter outlined Sumter's pressing need of being provisioned if it was to be held in the face of growing South Carolina belligerence. In effect, though, Anderson was advising his chiefs to give up the fort, since the massive infusion of men and materiel that Sumter required would be impossible to manage under the circumstances.

Lincoln decided to make a test case of Sumter, and wrote to South Carolina Governor Francis W. Pickens that he planned to provision the fort peacefully, with non-military supplies only. Pickens responded by instructing the Creole general, Pierre G. T. Beauregard, to demand the fort's surrender before the arrival of the Federal supply ships. Major Anderson would have until 4:00 A.M. on April 12 to carry out a peaceful evacuation.

When the deadline passed with no action having been taken, shore batteries were manned, and at precisely 4:30 A.M., South Carolina forces opened a bombardment that lasted until Fort Sumter was leveled and Anderson had surrendered, thirty-four hours later. Closing the breach laid open by Southern cannon would take four years and the sacrifice of over half a million lives.

In response to the attack, Lincoln—President now for only six weeks—called for 75,000 three-month volunteers, and it was this call to arms that had come clicking over the wires into Abingdon in mid-April. Virginians were being asked to shed blood, if necessary, for the Union which they, largely, had founded.

As he left Floyd's house that day, Mosby knew he had little time left to decide for or against a *united* States.

His decision, however, was already partly made. In spite of his Unionist sentiments, and solely to please an old classmate named William W. Blackford, he had allowed his name to be added the previous summer to the muster rolls of the Washington Mounted Rifles, a company Blackford was trying to raise from among the mountain men around Abingdon. Blackford had no cavalry training himself, but with the assistance of Hardee's *Tactics* and a little nerve, he himself drilled the few patriots who showed up every court day on the Abingdon green.

The man Blackford wanted to command the Washington

Mounted Rifles was at first uninterested. A West Point graduate, the thirty-seven-year-old William E. "Grumble" Jones had retired from the army four years previously, after having lost his wife at sea, and had been living the life of a mountain recluse ever since. He was a topnotch soldier, if an odd duck. At length, however, he agreed to take over the company—around the same time that lawyer Mosby decided to show up for a cavalry lesson.

Mosby took one lesson and vowed never to come back.

It was hard for him to believe that a man who looked like a tramp and acted like a lunatic had been a career officer. A small creature with darting eyes and considerably more hair on his chin than his head, Jones was dressed that day in faded blue jeans and a tattered old homespun coat, with officer's insignia straps tacked on in apparent afterthought. With every gust of wind the coat flapped open to reveal a common hunting shirt beneath. If he looked like a clothes tree, he carried on more like a maniac. Cursing, raving, screaming, he struck terror into his humble volunteers. Mosby endured Jones's bellowing, his demands for repetition of apparently mindless exercises, his eccentricities, just long enough to convince himself that soldiering was probably not for him after all.

Mosby's attitude toward military matters made an impression on Blackford. "There was nothing about [Mosby] then," said Blackford, "to indicate what he was to be—he was rather a slouchy rider, and did not seem to take any interest in military duties. . . . We all thought he was rather an indifferent soldier."[7]

For more than two months prior to the attack upon Sumter, the Virginia State Assembly had been in session, debating whether to follow its seven sister states out of the Union. Union feeling still ran high in Virginia, especially in the northwestern parts, and the discussion dragged on for weeks. As William Blackford's sister-in-law Susan wrote:

> The sentiment of the Virginian people was strongly against the violent action of South Carolina and the other Southern States in withdrawing from the Union merely because a sectional President had been elected. They thought that the South

should wait and take no action until its rights were so violated that forebearance would cease to be a virtue. . . . Virginia . . . refused to pass an ordinance of secession until Lincoln called upon her to furnish eight thousand troops to make war upon her Southern sisters and was preparing to march an army over her soil to subjugate the Southern people.[8]

Lincoln's call for troops galvanized the vacillating parliament: two days after the presidential summons, the assembly voted eighty-eight to fifty-five "to repeal the ratification of the Constitution of the United States of America by the State of Virginia, and to resume all the rights and powers granted under said Constitution."[9] May 23 was the date set for approval by the Virginia people—who, when the date arrived, voted to accept the assembly's decision and secede from the Union. The vote proved academic, however, for by that time jumpy Virginia State forces had already seized the Federal installation at Harpers Ferry and the Norfolk Navy Yard.

About these days of confusion and decision, Mosby wrote that a few scattered individuals made an effort to "breast the storm of passion," but that their fate did not encourage imitators. They were like "ocean wrecks," he said, which served to "illuminate the storm."[10]

"In the delirium of the hour," he wrote, "we all forgot our Union principles in our sympathy with the pro-slavery cause, and rushed to the field of Mars."[11]

"Virginia," said Mosby, "went out of the Union by force of arms, and I went with her."[12]

While the young attorney was returning glumly to Jones's drill field, official Washington was dissolving into a kind of apoplexy. The thin ribbon of the Potomac was now all that separated the capital from supposed hordes of malevolent Southerners. To the northeast, no barrier at all existed against the hotly secessionist mobs of Baltimore, whose character was soon made clear. On April 19, two days after the Virginia Assembly had voted secession, nervous young troopers of the Sixth Massachusetts Volunteers were changing trains in Baltimore, on their way to reinforce the capital. They were stoned and fired upon by an angry mob in an action that left four of them dead and over thirty wounded. It looked as though the nation's capital was to become an island if Lincoln did not take swift action.

He did. By April 27, Lincoln had threatened suspension of the writ of habeas corpus in Maryland and shortly thereafter sent the heavyhanded Benjamin Butler to enforce what was to become a harsh martial law. General Butler almost at once jailed the mayor of Baltimore, nineteen members of the state legislature, and many common citizens. He was eventually recalled, but Lincoln did not hurry to undo what had been accomplished.

By the end of April, 11,000 troops were bivouacked in Washington, and Lincoln, expecting imminent invasion, was practically gnawing his nails waiting for more.

Mosby had a second child now—a boy named Beverly—but by early May his cavalry lessons were beginning to interfere so much with family life that he saw little of his new son. Jones had moved the company into camp on the grounds of the Martha Washington College, near Abingdon, where several other companies were also quartered, and he worked the men without pity under the waxing summer sun: "Stand to horse! . . . Prepare to mount! . . . No, no, no. Ragged. Ragged! You farmhands haven't gotten out of the bullrushes yet! It must be *smooth*. . . . Now—prepare to mount. . . . Mount! . . . Count off by fours! . . . Fours ahead—gallop!"

Mosby the lawyer was allowed to live out of camp until he could close down his business, but he drilled almost daily. He, the "slouchy rider," the "indifferent soldier," had to endure something extra at the hands of the perfectionist Jones. But under Jones's harsh discipline a change was beginning to take place: he was starting not only to admire his stern commander but actually to take to the idea of soldiering.

Before long he had made his final courtroom appearance, said preliminary goodbyes to his family, and moved with his company into some half-finished buildings on campus. Here he was introduced to camp cookery and to some hitherto undreamed-of aspects of military life, the most startling of which was the necessity of standing guard.

The new man was ordered out on his first night, an experience that took some of the edge off his growing zeal. The night was cold and windy, and he had brought with him only an old hunting shirt. After being given the countersign and some quick instruction in the duties of a sentinel, he was sent to walk his round for a couple of hours under the stars. He was, he said, the "frailest and most delicate man in the company" at this time; and, he added, no service he ever had to perform during the war "went as much against the grain" as this first night's duty.[13]

Toward the end of the month the company was moved to another campground where plank sheds were available for shelter, and the instruction continued. Bottoms were hardening to the saddle, legs getting stronger, response time to orders was shortening, and the Washington Mounted Rifles— still without a uniform among them—were beginning to think and act like a military unit.

By the time Mosby had gone into camp with his company, Robert E. Lee had been offered command of the expanding Federal armies, but had quietly declined, preferring to accept a command in his native state. Lee, an engineer by training, and a graduate of West Point (its superintendent from 1852 to 1855), had won plaudits in the war with Mexico. Until the previous February he had been mainly on cavalry duty in Texas. He was fifty-four years old.

One of Lee's first acts on assuming command of the state militia had been to begin posting men across the river from Washington. In mid-May, when it was decided by Confederate authorities to shift the capital from Montgomery to Richmond, he took the further step of moving a battery into position at Aquia Creek Landing on the lower Potomac, to guard the northern terminus of the railway to the new Confederate capital.

Serious preparations were under way throughout Virginia; in Richmond, especially, they were in deadly earnest. Machinists at the old Virginia Armory worked night and day converting old flintlocks to cap-and-ball; at the great Tredegar Iron Works old cannon were being rifled and new ones forged. Troops were arriving from all over the South, and throughout the city could be heard the rhythmic shouts and frequent profanities of drillmasters at work with their charges round the clock.

In Washington mild panic reigned. To strengthen the city's almost nonexistent defenses, government clerks were called upon to enroll into "companies," and arms were distributed—stacked in almost every office for instant access. With a pack of what most Washingtonians would have labeled "desperadoes," a Kansan named Jim Lane bivouacked in front of the Executive Mansion, self-appointed guard to the President. Men worked all day in the bowels of public buildings, carving niches for mines that would be used to blow up both buildings and records in case of necessity. A gunboat lay off the Navy Yard with steam up day and night, ready to whisk away the President and his advisers at a moment's notice.

Many Southerners who had held Federal jobs were caught in Washington by force of circumstance, but a large number left as soon as possible to join the regiments forming in their respective states. To the men who remained, loyalty oaths of questionable constitutionality were administered by department heads, and those who would not take them were summarily dismissed. Even those who took the oaths did not last long, being easily evicted by the hordes of office-seekers arriving daily from New England.

If anxiety was the prevailing sentiment in Washington City, gaiety and animation filled the air to the immediate south. In Alexandria, a scant ten miles from the Federal capital, the Confederate Stars and Bars floated from the housetops, filling with pride a people who were already brimful of energy and determination.

Lincoln looked with apprehension upon the buildup of arms in Virginia, and the seizure of Federal property, but refrained from making any move southward until the results of the state's secession referendum should arrive. On May 23 the ordinance passed, and on May 24, at 2:00 A.M., Federal troops advanced across the Potomac, taking both Arlington Heights and Alexandria with little difficulty. In a series of skirmishes in late May and early June the first harvest of dead was gathered from both North and South. The Federal foot, firmly set upon Confederate soil, would not easily be dislodged, and Virginia, laggard in secession, was fated now to become the major battleground of the war.

As the month of May wore on and the hot sun bore into the backs of men in training on dust-choked fields across the South, it began to dawn on Mosby that he was about to leave his wife, family, friends, and all that was familiar. Since the few close friends he had were not in the cavalry but part of an infantry company slated for addition to a Colonel Jackson's brigade, he made an impulsive, last-minute effort to transfer to this group. On the very day of making the request, however, his own company was mobilized—ordered to Richmond, over four hundred miles to the northeast. He was bitterly disappointed; he had made his move too late.

"I remember distinctly, now," he said, "how with a heart almost bursting with grief, in the midst of a rain, I bade my friends in the infantry company farewell just as they were about getting on the train. I had no dream then that I would ever be anything more than a private soldier." [14]

Mosby's own company then left, its horses ankle-deep in a thick, sucking mud. Those men who had them wore oilcloths; others had to suffer the discomfort of cold rain streaming off hat brims to soak them through. Abingdon's women, children, and old men came out in the drizzle to see the company of a hundred or so men march off to war, yet all their good wishes proved small consolation to one who was leaving his wife and young children for unknown hardships. The men were to stay with families along the way to Richmond, and did so, but Mosby recorded that he was so depressed on the first day out that he spoke scarcely a word to his hosts that night.

As the march progressed, wrote Mosby, "gloom was succeeded by mirth and songs of gladness, and if Abraham Lincoln could have been sung out of the South as James II. [sic] was out of England, our company would have done it and saved the country all the fighting." [15]

A few days out, news arrived of action in Fairfax, with the information that the first Confederate soldier had fallen. Spirits became fiery. The march, despite the weather, began to resound with boasts of naive patriotism and cheers of the Virginia country folk who lined the roads. Bouquets were flung, garlands were plaited for horses and men, kisses were thrown or stolen, dozens of cakes and pies were washed down with hundreds of gallons of buttermilk, and gradually the Washington Mounted Rifles rose to the task before them, secure in the knowledge that their cause was popular, just, and right. The men sang their hearts out—mostly sentimental songs, sometimes comic. One particular ditty was always called up when passing a farmhouse:

> He who has good buttermilk a plenty,
>   and gives the soldiers none,
> He shan't have any of our buttermilk
>   when his buttermilk is gone.[16]

On June 18, an exhilarated Mosby wrote his mother that he had arrived in Richmond after eighteen days on a rainy road. He informed her that he had "no sign of a cold," but that his clothes, sent ahead by rail, unfortunately had not arrived. "I wish you wd send me something to eat," he added.

> The food here is very rough. Nothing but fat salt meat and cold hard bread. . . . I am writing in Mr. Palmer's store. He is very anxious for me to go with him now, but I have nothing but dirty clothing—a blue jeans hunting shirt over a blue flannel one. . . . Mr. Palmer says ours is the finest company that has come to Richmond, not in dress . . . but in fighting qualities.[17]

The motley company rested with hundreds of other raw troops at the fairgrounds; then after a few days the men were ordered to a training camp at Ashland, a few miles to the north. On the day before leaving, however, Grumble Jones pulled a coup in somehow finding uniforms for his ragged troops. He was in turn nearly victimized by a coup of another sort when the men laid eyes on the "uniforms" he had gotten—a dun-colored rough homespun, obviously from the looms of the state prison. They were heavy, ill-fitting, and ugly, and on the very day of issue were heaped up in disgust in front of Jones's tent. Only two men did not join in the mutiny: John Mosby—perhaps because he had nothing else to wear—and his new friend, Fountain Beattie. Both in fact wore their new "prison cloth" into Richmond that day.

Mosby's last letters before leaving for the front were written to his wife in the final week of June, from Ashland. "My dearest Pauline," he wrote:

We reached this place last Saturday. Tomorrow we are ordered to leave for Winchester. We will go there by R. Road. Ma and Pa came down to Richmond Sunday and came out here to see me. Left yesterday evening. Ma brought me a box of nice things to eat. . . . My health is just as good as it can be. There are eight other cavalry companies here. . . . I like a soldier's life far better than I ever dreamed I would. And were it not for the uneasiness and anxiety of mind which I know it gives to those who are near and dear to me I would be perfectly happy. The soldiers say that May's picture is beautiful. I wear it in a pocket in my shirt. . . . Kiss my babes a thousand times for me and tell precious May to dream about me every night until I return.[18]

A few days later he added to the same letter:

Since writing the above we have been ordered to march to Winchester on horseback. We start tomorrow. We'll soon be among the Yankees. . . . I wear the little cross around my neck. . . . Excuse this miserable scrawl. While I write a man is blowing a bugle on one side of me. I am sitting on a pair of saddlebags writing on a board. We are armed with sabres, pistol, and Sharps carbines—a short rifle three feet long. Can shoot ten times a minute with it. It will take more than a week to get to Winchester. . . . Kiss my babes for me.[19]

That Jones had been able to equip his ill-garbed bunch of ragtags with Sharps carbines was testimony to his influence with the Confederate authorities. "We considered this a great compliment," wrote Mosby, "as arms were scarce in the Confederacy. We had been furnished with sabres before we left Abingdon, but the only real use I ever heard of their being put to was to hold a piece of meat over a fire for frying."[20]

On May 23, the day set for Virginia's secession referendum, rebel troops seized all trains coming past Harpers Ferry, at the mouth of the Shenandoah. More than three hundred cars and fifty-six locomotives were captured, many to be routed south to Winchester—and then, incredibly, hauled by horse over deeply rutted roads to Strasburg, railhead of the Manassas Gap line and gateway to the Confederacy.

Apart from the value of the rolling stock seized there, Harpers Ferry was of great strategic value to the Confederacy, as it commanded both the railroad to Baltimore and the canal that ran for sixty miles along the Potomac to Washington City. On May 24, Maj. Gen. Joseph E. Johnston assumed command of the forces at Harpers Ferry, and on June 14, without yet having faced a real threat from Union troops, he took the astonishing step of ordering the Ferry abandoned. Federal officers, certain that the move was a prelude to a massive attack upon Washington, scurried back to protect the capital. Johnston, however, had no such lofty intention, and remained largely oblivious of the consternation caused by his simple retreat to Winchester.

The entire country was taken aback by the news that the Ferry had been abandoned. As it turned out, Johnston had acted on his own initiative, against the wishes of Lee and others, who had intended to hold it, not necessarily as a fortress but as a salient for an active force to threaten the flank of an invading army, and to interrupt communications with the West. Johnston was a cautious man, however, with little confidence in the skills of the new troops under his command, and he thought he had inherited an ultimately untenable position—so he gave up the prize to incredulous Union forces.

Johnston's evacuation of Harpers Ferry was regarded by many as one of the greatest blunders of the war.

One day in the first week of July 1861, Pvt. John S. Mosby of the Washington Mounted Rifles packed his duffle on a parade ground in Ashland, stood a final inspection, mounted up, and rode off with his company toward the Shenandoah Valley. His unit and others had orders to report to a Lt. Col. James Ewell Brown Stuart, commanding First Virginia Cavalry at Bunker Hill, between Winchester and Martinsburg.

Within three weeks the twenty-seven-year-old Mosby would have his first taste of war.

2

IN THE FORGE

[Young Mosby's] peculiar complexion and conformation, and
his spare and delicate habit, are such as to have excited in my
mind almost as often as I have seen him the serious apprehension of his premature death with tubercular consumption.
—Dr. Hughes, family physi-
cian, June 11, 1853

I F THE FAMILY from which John Mosby sprang was
not quite aristocratic, neither was it common. Mosby's father, Alfred Daniel, was a university-educated
planter (Hampden-Sydney College), had "connections"
throughout the Commonwealth, and was reasonably well off,
holding a small number of slaves. He could trace his Virginia
lineage back to one Edward Mosby, who had come from Britain prior to 1655. The original family name was apparently de
Moresby.

Virginia Jackson McLaurine, Mosby's mother, was closer to
the immigrant ships, her line having taken hold in America
with the arrival of her grandfather, the Rev. Robert McLaurine, an Episcopal minister come from Scotland two decades
before the American Revolution. Virginia, a small, fiery
woman, lived on almost into the twentieth century, and seems
to have been the family's driving force.

Alfred and Virginia's first child, Cornelia, was born around
1830, but soon died, cause unknown. On December 6, 1833, a
second child was born, a boy who was given the name John
Singleton. The house in which he was born, situated forty
miles west of Richmond, in Powhatan County, belonged to
his maternal grandfather, James McLaurine. It had, no doubt,
been arranged for the birth to take place here because the
family's own home, off to the west in Nelson County, was
fairly isolated—far from competent medical assistance.

Virginia Mosby remained at her father's house probably until some time after Christmas, before taking her new baby to

their own home in the woods. Here the center of civilization was a crossroads known as Murrell's Shop, and it was from this place that Virginia posted a letter to her sister-in-law, Virginia Cabell Mosby, as soon as she had gotten settled. Naturally the letter was about her son. "He is a remarkably fine child," she wrote, "larger now than my dear little Cornelia was at her death. I have named him John Singleton after your old man and his grandpapa. He claims a present from both for his name." She continued with a description of the boy: "He has fair skin and hair and very dark blue eyes. Some say it will be black but I don't think so myself. He is right pretty, but not as much so as my other baby was."[1]

A few years later the growing family—two or three little girls had been added in the interim—moved to a farm in fertile Albemarle County, an area still heavy with the presence of Jefferson, dead less than two decades. The farm lay only a few miles out of Charlottesville, and the Mosbys would be able to see from their peach orchard what many rode miles to see: the great Virginia shrine of Monticello.

Just before moving, probably in 1839, Mosby came of school age, and although his parents knew his scholastic career in Nelson County would be short-lived, they decided to begin his formal education. In the brief weeks he attended classes here, he learned the basics of spelling, but picked up some sterner lessons as well.

One autumn day when Mosby would have been about five, he saw his first drunk. What made the occasion especially memorable was that the sot happened to be his new schoolmaster. "[My schoolmaster] went home at playtime to get his dinner," wrote Mosby, "but took an overdose of whiskey. On the way back he fell on the roadside and went to sleep. The big boys picked him up and carried him into the schoolhouse. . . . The school closed soon after."[2]

Earlier on, he had had another lesson of a more practical than scholarly nature. "As I was so young," he recalled,

my mother always sent a negro boy with me to the schoolhouse, and he came for me in the evening. But once I begged him to stay all day with me, and I shared my dinner with him. When playtime came, some of the larger boys put him up on a block for sale and he was knocked down to the highest bidder. I thought it was a *bona fide* sale and was greatly distressed at losing such a dutiful playmate. We went home together, but he never spent another day with me at the schoolhouse.[3]

He continued his education in Albemarle, accompanied to school now by a sister, Victoria, and later by a second sister as well. Increasingly hampered by ill health, he nevertheless walked in all weather to a log schoolhouse in the woods adjoining his father's farm. The widow schoolmistress here in Fry's Woods ran three sessions a day, and drilled her charges from the "Peter Parley," a standard schoolbook of the day. Fry's Woods was also an attractive spot to the Mosby children outside their school hours; they frequently walked there on hot summer evenings to drink from the cool spring that bubbled up near the schoolhouse.

By the fall of 1844 Mosby was ten, and off to a third school: the Male Academy at Charlottesville. Since the new school was miles from home, and perhaps since the child was showing more marked signs of chronic pulmonary illness, he was allowed sometimes to take a mare, packing feed in one saddlebag and his own lunch in the other. By this time not only was his poor health becoming more evident but the edges of a difficult character were beginning to cut through. "Mosby and I," wrote Charlie Wertenbaker, a classmate from these days, "were school and desk mates at a school kept in the 'Grove.' . . . He was a hard student, and not in very good health, and that made him a little crabbed, and he was consequently not very popular with the boys."[4] This is the earliest reference to Mosby's poor health and lack of popularity, two problems that would dog him throughout his youth.

If young Mosby had been blessed with a stronger body or a less "crabbed" character, his school years might have been more pleasant. He was, however, not only a physical weakling but a hardhead, whose most pronounced trait was a willingness to fight. Unfortunately, he never succeeded in beating anyone. In later years he could remember only one childhood scuffle he'd not gotten the worst of, and even in this case was forced to attribute "success" not to his own prowess, but to an adult who had intervened. His mind was filled with Walter

Scott and tales of chivalry, but his body ill-suited to carry out his fantasies. Not surprisingly, his childhood memories were tinged with bitterness. "Boys," he once noted, "are the meanest things in the world. . . . The larger ones invariably take advantage of the smaller ones." Emphasizing that as a boy he was "very spare and delicate," he unhesitatingly lumped himself with the prey, not the predators, among children. "When the war broke out," he said, "I was glad to see that the little men were a match for the big men through being armed."[5]

With a Navy Colt filling each hand, he was to prove himself more than a match for "the big men."

Despite fears among those who had heard his stubborn cough that he would "never live to be a grown man," the boy pursued a fairly well-rounded life. He read with enthusiasm, favoring romantic works by Scott, or Irving's tales of the Moors in Granada. He rode regularly, and on Saturdays was usually up and afield with his gun before the sun rose. Nourished by romantic literature, he persevered in the knee-jerk defense of his "honor." He abhorred athletics, however, an attitude that may say more about his lack of social than athletic abilities. One pictures him as a student, looking down his nose at athletic, well-socialized boys while at the same time secretly measuring himself against them, probably with as much anxiety as disdain. But with books he was comfortable, and by late summer 1849, when he was fifteen, his report card attested that he was "well-prepared" or "very well-prepared" in spelling, reading, Latin, Greek, French, algebra, and geometry, and that his deportment was "very good."[6]

About this time the boy came into close contact for the first time with a non-Southern viewpoint, in the person of a young woman Mosby's father had employed to help care for his growing family of daughters. She was Abby Southwick, a Northerner, and a quintessential Northerner at that: she'd come from the very birthing place of anti-Southern radicalism, Massachusetts, and even claimed acquaintance with two of abolitionism's demigods, William Lloyd Garrison and Wendell Phillips.

The thoughtful and introverted Mosby was an apt target for Miss Abby's abolitionist gospel. He spent long hours with her discussing a range of political issues, notably slavery. One can only speculate on the effect his mentor's sex might have had on the discussions, but, for whatever reason, Mosby—his basic prejudices notwithstanding—always showed resilience in racial matters. Like most Southerners of the day, he was no friend of the black man, but he was never a defender of slavery and treated blacks with consideration.

He himself, he said, cherished "a strong affection" for the slaves who nursed him and played with him in his childhood. "That was," he added in later years, "the prevailing sentiment in the South—not one peculiar to myself—but one prevailing in all the South toward an institution which we now thank Abraham Lincoln for abolishing."[7]

"In retrospect," he said, "slavery seems such a monstrous thing that some are . . . trying to prove that slavery was not the cause of the war. Then what was the cause?"[8]

His personal servant, Aaron, who attended him throughout much of the war, was himself recipient of Mosby's continuing generosity half a century after emancipation, when both were white-headed and slavery a dark memory.

Abby Southwick moved back north, where she eventually married and settled down. By this time, though, she had become a part of the Mosby family, and agonized for it throughout four years of war. She sent money and clothing to Mosby's mother almost as soon as the cannons fell silent.

When the curtain drew back on the turbulent fifties, Mosby was sixteen. He'd completed enough courses at the academy to qualify for the university, and in the fall of 1850 enrolled at the institution founded by Jefferson only thirty years earlier—the University of Virginia, in Charlottesville. By this time it was becoming more evident that the young man would have some difficulty in making a mark in the world. He was handicapped by chronic illness, was small, and had few friends. He was irritable, due both to fragile health and to an awareness of his unprepossessing appearance, and this led to frequent difficulties with classmates. He was not totally without friends, and certainly not without attractive qualities, but he seemed possessed of a growing inwardness and an increasing tendency to let his darker fires burn.

Inwardness had its compensations, however, and he spent

as much time digging into the classics as he did in brooding. During his first term at the university he received a certificate for achievement of "first division" status in the School of Ancient Languages' senior Greek class.[9]

His intellectual efforts came untracked temporarily in the spring of 1851, when he was arrested and charged with assaulting a police officer in a typical "town vs. gown" melee. The cause of the outbreak is unclear, but Mosby was indicted for assaulting Charlottesville Constable George Slaughter with "fists, feet, and gun."[10] (He had actually broken a gunstock over Slaughter's head.) Fined $10, he was freed, no doubt leaving his name and face well engraved in the memory of the Commonwealth's Attorney, William J. Robertson.

The incident with Slaughter foreshadowed an event that brought Mosby's education in math, languages, and natural philosophy to a rude and final halt, and denied him a university degree. In the spring of 1853, during his third year of university studies, he shot a fellow student. Immediately following the shooting he was thrown into the Albemarle County Jail and expelled from the university. From the diary of a classmate, March 30, 1853:

> Yesterday was a day of some excitement in college. A student named Mosby—a graceless scamp—took some affront at some remarks made of him by Turpin, . . . also a student. [Mosby] had written demanding an apology which T did not give. Accordingly M met him as he was coming out from dinner at Brock's and leveled a pistol at his head. Turpin sprang forward to strike it up but only in time to receive the fire when it was almost against his face. The ball entered near the corner of his mouth and lodged in the muscles of his neck without injuring any important organ. Mosby was apprehended . . . in this county. The affair has made very little impression.[11]

The event may have made little impression on campus, but it caused a great upheaval in Mosby's life, the most immediate effect of which was to tear him out of the comfortable cocoon of the university and strip him of his liberty. It was a steep price to pay for having finally learned how to win a fight.

George Turpin was an athlete, probably well known at school. Being an athlete was itself enough to put him in a class alien to Mosby (who once boasted that he'd never even seen a ball game); but worse, Turpin was a bully. Son of a Charlottesville tavern keeper, he was enrolled in the university's medical program, but his interests seem to have run more to brawling than to healing. He was on record for several assaults upon classmates, some with weapons. He observed no niceties, did not believe in idle threats, and to run afoul of him was almost to assure oneself of a vicious beating.

Mosby, who normally would have had little to do with such a boy, did run afoul of him. The cause of the run-in seems trivial enough, but his stiffnecked nature virtually guaranteed that such a negligible incident would become overblown. Mosby had recently invited a few classmates to a get-together at his home. Soon after the party, one of the boys who had attended informed Mosby that Turpin had been heard talking about the affair, and making some uncomplimentary references to the host. According to Turpin, two of the guests had been invited not because of their friendship with Mosby, but solely because they played the fiddle and could offer some entertainment.

Mosby seethed when he heard this, and sent Turpin a note asking what he meant. The directness of the note no doubt annoyed Turpin, who was unaccustomed to being called out by anyone, much less by one of the least imposing creatures on campus. At any rate he was stirred enough to announce that he would soon be coming to see Mosby, and that Mosby could expect to be eaten up "blood raw."[12] The message would have caused any boy on campus to quail. Mosby resolved that Turpin would not get near him, but he knew the only means he could take to keep him away would be a firearm, and a willingness to use it.

He borrowed an old Allen pepperbox—a small, six-barreled revolver, highly inaccurate except at close range. He loaded it, slipped it into his pocket, and went to his boardinghouse to wait. Pacing nervously on the back porch, he poured out his problem to the landlord's son, Charlie Brock, occupied in cleaning a bird gun. A few idling students appeared in the meanwhile, coming up from dinner, and then Turpin came.

The air became immediately charged with enough ill will to melt a path through the small crowd, and the two were left facing one another on the porch. The smaller boy, one hand in his pocket, took the offensive. "I understand," he said, "you have been making some assertions . . ." Turpin, smelling easy blood, said nothing but came directly at Mosby. This proved to be a mistake, for Mosby immediately produced the revolver, pointed it squarely at the advancing youth, and fired once at point-blank range, driving the ball through Turpin's high-standing collar and into the back of his neck. Somehow it missed his spinal cord. Slumping to the floor, Turpin watched dazedly as first his arm, then the floor, was crimsoned with his blood. Mosby, agitated, made his exit during the ensuing hubbub and went home. He must have known he'd just pulled the world down around his ears.

By nightfall he had been arrested, charged with "malicious and unlawful shooting," and locked up in the county jail. A few days later he was expelled from the university. He felt greater distress over the expulsion than over its cause, writing in later years: "I have never done anything that I so cordially approve as shooting Turpin."[13] His parents were beside themselves with grief and shame.

On May 20, 1853, the nineteen-year-old youth was brought to trial, and five days later a verdict was reached: of "malicious" shooting, not guilty; of "unlawful" shooting, guilty as charged.[14] Sentence was pronounced by Judge Richard H. Field, the man who would eventually admit Mosby to the bar: one year in prison and a $500 fine.

In light of subsequent efforts to free the young man, many must have been astounded by both the verdict and the sentence. But the blow was especially crushing to the prisoner. His hope of being vindicated by a jury of fair and thoughtful men had not been realized. He was led back, sullen and dejected, to an airless cell, to begin passing the first hours of a most unpromising future. During his confinement he was visited by Aristides Monteiro, a friend who always seemed to bring out the brighter side of his nature, and who would one day serve as surgeon in Mosby's partisan rangers. "Of all my University friends and acquaintances," wrote Monteiro, "this youthful prisoner would have been the last one I would have selected with the least expectation that the world would ever hear from him again."[15]

While Mosby languished in jail during the first weeks after his trial, his parents were gathering evidence they hoped would convince Governor Joseph Johnson to extend executive clemency. Several types of evidence were finally presented: poor health of the prisoner, self-defensive action, prejudiced jury members. There was substance to all three arguments, including the last. Several jury members had complained of prejudice toward the Mosby family on the part of a fellow juror. The harsh verdict seems in fact to have been a sop to this and to another individual, who had been pressing for a felony conviction.

Three medical men who knew the family were unanimous in warning that young Mosby's poor health could convert his temporary imprisonment to a death sentence. Dr. J. W. Poindexter asserted that the boy was predisposed to pulmonary disease and had been troubled by a cough for his entire life. Two other doctors, Hughes and Bibb, attested to the possibility of the prisoner's premature death from tubercular consumption. These affidavits were sent to Richmond in early June. On their heels came a petition signed by no fewer than three hundred persons attesting that they knew the Mosby family and desired the pardon of young Jack Mosby. His parents must have spent weeks scurrying from farm to farm in the ovenlike heat of the Virginia Midlands, pleading for these signatures. The petition in fact alluded to the heat, and how it might "[conspire] with the close and impure air of a prison" to "fatally impair a system naturally feeble, and now greatly unnerved by mental dejection."[16]

If the governor took any note at all of his mail on the subject, he must have at least raised an eyebrow when a petition for clemency arrived over the signatures of a majority of the jury that had convicted the young man. But the final push was supplied by Lieutenant Governor Shelton F. Leake. In a lengthy letter to the governor, Leake pieced together all the eyewitness accounts of the incident, going so far as to affirm that in Mosby's place he would have done exactly the same. He, too, elaborated on the extenuating circumstances of Mosby's health and social position. It was a strong case for executive clemency, and there seemed every reason to believe the prisoner would be pardoned.

Governor Johnson denied all requests for clemency, offering no explanation for his decision. The family, at first stricken, soon redoubled its efforts, and by December the governor had yielded. On the twenty-first of the month, two weeks after Mosby's twentieth birthday, Johnson signed a pardon; two days later young Mosby was freed. The Virginia Assembly then acted to remove his obligation to pay the fine.

Although Mosby was now free after nearly a year in jail, it is debatable how much he noticed his liberty since, between May and December, he'd developed a new and consuming idea that he'd begun to pursue even while behind bars.

For all his observable plainness, Mosby was an impressionable youth, with determination enough to carry out almost anything he took into his head. He had evidently been struck at his trial by what might be called the power of words. He'd been locked up, after all, by words, not by pistols or swords. Very quickly he who had never before shown the slightest inclination to legal matters—quite the opposite, in fact—conceived a deep interest in the cool workings of law.

He asked his jailer for a law book, but, not surprisingly, got nowhere. As he sat brooding in the hot cell, breathing air that was ripening with the advancing season, he could think of only one other person to ask: an attorney he had seen frequently at the jail that spring, William J. Robertson, prosecutor for the Commonwealth, and the man who had put him behind bars. He resolved to speak to Robertson, distasteful though this might be.

The older man listened dubiously, one imagines, as Mosby spoke—probably in the haughty manner of one needing a favor from an enemy, and not wanting to act as though it were being asked. He described his interest in the law, his lack of success in finding appropriate reading material, and wondered if Robertson could see his way toward loaning him a book.

Soon afterward a copy of Blackstone's *Commentaries* was passed between the bars, and while Mosby's parents outside were shaking the temple pillars for his release, the young man was moving toward his straw mattress, oblivious of the heat and the stench, to lose himself for the first time in the murky depths of the law. His legal career had begun.

Robertson dropped by again and they began to talk, no doubt guardedly at first, but then more freely. Mosby had shed all animus toward the older man, and Robertson himself must have begun to appreciate that he had locked up a rare bird. He determined to devote some attention to this lad, and eventually made his entire library available to him.

Mosby, who conceived passionate loyalties to a few people in his life, quickly became as much attached to Robertson as to the law—they in fact became lifelong friends—and when he stepped out of his cell it was to step almost directly into Robertson's library, to continue what he had begun.

The university, with its mathematics, Greek, and philosophy, was forgotten by the former humanities student, so wrapped up now in his new profession that he had no time to worry whether or not there were bars on the windows.

3

MANASSAS

War loses a great deal of its romance after a soldier has seen his first battle. I have a more vivid recollection of the first than the last one I was in. It is a classical maxim that it is sweet and becoming to die for one's country; but whoever has seen the horrors of a battlefield feels that it is far sweeter to live for it.

—John S. Mosby
War Reminiscences

H E WAS LIKE A GOD. Mosby and his companions, fresh from the training camp at Ashland, had heard of him, as they had heard of Lee, Lincoln, and Davis. But hearing was not at all the same as seeing.

He came out to them at Bunker Hill, in the Shenandoah Valley, riding a prancing bay hunter whose flanks he touched with delicate spurs of gold. From his soft buff gauntlets to wrinkled cavalry boots; from the light French saber swinging easily over his yellow silken sash; from the rows of sparkling buttons to the polished black pistol holster, J. E. B. Stuart looked the commander. Only ten months older than Mosby, he was already a lieutenant colonel and veteran Indian fighter. On the day that Mosby first saw him, his bright blue-gray eyes, flaring nostrils, and spacious forehead were framed by a standard forage cap above and full chestnut beard below. Like his horse, Skylark, he bubbled with primal vigor and enthusiasm. His happiness was contagious. Plainly pleased with the arrival of his new recruits, he laughed uproariously, joked with privates, and backslapped officers. The new men could well believe that he sang on the march, even in the rain, and that he could go for days without rest. They could also believe he was a practiced judge of womanly attributes, and that he probably had numerous female admirers.

"Beauty" Stuart they had called him at West Point, apparently because his arms were too long for his relatively blocky frame. Some called him a fop. Such epithets took little root, however, among men who had ever seen him sit full face to a storm of lead without blinking. It was known that, unlike Grumble Jones, he took no oaths and allowed none to be taken in his presence, that he played no cards, and drank no liquor. Except for singing, he had few skills outside the military sphere, and showed little interest in developing any. He wrote well, but read almost nothing. Despite an impossibly sunny temperament, he had his dark side, but those who learned to accept his prejudices and to obey without question would never have occasion to experience it.

Stuart's immediate task was to turn relatively skilled horsemen into cavalry troopers—into men who could spend twenty hours in the saddle, choke down a piece of half-fried dough, then sleep on the ground with an open eye and one leg tied to a grazing horse. Since there was only one way to accomplish such a transformation, Stuart himself, on the day after the new companies' arrival, led them north into the Union lines at Martinsburg. Within sight of the tent-covered green hills, they surprised a Yankee foraging party, which was captured after a short chase. The eager Mosby jumped into the thick of the fray and emerged with his first war booty—a U.S. Army canteen. He wrote home proudly about his "first adventure with the Yankees."[1]

In the following days, Stuart pushed the men through punishing drills and reconnaissances over a fifty-mile front. Since the First Virginia Regiment of cavalry was to be the antennae of Johnston's division—which lay a few miles to the south, at Winchester—it was expected to keep close tabs on Gen. Robert Patterson's 14,000-man Federal command at Martinsburg. Something was obviously brewing behind Union lines (Patterson had in fact been ordered to "feel strongly" Johnston's army), but the eventual summons to battle for Mosby's company was not to issue from a misty glade in the lower Shenandoah.

It was to come instead from a steamy plain sixty miles to the southeast, near a little town called Manassas.

If Lincoln's growing army planned on "pushing on to Richmond," as it was being exhorted to do on many a journalistic front, the most obvious first step was the seizure of Manassas Junction, the railhead whose possession would assure the Yankees of control of all rail traffic between Alexandria and the Shenandoah Valley. In anticipation of a Federal move against Manassas, the "hero of Sumter," Pierre G. T. Beauregard, had been quietly building up a force around nearby Centreville, and by mid-July had assembled some 22,000 troops—all, unfortunately, green as grass. In Arlington, Union Gen. Irvin McDowell fretted with his force of 30,000 equally green recruits. Lincoln, in the meanwhile, knowing that his increasingly restive three-months volunteers would soon be abandoning the army en masse, decided he could put off action no longer, and on July 16 ordered McDowell to move against Beauregard.

Thanks not only to Confederate spies in Washington but also to detailed accounts of McDowell's advance in the Northern papers, Beauregard was kept fully informed of the Yankees' ponderous progress and fell back gradually before him, feeling for advantageous ground near Manassas. By July 20 he had settled himself on the southwest bank of an indifferent stream called Bull Run, awaiting McDowell's uniformed mob, which had taken two and a half days to advance only twenty miles—partly because of the many tempting berry patches that lined the roads.

Despite his outnumbered and inexperienced troops, Beauregard waited with some confidence. He had not only chosen the ground, but had successfully beaten back two sallies by advance Yankee units on the eighteenth. More importantly, he knew that Joe Johnston had succeeded in slipping away from Patterson's front in the Valley with 9,000 men—including Gen. Thomas Jackson's brigade—and that these men were even now detraining at Manassas. If Patterson did not realize an army had evaporated before him, McDowell had even less suspicion that one was materializing on his own front. The fact was that hundreds of Confederates were arriving in Manassas every hour.

That Johnston had been able to slip away unnoticed was due to strenuous activity on the part of Stuart's cavalry. For an entire night and day, as Johnston marched his infantry and artillery out through Ashby's Gap to entrain at the hamlet of

Piedmont Station, Stuart's men made themselves as conspicuous as possible across Patterson's entire front. Then, on the evening of Thursday, July 18, they too vanished, leaving only a thin screen of horsemen to occupy the confused Union forces. Desperate to reach Manassas before the fighting began, they pushed their way through and around Johnston's infantry and artillery, strung out now between the Valley and Manassas by highway and rattling flatcar.

Stuart's cavalrymen arrived exhausted on Saturday afternoon, July 20. In thirty-six hours they had covered more than sixty miles, over roads alternately dust-choked and muddy but always thick with white-topped supply wagons, jostling infantrymen, and lumbering artillery caissons. In an attempt to save time by taking to the fields on the night of the eighteenth, they'd nearly trampled hundreds of unseen infantrymen, asleep in the tall grass. Supplies were short, and on the day they left they'd been reduced to chasing down Shenandoah bullfrogs for supper.

The dusty, mud-caked cavalrymen, fatigued by almost an entire week in the saddle, had seldom seen such a display of martial bustle as they met in Manassas. Railway cars were in constant motion—coupling, uncoupling, hastily depositing cargoes of nervous young infantrymen and shuttling back for more. Disembarking men were marched immediately to the Confederate lines forming along Bull Run, past great trains of wagons creaking under heavy loads of food and ammunition. Hundreds of other men with apparently nothing to do stood as spectators to a procession of self-important orderlies, commissaries, and quartermasters, who scurried past endlessly with messages or shouted orders. A wagonload of sorry-looking vivandieres—accoutrement of Rob Wheat's scruffy Louisiana Tiger Zouaves—were passing through on their way to the rear; they were dressed as men. Clouds of dust hung over the roads for miles around.

Before sundown Stuart moved his men into bivouac about a mile from the Stone Bridge at Bull Run, on the left of and behind Beauregard's line. The enemy would be coming at them from across the stream.

With their blankets unrolled in the tall broom sedge at the edge of a pine grove, the cavalrymen relaxed now under the stars, enjoying their first good food and tobacco in several days. Persistent firing along the line, however, and a tense awareness of what was to happen at daybreak, spoiled what might otherwise have been a splendid summer night. "I shall never forget my sensations," wrote Mosby, "when Fount [Beattie] and I spread our blankets on the ground and lay down to sleep under the Sentinel stars. I said to Fount, *'This may be the last night we shall sleep together.'"* 2

Before dawn on Sunday morning, Confederate bugles sounded along the line. As the sleepy men gulped hot coffee, buckled on sabers and sidearms, then drew water for canteens and rations for horses, the intensity of musketry and artillery fire increased. Dense smoke, punctuated by cannon flashes, could now be seen hanging over the oaks to the north. "We knew," said Mosby, "the tremendous issue to be decided that day." As the battle noises grew louder, "Boots and Saddles" was sounded, and the troopers silently mounted before falling into ranks. Mosby's blood was up. "Although my name afterward became better known than it was then," he said, "there is really nothing in my military life that I remember with so much satisfaction as that on the eventful day—big with the fate of the Confederacy—when we had fallen into ranks and were calling off, I was number one in the first set of fours, and rode all day that way." 3

Despite this forward position in his company, Mosby was to see no more than the fringes of the fighting, since Stuart early in the day divided his regiment, detailing the Washington Rifles and another company as reserves. No use was made even of Stuart's main body during an entire morning of savage engagement, and the young commander was furious. His stream of couriers to General Jackson, who by now had had a finger shot off, could elicit no command to move. The Yankees had earlier forced a crossing on the Confederate left, and by 1:00 P.M. the line was taking a severe pounding and beginning slowly to unravel. Yet Stuart's men still waited—shirts sticking to their backs in the sultry July sun, breathing air that was sweetening hourly with the smell of blood and powder. Yankees were soon pouring across the Sudley Road in alarming numbers, pursuing whole ranks of Confederates who suddenly would not stand. Jackson's brigade, lying in tall grass at the edge of a wood, was the only Confederate unit not to crack. In the hellish din created by musketry and great projectiles whistling and cracking overhead, the long-awaited order finally arrived: "Tell Colonel Stuart he may engage."

As Stuart hurriedly assembled his men in a wood atop the rebel-held Henry House Hill, a thick fringe of Yankee bayonets was beginning its advance upward, followed by rapidly moving artillerymen unlimbering as they came. At last, saber up, Stuart burst from the wood at the head of his eager horsemen. Battle flags were snapping, and all riders were high in the stirrups—some brandishing pistols, others sabers, shotguns, or repeating rifles. After a moment's hesitation to take in the field, the cavalrymen started their downhill run, full tilt through the yellow smoke and fire, straight at the advancing Federal line: the scarlet-fezzed and pantalooned Eleventh New York Zouaves.

A double sheet of flame erupted from below as two lines of 250 infantrymen each opened on the charging horsemen at thirty yards. A few troopers fell, but Stuart did not break stride, smashing the Yankees while they reloaded. Before the bloody melee was over, he had seized two light batteries and wheeled them into a clump of pines to the right of and a little behind the advancing Yankees, where he proceeded to work them with deadly effect.

The two reserve companies, Mosby's among them, were brought up now, under command of a Marylander, a Major Swan. Yankees still poured across the road, and the outcome was far from certain. As Mosby recounted: "We were posted . . . in rear of our artillery and directly within range of the hottest fire of the enemy. For two hours we sat there on our horses, exposed to a perfect storm of grapeshot, balls, bombshells, etc. They bursted over our heads, passed under our horses, yet 'nobody was hurt.'"[4]

Rebel troops had been arriving on the cars all day, and it was the arrival of Edmund Kirby-Smith's brigade late in the afternoon, coupled with Jubal Early's quickmarch to the besieged Confederate left, that finally stemmed the tide. Sheets of scorching fire suddenly exploded from the woods, to the consternation of Federal troops who were successfully rolling back the Confederate line. The confident Union ranks started to crumble under the rain of fire, then broke, and finally thousands of blue-clad soldiers began to run in terror, pursued now by the exultant Southerners. With a rising, terrifying wail—the "rebel yell"—they hurled themselves after the fleeing Yankees, across the silty stream that now ran red, past unseeing men in blue or gray who floated face downward, past littered heaps of corpses to whom victory no longer mattered.

When the Northern line broke, Private Mosby's company made ready for action, but Swan hesitated. Grumble Jones was furious. Up in his stirrups, reining his horse viciously, he was roaring: "Major Swan! You can't be too bold in pursuing a flying enemy!" (Mosby's own evaluation was that Swan "did a life insurance business that day.")[5] Swan at length ordered the squadron to pursue.

Mosby later wrote to Pauline:

In the evening when they gave way the order was given us to charge them. We were then in a distant part of the field. In a moment we were in full pursuit, and as we swept on by the lines of our infantry, at full speed, the shouts of our victorious soldiers rent the air. We pursued them on six or eight miles until darkness covered their retreat. An army was never so perfectly overwhelmed by defeat. . . . The whole road is blocked up with what they abandoned in their flight. . . . One of their surgeons told me that when our cavalry came down upon them it looked like they were riding over the tops of the trees.[6]

Pandemonium reigned. Anything that encumbered flight was discarded by the fleeing Yanks: muskets, cartridge boxes, belts, knapsacks, haversacks, blankets. But so terrified were the Northern troops that even men fully armed with muskets, bayonets, Bowie knives, and Colt's revolvers were taken like sheep. Dozens of Yankee artillery pieces were captured, and some used against the retreating columns. Horses screamed and reared, mules brayed. A shell exploded on a team crossing Cub Run, to the east, and blocked the bridge. Carriages, which had come out from Washington with the curious, further obstructed orderly retreat and heightened the panic.

Half-finished lunches and champagne bottles lay in the dusty roadside amid castaway parasols and ladies' shawls, as clerks, congressmen, and ordinary citizens were caught up in the press of the terror-stricken troops.

There were, of course, many who could not leave, and as night fell they sent up an unnerving chorus of groans, weeping, prayers, and curses. Unknown men skulked about the darkened field, stripping the dead, not balking at a surreptitious murder when a body resisted. Trains of wagons were shuttling in with supplies and out with the wounded and dead. They threaded their way past ambulances, horsemen, captured artillery, and long lines of prisoners. The high-pitched shriek of locomotives vied all night with the cursing of teamsters and the sounds of agitated cattle, horses, and mules.

By morning a cool rain had begun to fall, and after daybreak the exhausted Mosby was sent across the muddy battlefield with a message to Stuart, at Sudley. Broken caissons and other paraphernalia of war littered the stinking ground, washed now by a rain that fell indifferently upon dead horses, blasted trees, and headless men. Everything had been shot through and through with musket balls. Bodies of men cut down by infantry fire were lying in windrows, like harvested corn; other bodies had been arranged more casually, distributed in fragments by artillery fire. "Human imagination," wrote Mosby to Pauline,

> cannot picture the harrowing scene. In confused heaps were lying men and horses, adversaries and friends. But to hear the groans of the wounded and to see their ghastly wounds was more heart-rending than to look on the dead whose sufferings were over. They were strewn over a space of five or six miles. All over the field were gathered groups of men performing the last sad office for the dead—away from home and friends and kindred. They buried them without a stone to record the memory of their names, but to sleep in unknown graves until "the archangel's trump, not glory's, shall awake them."[7]

Tired rebel surgeons persevered in their grisly work. Most Yankee surgeons had fled before the stunning Confederate onslaught, and when finished with their own wounded, Confederate surgeons attended to Yankee survivors as well. Victims screamed and begged to die. In the dim light of the surgeons' tents could be seen blood-stained men, stripped to the waist, one or more kneeling upon a struggling patient, another probing or sawing. Fly-covered piles of limbs were rising outside the tents, and men who had somehow survived their surgery lay about in the mud, weeping, staring, vomiting.

Richmond was aghast at the price of victory, as trainloads of wounded began to arrive. Jefferson Davis himself had been on the scene to witness the carnage. Perhaps partially because of the horror, stricken Confederate authorities had little stomach to pursue the flying Northerners; they thus let pass an outstanding opportunity—if not to seize the Northern capital, at least to isolate it and dictate terms. Failure to grasp this opportunity was to have deadly consequences for the Southern cause. Mosby himself later observed: "It is paradoxical but true that the Confederate cause was lost at Bull Run."[8]

Manassas had been the first great conflagration in the ripening hostility between the sections. It had been so vicious and intense, and the outcome so unexpected, that neither side was eager to engage again. The remnants of a broken Union army limped back to Washington, and when satisfied that no pursuers threatened, settled down to lick their wounds, protect themselves, and plan for the future. Lincoln's first important move was to get rid of McDowell and the bungling Patterson. In Patterson's place he put Gen. Nathaniel Banks, and in McDowell's, a thirty-four-year-old dapper little gamecock from the West named George Brinton McClellan. General McClellan was given the task of creating from the rubble of Manassas an efficient fighting force, which would bear the name of the Army of the Potomac, and which would be responsible not only for carrying the war to Richmond but for keeping it away from Washington.

McClellan set about fulfilling his duties as defender at once, ordering the construction of a thirty-seven-mile system of fortifications around the city. Throughout the fall and early winter the woods along the Potomac rang with the sounds of axes and spades, as men feverishly worked to create these defenses. Most of the system was in place by Christmas. Mc-

Clellan was a popular man with the troops, and despite the formidable challenges of morale and organization he faced, many Northern leaders felt that if anyone could whip a fighting force into shape it would be George McClellan.

If the rebel army did not pursue, it was at least not slow to fill the void left by the retreating Yanks. Stuart's troops, after resting a day at Manassas, pushed on to the Potomac, where their presence and unknown intentions proved a source of anxiety to McClellan throughout the rest of the summer and early fall. Stuart set up his headquarters on Munson's Hill, within sight of the capital, awaiting the order to advance. He was clever enough to ring his outpost with black-painted logs, and it was only weeks later, when ginger Yankee advances were again being conducted, that chagrined Federal troops who had been watching the position through glasses realized they'd been looking at "Quaker guns," not cannon.

Mosby was detailed to ride picket along the Potomac, a duty which he carried out three days a week until the following spring. He found it "more agreeable . . . than the routine of a camp," he said, and since his post was well in advance of Confederate lines, he had his share of enemy contact.[9] In one of his first nights out his company was fired upon near Alexandria, and Grumble Jones's horse went down, shot through the head. In early August he was close enough to the Union camp at Georgetown to hear the morning drum beat. "Some of the Yankees came to my post under a flag of truce," he wrote to Pauline, "—stayed all night—ate supper with me; and we treated each other with as much courtesy as did Richard and Saladin when they met by the Diamond of the Desert."[10]

Fraternization during the fall and winter was common. Charles Blackford (William's brother), stationed at Leesburg that fall, wrote: "Everything here is very quiet. The pickets on the other side of the river are very friendly with our men, exchanging visits, papers, and other courtesies. Some of our men went over a mile into Maryland and took dinner with some officers in the Yankee camp." His conclusion: "A very dangerous and improper thing to do, I think."[11] When Blackford's wife toured the picket posts near Leesburg with her husband that winter, she reported that Yankees across the line touched their hats and presented arms as she passed.

In early August, Mosby's mother wrote to a relative for some tomatoes to send to her son, since her own were not ripening. "His fare is very coarse now and spare too," she said, "so I feel very anxious to get off a box to him, particularly as there are so many sick, and he divides all he has with them."[12] One wonders what kind of letters she was getting from her son, for Mosby was at the same time writing to Pauline:

> I am living first rate now. When I go off on picket I carry along . . . a small cart I took from a Yankee. The place where we go was a settlement of Yankees who have all now fled. . . . They left everything behind them. Aaron just comes home with his cart loaded down with vegetables, etc. we get from their gardens. That you may form some idea of our living I will give you our bill of fare for dinner for the last three days: chicken pie, green peach pie, stewed green peaches, corn, butter beans, tomatoes, potatoes. I made the sauce myself for a peach pie and all pronounced it the best they ever ate. Tell Mrs. Appling that the knowledge I picked up in her kitchen I now find very serviceable.

He mentions in this letter that he shares a tent with Fount Beattie and his brother, but declares that his scope of acquaintance is not great. "With the exception of two or three men I am almost . . . isolated from the rest of the company. Camp life has almost entirely destroyed my social feelings, and I have never gotten acquainted with anyone outside of my company." He complains about Wade Hampton's vaunted South Carolinians, now being lionized in the papers despite the fact that they'd actually fled the battlefield—he'd seen them fleeing. He boasts of his good health, and speaks of the lock of little May Virginia's hair that he carries in her daguerreotype.[13]

Except for a serious fall from a horse in late August, which incapacitated him for a short time (the animal actually tripped over a sleeping cow during a melee among Stuart's own men on a pitch-black country road), the final weeks of 1861 were not unpleasant for Mosby. The dangers of Manassas were past, but brushes with Federal troops were common enough to keep the blood up. In his off hours he found time for reading military works such as Napoleon's *Maxims,* Noland's *Employment of Cavalry,* and some books on partisan warfare. It was at Pauline's insistence, no doubt, that he was doing a bit of part-time proselytizing for the Church of Rome. On November 3 he wrote to her, "Fount Beattie is diligently reading your Catholic books and says he is convinced it is the true Church." Fount would, he added, still require a little push to bring him into the fold.[14] His friendship with the uncouth Grumble Jones was deepening. To his sister Liz, he wrote: "Although Captain Jones is a strict officer he is very indulgent to me and never refuses me any favor I ask him. I think he will be made a Colonel very soon."[15]

"Aaron," he noted, in reference to his servant, "considers himself next in command to Captain Jones."[16]

Jones was in fact made colonel shortly thereafter, and given command of Stuart's regiment. In a spate of promotions that fall, William Blackford was named captain of the Washington Mounted Rifles in Jones's place; Fitzhugh Lee (Robert E. Lee's nephew) was named lieutenant colonel of the Second Virginia Cavalry; and Stuart was promoted to brigadier general.

In anticipation of the long hours in winter camp, the irrepressible Stuart had by this time built a troupe of stringed instruments and singers around a man named Sweeny, a skilled banjo player. In the wink of an eye Sweeny could be ready for anything from "Sweet Evelina" to "The Dew Is on the Blossom," or "If You Want to Have a Good Time, Join the Cavalry." Stuart's servant, Bob, worked the bones, and others played fiddle, guitar, or sang. Most of these musicians had been taken onto Stuart's staff under the guise of couriers. Provided a man were reliable himself and had a reliable horse, it did no harm to him in Stuart's eyes to have some musical talent or other entertainment ability. Stuart watched for such men and absorbed many into his staff. It was, one imagines, his way of distancing himself from a brutish reality.

By mid-October the Union army had begun to probe again into Virginia, and in spite of a sharp setback at Ball's Bluff, near Leesburg, the Yankees easily laid claim again to the area east of Fairfax Court House. In response to the growing Yankee presence, the Confederate army fell back toward the Manassas battlefield to take up positions along Bull Run and around Centreville.

Many men now began to construct rude cabins for the winter, preparing to settle down for a few months of snow, cold, and inactivity. For those fortunate enough not to fall prey to serious epidemics of measles, mumps, typhoid, or smallpox, there was hunting, woodcutting, card and checker playing, letter writing, and regimental concerts. If a man were so inclined, there was an occasional prayer meeting in an artillery tent. There were always clothes to be washed and mended, and the ever-present Beadle novels to read. Soldiers wandered only infrequently on the battlefield nearby, where they might too easily see the puckered bodies of men and horses being washed out of shallow graves by the autumn rains.

On November 1 the final fossil of the Union old guard was cleared away when feisty old Winfield Scott retired as commander of the United States Army, to be replaced by none other than young George B. McClellan. To demonstrate his confidence in his new chief, Lincoln himself crossed the Potomac on November 20 to join his commanders in a review of 100,000 Federal troops at Bailey's Cross Roads, near Falls Church. This great show of force in Virginia, however, proved to be a rumbling mountain giving birth to a mouse, for McClellan seemed more and more content to build an army and less intent upon using it. To the President, "Little Mac" was a deepening mystery.

At the end of 1861 there occurred an event that gave the South a crumb of hope that the Confederacy would soon gain the help of England. James M. Mason and John Slidell had been designated Confederate representatives to London and Paris respectively, and in November were sent to Europe aboard the English packet *Trent* to present their credentials. Just off the port of Havana the *Trent* was halted by a U.S. man-of-war, and the two men seized, taken off, and without ceremony locked up at Fort Warren in Boston.

Far from being offended, the South was jubilant, since the

seizure of passengers from a British vessel seemed certain to ignite the expected British fire. Moreover there was little doubt in Richmond that Lincoln's Secretary of State, William H. Seward, would resist all pressure to release the captured rebels, further infuriating the English. "We could almost hear the roar of English guns," wrote Mosby, "dispersing the fleets which were blockading our coasts."[17]

But these expectations went unfulfilled when, within weeks, Mason and Slidell were turned over to the British, along with an apology from Washington for having violated British maritime rights. Thus evaporated the perfect *casus belli*. To wither Southern hopes even further, England and France refused to receive the Confederates in an official capacity, and persisted in a neutral stance.

In addition to lack of outside assistance, the South had at this time the more pressing problem of manpower. "In the opening of the year 1862," wrote Mosby,

> there was a great deal of depression in the Southern Confederacy. A considerable amount of this was due to the failure of our hopes of having England as an immediate ally, but most of it was on account of the expiration, in the coming spring, of the terms of enlistment of most of the regiments and the reluctance of the men to reenlist before going to their homes. General Joe Johnston issued an address urging the twelve-months' volunteers to reenlist, but it had little or no effect.[18]

To deal with this problem, a Conscription Act was passed by the Confederate Congress, making all white men between the ages of eighteen and thirty-five subject to military service. "The conscription law," commented Mosby, "increased the numbers but impaired the *esprit de corps* of the volunteer army that won the victory of Manassas—the flower of Southern manhood had been gathered there. But the law saved the Confederacy from the danger of collapse . . . through the disbandment of its army."[19]

Prior to the passage of this act in April 1862, Stuart himself did his share to encourage reenlistment by making the rounds of Confederate camps. In January, after delivering a short speech to assembled companies at the First Virginia's encampment at Bull Run, he asked all to step forward who would be willing to reenlist unconditionally without first receiving a furlough. Out of the hundreds of men present, Mosby claimed, only two stepped forward—the same two who had without murmur worn Grumble Jones's "prison cloth" the previous June, Privates Beattie and Mosby. This fact may have had something to do with Jones's glowing endorsement, a few days later, of Mosby's request to visit his family, which he had not seen in nearly a year. It probably also had some bearing on other events soon to follow that were to lead to far broader opportunities for Private Mosby.

In early February, after his visit home, Mosby stood picket for what proved to be the last time. But the night proved memorable for other reasons as well.

The men performing picket duty were accustomed to hearing unexplainable sounds in the dark—sounds that frequently turned out to be the false alarms of a rabbit, cow, or rooting hog. In fact, some animals would sometimes draw the fire of a whole line of pickets, and occasionally even bring in the reserve videttes from camp. There was an old gray horse near Fairfax Court House that had been fired on so many times in the night—always without effect—that Mosby wondered whether the government had ever allowed it a pension.

On this particular night the snow was deep and hard frozen. "I wore a woollen hood," said Mosby,

> to keep my ears from freezing, and a blanket thrown around me as a protection against the cold wind. The night was clear . . . and bright. I sat on my horse under the shadow of a tree, both as a protection from the piercing blast and as a screen from the sight of an enemy. I had gone on duty at midnight, to remain until daybreak. . . . The swaying branches of the trees in the moonlight cast all sorts of fantastic forms on the crystal snow. . . .
>
> Now I confess that I was about as much afraid of ridicule as of being shot, and so, unless I got killed or captured, I resolved to spend the night there. . . . I was suddenly aroused by the crash of footsteps breaking the crust of the hard snow. The sound appeared to proceed from something approaching me with the measured tread of a file of soldiers. It was screened from my view by some houses near the roadside. I was sure that it was an enemy creeping up to get a shot at me,

for I thought that even the old horse would not have ventured out on such a night, unless under orders. My heart began to sicken within me. . . . My horse, shivering with cold, with the instinct of danger, pricked up his ears and listened as eagerly as I did to the footsteps as they got near. I drew my pistol, cocked it, and took aim at the corner around which this object must come. I wanted to get the advantage of the first shot. Just then the hero of a hundred panics appeared—the old gray horse! I returned my pistol to my belt. . . . My credit as a soldier had been saved.[20]

Spring began to break, and with the spring came news of yet another setback for the Confederacy. A little-known Yankee general named Grant had just succeeded in taking Forts Henry and Donelson in Tennessee. In the thick of the fighting at Fort Donelson, Mosby's one-time hero, John B. Floyd—director of the fort's defense—had escaped by night with his brigade on two steamboats, sent from Nashville with supplies. Floyd was largely blamed for loss of the fort, and relieved of his command. The event was far more than one man's personal crisis, however, since with the fall of Donelson were lost not only some 16,000 Confederate troops but also all further hope of Southern control over Kentucky and most of middle Tennessee.

4

SUNRISE

So here began my friendship for Stuart which lasted as long as he lived.

—John S. Mosby, *Memoirs*

A S THE CARRIAGE bumped and splashed out of Fairfax Court House through a melting crust of mud and snow, Mosby, reins in hand, felt like a lucky man. A handsome young woman to either side, a barrage of good-natured jibes from his comrades at roadside, and finally the open road. Not an hour before, Stuart had ridden into town leading an empty carriage, had requested a man to move two of his young lady friends in it to a safer place behind the lines, and Blackford, aware that Mosby knew one of the women, had detailed him to the job. After turning his horse over to Fount Beattie to lead back to camp, he'd climbed into the carriage, picked up his passengers, and was presently rolling along to Frying Pan, with a fresh snow beginning to whiten the landscape. He would be able to drop them off by late afternoon, he calculated; then, after a hot cup of coffee, he'd return the carriage to Stuart's headquarters at Centreville and head back to camp.

He completed his pleasant assignment more or less on schedule, but by the time he drew up before the Grigsby House, which Stuart shared with Generals Johnston and G. W. Smith, it was dark and snow was still falling. After seeing to the horse, he reported to Stuart and requested a pass to return to camp, a few miles off on Bull Run. Stuart said it was nonsense to think of walking four miles on such a night and told him to plan on staying for dinner with him and the other generals.

Private Mosby had not reckoned on this. Accustomed to the cold pleasures of a cavalry camp, he now found himself being ushered to a fireside seat beside Joe Johnston himself, commanding the Department of Northern Virginia. As the

47

three generals chatted among themselves in the firelight, Mosby did his best to make himself invisible, speaking not a word, staring straight into the fire. After a brief agony, supper was announced and the generals moved to table, still chatting as they went. Mosby, despite a ravenous appetite, did not budge. Finally Stuart sent for him and he reluctantly took a place, neither raising his eyes from his plate nor speaking a word during the entire meal. "While I felt so much oppressed by the presence of men of such high rank," he explained, "there was nothing in their deportment that produced it." [1] Having passed a miserable hour at table, he was released to spend the night on some blankets Stuart had spread for him at fireside, and all went to bed.

Next morning the torture was repeated: a private breakfasts with three generals. With the conversation turning on a serious difficulty General Jackson was having with the Secretary of War, Mosby somehow found himself conversing with Joe Johnston, who, in his words, he "would have regarded it as a great privilege the day before to view through a long-range telescope." [2] Following breakfast, Stuart provided Mosby with a horse to take him to camp, and the greatly relieved private wasted no time in getting there.

His head was swimming as he dismounted before his tent, but the best—or worst—was yet to come. No sooner had he arrived in camp than he was summoned to Grumble Jones's tent. Expecting to be dressed down for his absence the previous night, he was totally unprepared for what the new regimental commander said to him.

"Private Mosby," roared Jones, "how'd you like to be my adjutant, starting, say, in a couple of days?"

Exactly two days later—February 14—Adjutant Mosby was installed in his new office, and, his humble past forgotten, was excitedly writing to Pauline for the necessary trappings of rank:

> You could buy the cloth [at Crenshaws], have it cut by a coat of mine, and then have it made near home. All I want is something neat, but nothing fine. Get me a pair of shoulder straps, and a blue cap. . . . I want a pair of pants also and vest. . . . Send my clothes as quickly as possible, as I have nothing de-

cent to wear and my present position requires that I should.
. . . Enclose to me also some socks.

He promised to send her $100 shortly (he sent her $150),
with more to follow. "I am very fortunate in getting the office
. . . ," he told her. "I can hold [it] during the war and it is a
good stepping stone." He was to be paid $110 per month. His
rank and pay were now just below that of a captain.[3]

Mosby was not to serve as adjutant for long—about two
months, to be exact—because he proved not to be the stuff of
which adjutants are made. Jones, no doubt, had meant the
promotion as a favor to a promising soldier, but the time
Mosby spent in this largely ceremonial office was reminiscent
of his two uncomfortable meals with the generals. "I have
always had a repugnance to ceremonials," he admitted,

> and was not half so much frightened in the battle of Bull Run
> as I was on the first dress parade I conducted. On such occa-
> sions the adjutant is the most conspicuous figure. I never could
> repeat the formulas of the regulations, and for this reason I
> remember the few weeks I served as an adjutant with less sat-
> isfaction than any other portion of my life as a soldier.[4]

He did, nonetheless, enjoy the privileges of rank throughout March and most of April, and with the confidence in-
stilled by his new position, took delight in bedevilling the
pompous Fitz Lee, who had always seemed to find Mosby's
satirical smile, slightly stooped neck, and strange, roving eyes
somewhat annoying. Lee, who commanded the Second Virginia, had for some time been bothered by other Mosby
quirks—a recently acquired preference for a civilian to a military saddle, for example, and his defiance of regulations in
wearing the red uniform facings of the artillery instead of the
buff of the cavalry. He had been irritated by Mosby's passion
for having the very latest news, and having it first.

But one day when Jones was away, and Lee had command
of Mosby's regiment, the last straw fell. It was time for dress
parade, and Colonel Lee had apparently not heard the bugle.
Mosby sauntered up to him, and affecting the deepest drawl
he could muster, said: "Kunnel, suh, de ho'n has blowed fo'
dress parade." The punctilious Lee exploded. Looking furi-

ously at Mosby, he burst out: "Sir! If I ever again hear you call that bugle a horn, I will put you under arrest!"[5]

The man in the White House was also growing impatient with a cocky deputy. Lincoln, to compensate for the increasingly apparent inadequacies of his new general, was by now studying military strategy himself, bringing to it a freshness of viewpoint unencumbered by military tradition. As Grant and others fought on in the West, George McClellan did little but organize. He stood on his need for more men and more time. He was immovable, unflappable. Against Lincoln's wishes for a frontal assault upon Richmond from the north, he strongly advocated approaching from the east, from the peninsula that lay between the York and the James rivers. At length he won the point. Lincoln was so pleased that "Little Mac" was at least proposing *something* that he relented somewhat on the details, insisting only that in any move southward McClellan leave behind a sufficient force to protect Washington, still under threat from Confederate troops near Manassas.

On March 9, just as McClellan was preparing for his cumbrous advance, the South presented him with an astounding gift: Manassas. In order to protect the Confederate capital from the expected Federal movement southward, Johnston had ordered a withdrawal to Richmond. Lee, adviser to President Davis, was against the move, but Davis and his cabinet were for it. As in the previous June, when Johnston had presented the dumbfounded Yankees with Harpers Ferry, Federal troops were jubilant, if mystified.

Southern troops remained mystified only, since Johnston, prior to evacuation, ordered the burning of Confederate stores, including all the troops' baggage. Huge quantities of food and clothing were lost—many soldiers had stored enough clothing at Manassas to carry them through the entire war. Blackford, for one, was furious. Johnston, "great on retreats," in his mind, had ordered the cavalry in a rearguard action to set fire to all corn cribs. "Here, right within our lines and close to the camps," he said, "quantities of grain were stored on the farms and we, all the winter, were drawing from Richmond and the interior; and it had all to be burned." Grain was not the only food destroyed. Piles of bacon as high as a house sent blue and yellow flames skyward, and the smell of frying bacon was wafted nearly to Washington.[6]

As McClellan's main force now crowded onto the wharves at Alexandria, preparing to move downriver to the Peninsula, detachments of Federal cavalry began probing further into Virginia to monitor the rebel withdrawal. They found Johnston, in a foul mix of snow, sleet, and a cold March rain, retreating along the Orange and Alexandria railroad between Manassas and Bealeton. Stuart's cavalry fought a running rearguard action against the Federal force, without knowing whether it was an isolated body or the advance of McClellan's entire army. The retreating Confederates knew nothing about the crowded Alexandria wharves or the imminent Peninsular campaign.

It was here that Adjutant Mosby attracted attention, by volunteering to find out for Stuart exactly what force was in pursuit. He was given three companions, one of whom was familiar with the roads. They quickly forded Cedar Run, and carefully skirted the advancing Union column. Due to a drizzling rain and dense fog, it was at first almost impossible to make out what the Yankees were doing or how large a force was involved. But by the time the Yankee column had reached the Rappahannock and begun shelling the rebels, who had just crossed, Mosby's small party was behind it and finally got the information it sought: this was an isolated body, not McClellan's advance. It maintained no communications with Washington, was in fact preparing to fall back, and could easily be routed by superior Confederate numbers.

The men took all night to get back to the river. At dawn Mosby plunged into the icy water alone—coming close to being shot in the morning fog by a suspicious rebel picket—and raced off to find Stuart. When he poured out his news, Stuart was elated. "In the rapture of the moment," recalled Mosby, "he told me that I could get any reward I wanted for what I had done. The only reward I asked was the opportunity to do the same thing again. In ten minutes the cavalry had crossed the river and was capturing prisoners. . . . This was the first cavalry reconnaissance that had ever been made to the rear of the enemy, and was considered as something remarkable at that time."[7] Stuart's report on the event sin-gled out Adjutant Mosby and Principal Musician David Drake, recommending both for promotion.

McClellan's first contingents were landed on the Peninsula on April 4, as Johnston's army hurried to join Gen. John B. Magruder's, forming to meet the enemy on the historic plain at Yorktown. It was at Yorktown that the roof would fall in on Mosby's adjutancy.

In late April, with battle lines in place around Yorktown, the army was, incredibly, "democratized." By a long-awaited act of the Confederate Congress, the entire rebel army was to be reorganized along democratic lines. Officers would from now on be elected, not appointed, and said elections were to be held at once. Discipline fell apart following this announcement, and McClellan would have had a great advantage had he begun to move at this time. Every company became a study in demagoguery and politics: men would not obey. At one morning's roll call an entire company answered from their beds. Would-be officers vied for votes, even to the point of promising "not to expose" the men, in other words, not to make them fight.

Blackford was voted out, and went to Richmond as a captain of engineers (eventually returning to Stuart). Grumble Jones was voted out as well—he, too, left for Richmond— and Fitz Lee elected in his place. Mosby immediately offered his resignation to Lee, and—not surprisingly—it was accepted. With a fine melodramatic touch Mosby noted, "I lost my first commission on the spot where Cornwallis lost his sword."[8] But Private Mosby, again at the bottom of the ladder, had a fallback: Stuart quickly invited him to take up residence with his couriers, and assured him not only that he would have work to do but also that he'd not be long without a commission.

The brilliant Jackson, during May, was methodically grinding up Union armies in the Valley, and by the final week of that month had so macerated the Federal forces there that Washington had good reason to fear for the capital's safety. Nearly 40,000 troops were kept back from McClellan because of the unpredictable ramblings of Jackson's small but well-disciplined force.

While Washington scrambled to protect itself, the cautious McClellan inched toward Richmond with his 110,000 men, giving Johnston ample time to fall back and prepare a reception. At the end of May, Johnston struck him at Seven Pines, nearly at the city's gate. Watercourses ran high on the low-lying Peninsula, and amid swarms of mosquitoes and peeping frogs, thousands of men grappled and died in the swamps and mud of the Chickahominy, east of the city. As the roar of battle grew stronger, Richmond citizens flocked to the Capitol roof for a sight of the bursting shells, arcing over blasted and burning trees. Richmond's largest wholesale stores were converted to hospitals to receive the wounded.

When at the end of this largely indecisive battle, Johnston himself was borne on a litter into the city, wounded, the worst was feared. Robert E. Lee was quickly put in charge, but to many it seemed virtually certain that McClellan himself would shortly be riding into the city. McClellan could force his way no further, however, and in succeeding days Lee took a firm hold, enforcing discipline, recruiting troops, fortifying the capital, and keeping the Federal army bottled up. Most importantly, he sent for Jackson's army, now fighting the pitched battle at Port Republic that would temporarily break the Federal grip on the Shenandoah Valley. McClellan fell back to the Pamunkey to regroup, leaving behind a 25,000-man siege force under Fitz-John Porter.

Since the armies had been lying so close to one another, there was little for the cavalry to do after Seven Pines. Mosby, in Richmond shortly after the fighting, looked up John Floyd, the anti-hero of Fort Donelson, to talk about a commission—a favor that Floyd did not hesitate to promise. Mosby was bored with the recent inactivity of the cavalry, and wrote to Pauline, "I . . . was never so homesick in my life," but went back to Stuart while he waited for some result from Floyd.[9]

In the midst of these doldrums he helped launch an effort that did much to establish Stuart's reputation as a great cavalry leader.

During a private breakfast with Stuart one morning, Mosby was asked what the chances might be of probing McClellan's right flank to learn whether he was fortifying on the Totopo-

tomy, a creek flowing into the Pamunkey. It was on this side
of the Federal line that Jackson could most easily strike, and
it would be important to gain some intelligence on it before
his arrival. Mosby took four men and rode off to find out,
returning in a few days with more information than Stuart had
bargained for.

Exhausted, he stretched out in the grass at Stuart's feet as
he relayed what he had seen. Penetrating McClellan's line had
been easy, he told him, so easy that a large body of men could
probably slip in almost unnoticed and do extensive damage.
"I remarked," said Mosby later, "that as the cavalry was idle,
he could find on the Pamunkey something for them to do." [10]

Stuart listened closely, became gradually more excited, and
began to pace. When his scout had finished, Stuart told him to
write down exactly what he had seen, making a point of having Mosby sign the report himself. Ordering his horse saddled
at once, he snatched up the paper and galloped off with it to
Lee. On his return, orders were issued to the cavalry to prepare to move out for a period of several days.

On the sticky morning of June 12, therefore, 1,200 gray-
clad troopers of the First, Fourth, and Ninth regiments of Virginia cavalry, plus elements of the Jeff Davis Legion and two
pieces of Stuart's own light artillery, headed north to skirt
McClellan's right, then plunged eastward onto the Peninsula.
In fewer than four days the tiny force described a complete
circle around McClellan's leviathan—a route of over a hundred miles—pillaging Union camps, taking large numbers of
prisoners, burning supply wagons and even ships tied up in
the James, and in general behaving as though unaware of
being outnumbered by a hundred to one or of being trapped
on a peninsula between a huge army and unfordable rivers on
all sides. The Confederates traversed swamps up to their saddle girths and made one twenty-mile passage along a riverside
road in full view of Federal gunboats on one side, with Mc-
Clellan's entire army close by on the other. The confused Mc-
Clellan offered them only the slightest opposition.

It was a revel. Appropriated Federal champagne and Rhine
wine flowed copiously. One trooper was captured because he
was too drunk to get away; another was killed. These were

the only losses. At Stuart's command, Mosby and two other men rode advance for the entire operation.

The ride around McClellan was widely regarded as an insult to the Federal army, and was the stuff of instant legend. It had been carried off with McClellan's own headquarters at no time further away than half a dozen miles. McClellan tried afterward to make light of what had happened, but his reputation had been struck its first serious blow. One of his staff officers, the Count of Paris, said of it: "[The Southern cavalry] had, in point of fact, created a great commotion, shaken the confidence of the North in McClellan, and made the first experiment in those great cavalry expeditions, which subsequently played so novel and important a part during the war."[11]

Stuart's stock shot upward, and Mosby, terrifically bored since his arrival in Richmond, was suddenly very pleased to be where he was. Stuart, knowing that Mosby had been restless, asked him to stay—not to go with Floyd—and promised that he would now have no difficulty in securing a commission. "Stuart's name," wrote a rejuvenated Mosby to Pauline, "is in everyone's mouth now. . . . Richmond in fine spirits— everybody says it is the greatest feat of the war. I never enjoyed myself so much in my life."[12]

Stuart was so pleased with his little scout that, before the month was out, he renewed his efforts to dig up a commission for him, writing an introduction for Mosby to the Secretary of War himself, George W. Randolph: "Permit me to present to you John S. Mosby, who for months past has rendered time and again services of the most important and valuable nature, exposing himself regardless of danger, and, in my estimation, fairly won promotion. . . . I commend him to your notice."[13] He recommended Mosby to Lee at the same time, and Lee in turn specifically named Mosby in General Orders No. 74, written to publicize the recent "brilliant exploit" of Stuart's cavalry.[14]

Mosby was not to get the promotion he sought, but his name stuck with Lee, as he would find out later.

In the final week of June, with his army advancing upon Mc-

Clellan at Mechanicsville, "Stonewall" Jackson made his first appearance among the troops defending Richmond. Those who had never seen him had to blink and look twice. The great commander came mounted upon a dingy cob, and was dressed in a faded, threadbare, and patched-together old uniform. His head—and most of his bearded face—was covered by a beat-up yellow forage cap bearing the insignia of the Virginia Military Institute, whose faculty he had left the year before to take a field command. The cap's peak was pulled so low that he had to ride with lifted head to see where he was going. He sat his horse like an automaton: stiff, angular, unbending.

He was thirty-eight years old, of medium height, with dark hair and eyes, and he looked as though his clothing formed no part of his thoughts. He was covered with dust, and easily the most unmilitary-looking man of his command. Stuart's men had heard that he was their commander's opposite in almost everything. Stuart, said Blackford, "loved a joke, and would ring the changes on one until a better one turned up."[15] They'd heard that Jackson was different, however—a man to whom a joke was a mysterious affair. He was said to be deeply religious, and in fact could discourse for hours on religion. He had even organized a Sunday school for black children. At ease mainly with clergymen, elderly women, and children, he was shy with young women and deferential to his troops, who idolized him. "Fool Tom" Jackson his men called him, but with no edge of ridicule.

During the days Jackson spent about Richmond, his men noted a gradual improvement in his wardrobe and cheered lustily with every addition he made to his outfit. Cheers for Jackson grew in fact as commonplace as the wild cheering that accompanied a rabbit chase, and whenever cheering was heard in the rebel army around Richmond, the saying was: "Well, it's either Jackson or a rabbit."

Although Jackson's mind seemed always on vacation from the present moment, when the time came for action he knew exactly what to do.

The combined armies of Lee and Jackson, on the offensive now, advanced upon McClellan like a machine: Mechanicsville on the twenty-sixth, Gaines's Mill on the twenty-seventh.

McClellan struck back, viciously, all the while backpedaling toward Harrison's Landing on the James, where his barges could take him off if necessary, and explaining his retreat to the press as a mere "change of base." The remark was taken up with glee in the Confederate army. In the midst of the blood and horror, "changing one's base" became a catchword. If a man slipped and fell in the mud, he was changing his base; if the rain flooded out a campsite, the men changed their base; if one dog was beaten by another in a fight, the loser was merely changing his base. When Blackford, by now returned to Stuart's command, was sent to advise Jackson that Stuart was en route to see him, Jackson replied, in a rare attempt at humor, "That's good! That's good! Changing his base, is he? Ha, ha . . . Changing his base."

On July 1, after seven days of savage action, the firing ceased. Stinking carcasses of men and horses littered the ground for miles around Richmond. McClellan, with 15,000 casualties, regrouped and rested his men at Harrison's Landing. Lee, who had lost 21,000, retired toward Richmond, which had weathered its first storm.

Lincoln was disgusted with his army's performance. He immediately relieved McClellan of most of his duties, putting Henry W. Halleck in his place as overall army commander, and John Pope at the head of a new Army of Virginia. Except for retaining command of the troops presently on the Peninsula, McClellan was finished.

With the advent of General Pope, and his initial comments to the press, Confederate ears pricked up. The general's first remarks in fact took on great entertainment value throughout the rebel army. Pope, newly arrived from the West, boasted that he would be moving so relentlessly against the rebels that he would not even have time to take care of his rear; it would have to take care of itself. He claimed to be a man who never rested, allegedly datelining his dispatches from "headquarters in the saddle." He would have no fixed base, he announced, and planned on seeing a large number of fleeing Confederate backsides.

To most rebels this was heady stuff, but Mosby was inclined to take the remarks more seriously. Pope, he felt, had opened a promising field for partisan warfare by this lack of concern for his rear. "I asked Stuart," he wrote, "for a dozen men to make the harvest where the laborers were few, and do for Pope what he would not do for himself, take care of his rear and communications for him."[16] Pope, he thought, could be forced to detail most of his cavalry to guard his communications and stores, seriously blunting his threat. But Stuart was recruiting cavalry at the time, and had no wish to release men for such extracurricular service. On the other hand, he knew Mosby was anxious for such duty, and believed in the idea himself, so he offered to write a letter of introduction for him to Jackson. Jackson, presently to the west at Gordonsville protecting the vital Virginia Central railroad, could probably supply Mosby with the men he had requested.

On July 19, Mosby left with a club-footed companion, a military exempt, to find Jackson. In addition to his letter from Stuart (which described the bearer as "bold, daring, intelligent, and discreet"), he carried with him a copy of Napoleon's *Maxims,* which Stuart wanted Jackson to read.[17]

He was never to reach Jackson.

After spending the night on a farm near Beaver Dam Station, Mosby decided to send his horse and gear on ahead with his companion and hop a train for a flying visit to his family. He unbuckled his pistols and sat down in the shade to await the cars. No sooner had he gotten comfortable when, in a cloud of dust, a detachment of Union cavalry burst into view. Mosby ran, but to no avail. Unmounted and unarmed, he was easily taken.

The Yankee cavalry—the Second New York—seem to have found the pint-sized Confederate more than a little amusing. (Mosby had by this time adopted the flamboyant dress of Stuart's cavalry.) "During an affray [at Beaver Dam]," wrote a regimental historian,

> we captured a young Confederate, who gave his name as Captain John S. Mosby. By his sprightly appearance and conversation he attracted considerable attention. He . . . displays no small amount of Southern bravado in his dress and manners. His gray plush hat is surmounted by a waving plume, which he tosses, as he speaks, in real Prussian style.[18]

His letter to Jackson was confiscated, and he was removed to a guardhouse near Fredericksburg, to be interrogated by Gen. Rufus King, commanding Union forces there. King treated him courteously, giving him time to write home and making good on a promise to send his letter through the lines. Mosby seems to have enjoyed his "interrogation," which included a convivial reading of captured Confederate mail with the Yankee officers. He must have made a favorable impression, for the officer who had captured him, Col. J. Mansfield Davies, offered to lend him Federal money for use in Washington, where he was to be sent. Mosby declined. He was then shipped off to the Old Capitol prison, where he found his confinement as enjoyable as his interrogation had been. On arrival, he had been advised that he would be part of the war's first prisoner exchange.

Ten days later he was issued a patent-leather Union haversack, $5 in greenbacks, and, with hundreds of other rebel prisoners, put aboard a southbound Potomac steamer.

The exchange steamer, after sliding downriver and out into the Chesapeake, moved into Hampton Roads near Fortress Monroe, where it lay for four days in the sweltering heat awaiting clearance to move up the James toward Richmond. While lying in the Roads, Mosby noted a large number of Federal transports at Newport News, chock full of Federal troops. He was mildly surprised that the Confederate officers about him seemed to take no notice, because the troops' presence seemed important to him. Whose were they, and where were they bound, he wondered. Would they be joining McClellan on the Peninsula, or heading north up the Chesapeake, ultimately to join Pope? In the latter case, he reasoned, the Peninsular campaign must have been canceled and McClellan himself would soon be pulling out, taking the pressure off Richmond. It could prove important to understand where the ships were headed.

Mosby had sized up the ship's captain as a Confederate sympathizer, and after learning that the troops were Gen. Ambrose E. Burnside's, up from the Carolinas, asked him to find out where they were going. He had judged his man correctly. Later in the day, passing close to the little Confederate on the crowded deck, the captain whispered, "Aquia Creek, on the Potomac." Mosby had his answer: the Union troops were headed north to reinforce Pope, and the Peninsular campaign must be on the verge of collapse. McClellan would not attack again without reinforcements; he too would soon be headed north.

He alternately paced the vibrating deck and leaned against the rail throughout the sticky night, as the ship moved slowly up the James to the exchange point. At 10:00 A.M., when it touched shore, he was the first prisoner on the pier. Seeking out the Confederate exchange commissioner at once, he explained that he had important information for General Lee and wished to be processed quickly. He was.

Without an introduction or a horse, bearing only his Union haversack and a few lemons he had purchased at Fortress Monroe, he set out along the dusty road to the commander's headquarters. It was an oppressive August day, and the thought of a twelve-mile hike in cavalry boots was distinctly unappealing, but he pressed on, sucking a lemon as he went. After trudging a few miles in the muggy heat, his uniform yellowed with successive layers of dust from passing horsemen, his feet were so sore he could hardly stand. He'd just crawled off the road to rest when a South Carolina cavalryman came by and Mosby begged him to stop, explaining that he had to get to Lee's headquarters with an important message.

With the help of the South Carolinian, he quickly arrived at the commander's front door. But Mosby had never met Lee, who by this time was held in considerable awe throughout the army, and his entry was not to be easy. He recalled the moment:

> The first [soldier] I met at headquarters, with a good deal of . . . insolence . . . told me that I could not see the general. I tried to explain that I did not come to ask a favor, but to bring him important information. Another one of the staff standing by told me to wait. . . . He . . . soon called me in. I now found myself for the first time in the presence of the great commander of the Army of Northern Virginia. He was alone and poring over some maps on the table. . . . His manner was gentle and kind. . . . With some embarrassment I told what I had learned about Burnside's troops. He listened attentively,

and after I was through called to a staff officer to have a man ready to take a dispatch to General Jackson.[19]

After awkwardly pressing the commander to accept his remaining lemons, Mosby headed for the door. But he had enough presence of mind to stop and tell Lee his name before leaving, informing him that he'd been with Stuart on the ride around McClellan.

"Oh, yes, I remember," answered Lee.

In camp again near Carmel Church, Mosby heard the distant roar of Jackson's guns as they opened on Pope's advance at Cedar Mountain, Jackson having been ordered to strike Pope before the arrival of the reinforcements from Burnside.

With some claim to truth, he remarked of this significant event to Fount Beattie, "I brought on that battle."

Following the action at Cedar Mountain, Lee quickly began to pull his army away from Richmond, and in a series of rapid moves had 55,000 men deployed by mid-August along the Rapidan, poised to annihilate the peripatetic Pope before Burnside could get there. McClellan, reluctantly preparing to evacuate the Peninsula by now, was unaware that Lee was actually leaving Richmond and not reinforcing it. Stuart's cavalry advanced across the Rapidan, engaging Pope in a series of skirmishes near Brandy Station, and spearheading a lightning Confederate thrust northward. In a matter of a few weeks, not only had Richmond been relieved of pressure but Lee had succeeded in tilting the balance in favor of the formerly beleaguered Southern forces. By the end of August all armies were, in an almost perverse twist of fate, converging on the bloody ground near Manassas. And thanks again to the cleverness of Jackson and Lee, when the clash came, the Southerners for a second time carried the day. (Mosby participated in this battle, getting a bullet crease in the head for his trouble.)

The smoke had barely cleared when Lee was again moving north for a first thrust at the Northern homeland, and as the gray horde moved toward the Potomac, Washington's pulse went up perceptibly. Clerks and government employees were pressed into service and pessimistic engineers shook their heads over the city's so-far untested defenses. With Pope's popularity having plummeted sharply after Second Manassas, McClellan found himself pushed again into the limelight, charged with Washington's defense. (Lincoln told someone: "If he can't fight himself, he excels in making others ready to fight.")[20]

By September 2, "Little Mac" was riding calmly among the city's apprehensive defenders, assuring them that all would be well. Yet even McClellan did not know precisely what Lee had in mind, or what he was capable of. In nine short weeks the Southern commander had transfered the war from the doorstep of Richmond to the threshold of Washington, and no one knew for certain what he would do next.

By September 3, McClellan was organizing a field force to pursue Lee and force him to a stand at some distance from Washington.

As Lee splashed across the Potomac north of Leesburg on September 4, still with 55,000 men in his train, he had no clear intention of either invading or investing Washington. He did know that his state was being devastated, his army was hungry, and the rich, golden fields of Maryland were close at hand. Whatever his other designs in heading north, he intended at least to replenish his stores in this paradise.

Mosby crossed the Potomac in Lee's advance guard and rode behind Stonewall Jackson in the now immortalized entry of Confederate soldiers into Frederick, Maryland. As the gray-clad troopers marched through streets lined with Yakee sympathizers, Jackson's band was playing "My Maryland." Mosby maintained that, despite having been there, he never heard anything about Barbara Frietchie shaking the Stars and Stripes in Stonewall's face until he later read Whittier's poem.

Following the passage through Frederick, Lee divided his force, sending Jackson with 25,000 men (half his army) to neutralize the 11,000-man Federal garrison at Harpers Ferry. Jackson recrossed the Potomac therefore on September 15, bombarded the fortress into submission, then led most of his force out to find the commander, anxiously awaiting him now on the southwest bank of Antietam Creek, near Sharpsburg. Lee's lean and berry-brown Confederates knew that Mc-

Clellan was advancing with a force of over three times their size; it was imperative that Jackson arrive.

The indefatigable Jackson in fact came in time to save Lee's force from annihilation, but more than 10,000 rebel casualties told the tale of a costly battle. Cannonballs had torn up with impartiality men, animals, and great tracts of real estate. Yankee losses, despite the overwhelming Federal advantage, were even greater than rebel losses. Never before or since during the war were so many men shot in one day.

During the battle, as Jackson's men were repulsing a final Yankee sally in the woods near the Dunkard Church, Stuart dashed out onto the field in advance of the infantry, with two men following: Jasper Jones and John Mosby. The ground was covered with the dead and wounded, and it was difficult for the three men to move without their horses treading on them. Although hundreds were lying on the field, Mosby's attention was drawn to a particular Federal officer who had been shot through the shoulder and seemed to be suffering considerably. He dismounted, leaving Stuart and Jones to continue without him, walked over to the officer, and rolled up a blanket under his head. He noticed a canteen attached to a dead soldier nearby, and under the questioning eye of the silent officer, retrieved it, having to step around a second wounded Yank to do so. He bent down first to this soldier, and held the canteen to his lips. "No, no." The man shook his head. "Take this to my colonel—he is the best man in the world."

Mosby, overwhelmed at such selflessness, put the canteen to the colonel's lips and asked the man his name. "Colonel Wistar, of the California Regiment." The Yankee and Confederate spoke for a few moments, and as Mosby turned to leave, Jackson's tremendous guns opened again on the retreating Union columns. Wistar, through teeth clenched in pain, asked: "Whose guns are those?" Mosby knew well whose they were, but later claimed he did not wish to add to Wistar's burden by telling him.

"I don't know," he replied, then mounted and rode off to join Stuart.

In a chance meeting with Wistar after the war (Wistar, a general now, was astonished to learn the identity of his benefactor), Mosby was told that the young soldier who had refused the canteen died later that night.

Before McClellan could bring all his force to bear, Lee slipped back across the Potomac in a treacherous night crossing and retreated up the Shenandoah. Stuart stayed behind for some raiding in southern Maryland before falling back himself. Mosby, during this time, made his way to his father's house (near Lynchburg now) to replace his horse, which had been disabled in the battle. Horses were a continuing problem for the Confederate army, since the animals were not considered "army issue," as they were in the North. A man was paid forty cents a day for the use of his own mount, and was expected to provide replacements as needed or he would be unable to ride. As the war dragged on, the scarcity of horses blunted somewhat the customary dash of the rebel cavalry. Men hesitated to expose their animals when it might mean a long period of inactivity, sidelined without a mount.

But Mosby seems to have had a dependable supply of horses, and when he rejoined Stuart in Fauquier County, it was to skirmish with McClellan's advance, now moving into the northern Virginia vacuum left by Lee. There is no evidence that Mosby was with the cavalry in mid-October when Stuart again unhinged Federal plans by making a daring sweep behind the Federal armies into Pennsylvania, doing extensive damage in Chambersburg, paroling hundreds of prisoners, and appropriating nearly 1,500 Pennsylvania horses.

As the Army of Northern Virginia fell back through the Valley to the familiar line of the Rappahannock, the cautious McClellan crept forward. He was actually closer to Richmond now than Lee was, yet made no move in that direction. Lincoln's patience was finally exhausted. On November 7, McClellan was in camp at Rectortown, Fauquier County, when notified that he had been replaced by Ambrose Burnside as commander of Union forces in Virginia.

Not wanting to be found guilty of his predecessor's sins, Burnside lost no time in moving his newly acquired army toward Richmond, concentrating his men at Falmouth, across the river from Fredericksburg where the fleeing Confederates were digging in. Despite some misgivings in Washington about attacking Lee's swelling forces here, Burnside seemed to see little reason for caution. Rations were meager in the cold Confederate camps, he knew; men were without cooking utensils or tents, many had no shoes or spare blankets, and their standard fare, it was said, was black bread and blue beef.

He would attack them at Fredericksburg.

Lee began in November to fortify the city, in an attempt to block the second Northern advance upon Richmond. He spread his cavalry along the river twenty or thirty miles to each side of town, placed cannon on the surrounding heights, and dug a system of rifle pits along the riverbank with deep, zigzag covered ways leading back into the town. Burnside, his shipment of pontoon boats delayed, spent two weeks positioning scores of cannon on the heights across the river. With over four hundred cannon between the two sides, the carnage promised to be of record variety.

Lee had a circular printed, urging all citizens to leave the town, and by December 8, with snow in the air, the exodus had started. Old men, women, and crying children streamed out of the city to camp in nearby woods. They crowded the frozen roads day and night. Carts, wagons, and carriages of every description pressed forward to escape the coming rain of fire. On December 11, in a thick morning fog, it began. Lee planned on offering only the resistance of William Barksdale's Mississippi veterans in the rifle pits during the expected laying of Federal pontoons, then a delaying action from the same contingent, forcing the confident Burnside to pay for his advance across the open ground west of the river.

Confederate resistance to the pontoon-laying was in fact stiff and extremely effective, forcing the Yanks to pull back and regroup, and leaving many a corpse sprawled upon the unfinished bridge or floating slowly down the icy river. But by 10 A.M. the fog had lifted, and the Federal bombardment began in earnest. Blackford described the Union cannonade as a Niagara of sound, with bursting shells and whistling rifle bullets flying literally everywhere. Heavy projectiles tore their way through rooftops and burst in bedrooms, parlors, kitchens. Dark columns of smoke began to rise in many parts of town, some colored with red tongues of fire. The ground shook for two hours as if in the grip of an earthquake, then abruptly ceased.

As soon as the Federal cannon were stilled, the effort to cross was renewed. The Southern riflemen, who had been well protected, again opened on the exposed Yanks; but Lee now ordered Barksdale to let them cross and to fall back through the trenches, just slowing their advance.

By the thirteenth, Burnside had succeeded in bringing across most of his more than 100,000-man army at three points, and assembling it west of the river for a direct assault upon the heights above the town. He was about to find out the seriousness of his misjudgment, for it was now that Lee opened with his own artillery and infantry, slowly decimating the near-defenseless Union forces on the open ground.

By December 15 the Yankees were beginning to recross the river.

They left behind them a town that looked and smelled like a butcher's shambles. Blasted walls were spattered with dried blood. Arms, legs, dismembered torsos lay everywhere in the streets. Death was wherever one looked. At the foot of Marye's Hill, near town, the field was as blue as if covered by a blue cloth, and might have been crossed at any point on the bodies of the dead and dying.

By mid-December, then, it was final: the Yankee army had again been repulsed. Lee had, in turn, broken McClellan, Pope, and Burnside. Confederate morale skyrocketed, high spirits buoyed even higher by the many acquisitions of Northern shoes, clothing, and equipment involuntarily left on Southern soil.

Mosby, posted with Stuart to the south of town, had seen little action. It had not been a cavalry battle. He seems actually to have anticipated inactivity around Fredericksburg, for prior to the battle he had written to Pauline requesting a dozen or so books—from Plutarch and Shakespeare through Scott, Hazlitt, Byron, and Macaulay. There is no indication that he ever received them, but the post-battle atmosphere might well have been conducive to reading. Pickets on opposite banks of the Rappahannock had again taken to swapping coffee and tobacco, passing goods and gossip to one another between crude canoes. Northern bands around Falmouth would play a popular Southern air, and in response a Confederate band at Fredericksburg would send back a rousing "Star-Spangled Banner."

The cavalry was not used for picketing, and was in fact sent to the rear, to put the horses closer to forage. Mosby, who could not abide inactivity, was crazy with boredom, as was Stuart, who decided that the cavalry might profitably take a jaunt northward at Christmastime. Its purpose would be to break up Burnside's communications with Washington and throw a little confusion into the Union camps, full now of turkey and Christmas cheer.

The raid proved to be more of a prank than an effective military action, but succeeded admirably in sowing confusion. No one knew where Stuart's rambling force of 1,800 horsemen and 4 artillery pieces was headed and so no concerted opposition could be made. Stuart struck as far north as Fairfax Court House, captured many sutlers' wagons, eluded Federal forces at almost every turn, and in general behaved like a Halloween funster. Sweeping into Burke's Station, on the Orange and Alexandria railroad, he took over the Federal telegraph office, listened in on Federal traffic for a while, then—just before cutting the wire—fired off a complaint of his own to U.S. Quartermaster General Montgomery Meigs about the low quality of Union mules, a number of which he was obliged to take back with him.

Stuart defied all attempts to intercept his force, making a daring escape not southward, as expected, but to the north and west. He swept around Fairfax Court House—less than two dozen miles from Washington—and along the way routed a regiment of Pennsylvania cavalry sent to cut him off. (This regiment was last seen "furiously charging to the rear," in the words of the Federal telegraph operator who witnessed its brief encounter with the Southerners.)[21]

Escaping successfully from Union lines, the raiding party rested near Middleburg, Loudoun County, before turning southward to the Rappahannock, and to a winter that promised to be as boring as the last. Stuart had put up for the night at the Rogers home, near Dover, and Mosby went after him next morning with his growing obsession. "I went to his room," said Mosby, "and asked him to let me stay behind for a few days with a squad of men. I thought I could do something with them."[22] To Mosby's great relief Stuart assented this time. There would be nothing useful for a man like Mosby to do in a winter camp, he reasoned. Neither singing nor flirting nor card playing seemed to interest him. He would probably go out of his mind.

"I got nine men," wrote Mosby, "—including, of course, Beattie—who volunteered to go with me."[23]

His career as a partisan had begun.

A teenage John Mosby as a student at the University of Virginia, early 1850s. He wears the medal of the Washington Society, a student club. *Credit: Manuscripts Department, University of Virginia Library*

Virginia Jackson McLaurine Mosby, mother of John S. Mosby. A woman resolute and strong, she lived nearly into the twentieth century. *Credit:* The Memoirs of Colonel John S. Mosby

Mosby's father, Alfred, and only brother, Willie, who later became his adjutant. This mid-1850s photo shows Willie in the uniform of a military school. *Credit:* The Memoirs of Colonel John S. Mosby

Aaron Burton, servant of the Mosby family until war's end. He accompanied Mosby throughout much of the war, and the two men maintained contact into the 1890s, when this photo was taken. *Credit:* The Memoirs of Colonel John S. Mosby

William H. Chapman, Sam's brother, as conscription officer for the regular army, at first rode only part-time with Mosby. By the end of the war he was Mosby's second in command. *Credit:* The Memoirs of Colonel John S. Mosby

Samuel F. Chapman, a divinity student before joining the Confederate army, was to become one of Mosby's most dedicated and capable followers. *Credit:* Mosby's Rangers

James Ewell Brown Stuart, legendary Confederate cavalryman, was Mosby's commanding officer until killed in the spring of 1864. *Credit: Cook Collection, Valentine Museum*

The action at Miskel's farm, April 1, 1863. Mosby's fledgling band—on this morning hardly as well mounted or uniformed as pictured—here turned the tables on a superior Union force that had surprised them. *Credit:* Munsey's Magazine

"Scouting," from an oil painting. Mosby is the rider at center. *Credit: Museum of the Confederacy*

A somewhat fanciful newspaper rendering of the pillaging of a
Federal wagon train by Mosby's men. Such looting enraged com-
manders of both North and South in the wake of Gettysburg.
Credit: Library of Congress

Mosby's attack upon Federal cavalry fighting from a house at Warrenton Junction, May 1863.
Yankee reinforcements here handed him his first rout. *Credit:* Munsey's Magazine

ABOVE: Mosby in action. The close-quarters combat pictured here was typical of the rangers' engagements. The combination of boldness and skill with a revolver accounted for much of their success as a cavalry unit. *Credit:* Munsey's Magazine

RIGHT: Mosby as a major, a rank he held from April 1863 until the following January. He had joined the army as a private. *Credit: Library of Congress*

Warrenton, Virginia, during the war. The courthouse at the right, portions of which stand today, was to serve as an arena for Mosby's peacetime career in the postwar South. *Credit: Library of Congress*

Ulysses Simpson Grant, photographed the year before the North's great campaign of 1864. Mosby was to be practically cast out of the South for his later attitude toward Grant and the Republican party. *Credit: Library of Congress*

Five of Mosby's riders. Walter Gosden *(standing, right)* was the father of Freeman Gosden, of subsequent radio fame. *Credit: Cook Collection, Valentine Museum*

Two views of Mosby's attack on Sheridan's supply train near Berryville, August 1864. With three hundred horsemen and two field pieces, this was the largest attack he had yet mounted in the war. *Credit:* Munsey's Magazine

Marylanders such as these, not subject to Confederate conscription, supplied a sturdy backbone to Mosby's command. Mosby stands hatless at center. *Credit: Maryland Historical Society, Baltimore*

A second artist's vision of Mosby's dawn attack upon Sheridan's train at Berryville. His relentless pressure upon Sheridan kept reinforcements away from Petersburg, and probably prolonged the Confederacy's life by several months. *Credit: Museum of the Confederacy*

Iron in the fire, a typical day's work for a Southern guerrilla. Ties were pulled up, splashed with turpentine, and ignited. Rails drooped into uselessness when thrown on top. *Credit: Library of Congress*

Mosby's men took credit for several incidents such as this, which were accomplished by prying a rail out of line near an embankment. A Federal crew attempts to right this engine. *Credit: Library of Congress*

Mosby as a full colonel, January 1865. Recuperating from his severest wounding, his neck does not yet fill out his collar. *Credit: Manuscripts Department, University of Virginia Library*

Colonel Mosby in 1865. *Credit: Cook Collection, Valentine Museum*

Mosby as a lieutenant colonel, a rank he held through most of 1864. *Credit: Manuscripts Department, University of Virginia Library*

Mosby as he appeared in 1866, in the last of his portraits in military uniform. *Credit: Manuscripts Department, University of Virginia Library*

"Mosby and His Men Returning from a Raid," by Armand Dumaresq. Mosby sits astride the white horse at right. *Credit: Museum of the Confederacy*

5

FOX IN THE HENHOUSE

I endeavored . . . to diminish . . . the aggressive power of the army of the Potomac, by compelling it to keep a large force on the defensive. . . . I wanted to use and consume the Northern cavalry in hard work. I have often thought that their fierce hostility to me was more on account of the sleep I made them lose than the number we killed and captured.

—John S. Mosby, *War Reminiscences*

WALTER FRANKLAND had just been discharged from Confederate service. Rather than reenlist with a regular unit, however, he and his friend, George Whitescarver, had decided to join Col. Elijah White's independent cavalry in Loudoun County, and were presently slogging—on foot—through oceans of northern Virginia mud to find him. But the two men and a rider they'd met at Salem, Joe Nelson, were at the moment being talked into something else.

The three had put up for the night at the home of one James Hathaway—known for his rebel sympathies—on an out-of-the-way road in Fauquier County, between Middleburg and Salem. It was a cold, wet February evening, and Hathaway—fire snapping cheerfully in the background—was presenting an interesting proposition. Why did they want to join up with Colonel White, he asked. If it was action they were after, there was plenty of that to be had right at the doorstep. A young private named Mosby, one of Stuart's scouts, had been in the area for a few weeks now, and was already raising Cain with the Yankee outposts toward Fairfax. In his first two days here, said Hathaway, he'd taken nearly two dozen prisoners and hadn't let up since. He was causing the Yankees plenty of trouble, and looked like he meant to cause a lot more. As Hathaway spoke, another horseman who'd heard of his hospitality splashed out of the falling night, drew up at the door, and was invited in. His name was Frank Williams, he said, and it turned out that he, too, intended to join an independent outfit.

Hathaway cemented the four men's interest when he informed them that Mosby was holding a meeting next day at a place called Rector's Cross Roads, not far away, and suggested they might want to drop by there before going off to look for White.

All four agreed to have a look at this Mosby.

When they arrived next day at the Cross Roads, doubled up on only two horses, the four civilians were met by the suspicious stares of a dozen weather-beaten Confederate cavalrymen, standing around in a snowy hollow near the turnpike. They hurriedly explained their presence, at the same time scanning the group for some sign of a leader. They found none. Someone finally pointed out the commander to them: a slightly built young man standing a little apart from the rest, picking his teeth as he watched them and from time to time glancing at the sky.

He shifted piles of snow around with his boots as they spoke to him, and when they'd finished, his reverie continued. The two with horses could stay, he said finally. The other two would have to get horses or wait until Yankee horses could be supplied.

His business with them at an end, he turned away and called the rough-looking assemblage to order.

The sudden appearance of a few Confederate cavalrymen in the Fairfax pine forests was something for which the Union army was unprepared. It was against the rules, which still declared that large forces move against one another en masse. But during January 1863 Federal commanders in Fairfax County had begun getting reports about nighttime assaults on their normally quiet cavalry outposts. Soldiers, horses, and weapons were disappearing on an almost nightly basis. The matter was especially galling to Col. Sir Percy Wyndham, of the First New Jersey Cavalry. Wyndham, an Englishman who presently commanded the cavalry outposts, was accustomed to doing things by the book, and was appalled that anyone would molest a dozing cavalryman or take his horse. He was most irritated at the thought of locals being so easily provided with weapons at the expense of the United States Army.

By the end of January, Wyndham was pushing out into Loudoun County with sizable search parties; but not knowing who he was looking for, he met with minimal success. "At first," said Mosby,

> they accounted for our attacks on the theory that the farmers and cripples they saw in the daytime ploughing their fields and taking care of their flocks collected in bands at night, raided their camps, and dispersed at daybreak. But when they went around at night searching the homes for these invisible foes, they generally found the old farmers in bed, and when they returned to camp, they often found that we had paid them a visit in their absence.[1]

On occasion, Mosby had in fact used Confederate convalescents from the hospital in Middleburg, but, he said, at last he "got one of the cripples killed," which "somewhat abated their ardor."[2]

The people of Middleburg were not pleased at the attention drawn to their quiet town by the rebel newcomers. Sympathies were divided here between blue and gray, and when, in late January, two hundred of Wyndham's troopers engaged Mosby's band in a running battle through the town's streets (Wyndham subsequently threatening to burn the place to the ground), an angry delegation came with a petition demanding that the Confederates get out. Mosby's written response: "Not being prepared for any such degrading compromise with the Yankees, I unhesitatingly refuse to comply."[3] Stuart, upon being informed of the citizens' hostility, helped stiffen Mosby's resolve by ordering him to stay where he was.

The defensive chain against which the Confederates were operating was forged of a series of cavalry posts set at half-mile intervals. The chain was anchored near Dranesville on the upper Potomac, and at Alexandria on the lower, with the center, appropriately, at Centreville. When Mosby, after his first few days of operations, returned to Fredericksburg to report to Stuart, he argued that, given a free hand, he could very quickly force the Yankees either to contract the northern half of this chain and thereby give up ten miles of country, or to reinforce it, taking troops away from the front lines to do so. He told Stuart that, for what he had in mind, quickness would more than make up for small numbers. Stuart, one of the few not to consider the plan a "quixotic enterprise," allowed him a total of fifteen men—many from Fitz Lee's regiment. Lee was less than ecstatic at having to give up his men to Private Mosby, but Stuart brushed aside his demands for their return, and Lee's men stayed with Mosby until the opening of the spring campaign.

It was in early February that Frankland, Whitescarver, Nelson, and Williams arrived. It was also around this time that one of Mosby's most valuable additions was made: a hulking sergeant from the Fifth New York Cavalry named Ames. Since Sergeant Ames had simply walked out of the Union lines in Fairfax to join the Southern guerrillas, he was without horse or arms, but lack of a mount or weapons was the least of his problems among the hostile rebel cavalrymen. They did not trust him. All the veterans except Mosby were for sending him back immediately. Mosby, however, after grilling the big Yankee about the disposition of Federal troops in Fairfax County, accepted him on the spot. "I never cared to inquire what his grievance [with the Yankees] was," he explained. "The account he gave me of the distribution of troops and the gaps in the picket lines coincided with what I knew and tended to prepossess me in his favor."[4]

Yet even Mosby felt that Ames should be tested. He told him that if he wanted a horse, he'd have to get it himself— even if it meant walking the thirty miles back to Germantown and taking it from the stables of his old regiment. And if he wanted to take that risk, added Mosby, he ought to take Frankland with him, since Frankland was now the only other dismounted man in the command.

In the last week of February the two men set off amid heavy rains to negotiate thirty miles of open road, dense thickets, and swollen streams before arriving in the pines behind the Union stables at Germantown. At midnight they looked on as two hundred troopers of the Fifth New York and Eighteenth Pennsylvania filed out to saddle their mounts.

Snatches of conversation told the intruders that they were watching a search party being formed to look for the "Loudoun guerrillas." When the troopers had left, the two men quickly slipped into the quiet stables, saddled and bridled two officer's horses, and rode out through the mud to warn Mosby of the coming clash.

They did not arrive in time, but it made little difference. Mosby, alerted to the Yankees' presence by the time the search party had reached Middleburg, rounded up a few men and galloped off immediately in pursuit. In Aldie—a few miles east of Middleburg—he caught up with what he took to be his quarry, all dismounted, relaxed, and feeding their horses at a mill.

In fact this was not the body from Fairfax, but the advance guard of the First Vermont, sent out from Dranesville on a similar anti-guerrilla sweep. Mosby burst among the lolling cavalrymen without warning, and what happened next came close to comedy. "I tried to stop [at the mill]," he explained,

> but my horse was high-mettled and ran at full speed, entirely beyond my control. But the cavalry at the mill were taken absolutely by surprise by the irruption; their videttes had not fired, and they were as much shocked as if we had dropped from the sky. . . . A panic seized them. Without stopping to bridle their horses or to fight on foot, they scattered in all directions. . . .
>
> Just as we got to the mill, I saw another body of cavalry [the main body of the First Vermont] ahead of me on the pike, gazing in bewildered astonishment. . . . To save myself, I jumped off my horse and my men stopped, but fortunately the mounted party in front of me saw those I had left behind coming to my relief, so they wheeled and started full speed down the pike. We then went back to the mill and went to work. Many had hidden like rats, and as the mill was running, they came near being ground up. The first man that was pulled out was covered with flour; we thought he was the miller. . . . I never got [my horse]. . . . In this affair I got the reputation of a hero; really I never claimed it, but gave my horse all the credit.[5]

Of the fifty-nine Vermonters who had come out to catch partisans, nineteen ended up in a Confederate prison.

By early March, Mosby had decided to try something he had been mulling over almost since his arrival. The presence of Ames, with his knowledge of troop distribution in Fairfax, would now make it feasible: he would infiltrate the vast Union encampment at Fairfax Court House and kidnap the annoying Percy Wyndham. If possible he would also take the brigade commander, Brig. Gen. Edwin H. Stoughton.

Mosby's dispatch to Stuart after the event tells how it turned out:

General:
  I have the honor to report that having accurately ascertained the number and disposition of the troops in Fairfax County, I determined . . . to reach Fairfax Court-House, where the general headquarters of that portion of the army were established. Sunday night, the 8th instant, being dark and rainy, was deemed propitious. . . . I . . . kept the pike until I got within about a mile and a half of the Court-House, when I turned to the right in order to avoid some infantry camps, and came into Fairfax Court-House from the direction of the railroad station. The few guards stationed around the town, unsuspecting danger, were easily captured. I then sent one party to the headquarters of Colonel Wyndham . . . , another party to Colonel Johnstone's, while with 6 men I went myself to Brigadier General Stoughton's. Unfortunately Colonel Wyndham had gone down to Washington, but his assistant adjutant-general and aide-de-camp were made prisoners. Colonel Johnstone, having received notice of our presence, made his escape. General Stoughton I found in bed asleep. . . .
  While these things were going on, other detachments of my men were busily engaged in clearing the stables of the fine horses with which they were filled. It was about 2 o'clock when I reached the Court-House, and I did not deem it safe to remain there over one hour and a half, as we were 10 miles within the enemy's lines, and it was necessary that we should get out before daylight, the close proximity of the enemy's forces rendering our situation one of great peril, there being three regiments of cavalry camped 1 mile distant, at Germantown, two infantry regiments within a few hundred yards of the town, one infantry brigade in the vicinity of Fairfax Station, and another infantry brigade, with artillery and cavalry, at Centreville. About 3:30 o'clock, therefore, I left the place, going in the direction of Fairfax Station, in order to deceive

the enemy as to my line of retreat. . . . When I came to within a half mile of Centreville I . . . turned to the right, passed so close to the fortifications there that the sentinels on the redoubts hailed us, while we could distinctly see the bristling cannon through the embrasures. We passed within a hundred yards of their infantry pickets without molestation, swam Cub Run, and again came into the Warrenton Pike at Groveton. . . .

The fruits of this expedition are 1 brigadier-general (Stoughton), 2 captains, and 30 men prisoners. We also brought off 58 horses, most of them being very fine, belonging to officers; also a considerable number of arms. We left hundreds of horses in the stables and other places, having no way of bringing them off, as I was already encumbered with more prisoners and horses than I had men. I had 29 men with me; sustained no loss. They all behaved admirably.[6]

The raid jolted the Union high command and proved downright embarrassing to a few. Col. Robert Johnstone, commanding cavalry at Fairfax, had escaped nude from his back door while his wife bit, clawed, and punched Mosby's men at the front door. The frightened colonel spent the rest of the night shivering in a privy. Brigadier General Stoughton—an up-and-comer from a wealthy Vermont family, and commander of Second Brigade, Casey's Division, of Washington's Defenses—had been whacked on the rump and pulled from his bed before being marched off. His career was ruined. Wyndham's pickets had been the ones who let the raiders through, while Wyndham was away in Washington. Wyndham's days, too, were numbered.

A cavalry pursuit was ordered, belatedly, but since no one knew the size of the force being pursued, the chase tended to be timid. Lincoln shook his head when he got the news. "Well," he said, "I am sorry for that—for I can make brigadier-generals, but I can't make horses."[7]

Secret Service men filtered into Fairfax now in search of an inside agent; the investigation centered upon a nineteen-year-old girl named Antonia Ford, known to have been friendly with Mosby when he was on duty in Fairfax, and friendly with Stoughton now. Miss Ford was a "decidedly good-looking woman," noted Secret Service chief Lafayette C. Baker, "with pleasing, insinuating manners."[8] Whatever her attributes, they were insufficient to prevent her being packed off with several others to the Old Capitol prison, where she was held for months. Mosby afterward maintained that Antonia was "as innocent as Abraham Lincoln," which was probably true.[9]

No one seems to have thought of a deserter named Ames.

By daybreak the party was outside of Federal lines, and the much-relieved Mosby allowed Stoughton to visit friends in Warrenton before taking him on to Fitz Lee's headquarters near Culpeper Court House. Lee, a classmate of Stoughton's at West Point, was astonished to see Mosby walk in with his old friend. Plainly embarrassed at having to take the Vermonter prisoner, he went out of his way to ignore Private Mosby. "I brought Stoughton to Fitz' headquarters at Culpeper," wrote Mosby in a letter describing the scene,

on the morning of March 10, '63. A cold rain was falling. I walked into Fitz' room with Stoughton and the other officers. Fitz was sitting at a desk writing. There was a big fire blazing. I presented Fitz' old classmate to him. If I had been an orderly who had brought him a morning report he could not have treated me with more indifference. You would not have thought from his manner that I had done anything more than . . . routine. Although I was cold and dripping wet he did not ask me to sit down and warm myself. It was plain that he was sorry for what I had done. I was very mad at such treatment— shook hands with the prisoners—told them that I would leave them with General Lee, and rode off in the rain. . . . I had hardly got back to Loudoun before I received a letter from him telling me to send the men who were with me back to their regiment.[10]

Before heading north again, however, Mosby got the recognition he sought. Immediately after leaving Lee's headquarters he spotted Stuart and John Pelham, Stuart's boy-genius artillery commander, stepping off the cars. He raced to Stuart and excitedly spilled out his story, easily infecting his effervescent commander with his own mood. Stuart clapped him on the back and, almost on the spot, began composing a public announcement of the raid.

Within a few days, the account of Stoughton's capture was read on dress parade to every cavalry regiment in the Army of Northern Virginia: "Capt. John S. Mosby has for a long time attracted the attention of his generals by his boldness, skill, and success, so signally displayed in his numerous forays upon the invaders of his native State. . . . His late brilliant exploit . . . justifies this recognition. . . . The feat [is] unparalleled in the war." [11]

Robert E. Lee, a few days after the event, wrote to Stuart, "Mosby has covered himself with honors," and later in the month, "Hurrah for Mosby! I wish I had a hundred like him!" [12]

The raid had occurred on a Sunday night. By the following Friday, Lincoln had summoned Maj. Gen. Julius P. Stahel to the White House, ordered him personally to take charge of the cavalry in Fairfax, and warned him that, in the future, successful guerrilla raids would be cause for his deep displeasure. Both Johnstone and Wyndham were reassigned.

The Stoughton affair was Mosby's "Open Sesame." On March 16, back in Loudoun, he wrote to Stuart: "Public sentiment seems now entirely changed, and I think it is the universal desire here for me to remain." [13] On the twenty-first, Robert E. Lee was writing to Jefferson Davis in search of a commission for Stuart's now-famous scout, whose rank was still somewhat indescribable. "I wish I could receive [Mosby's] appointment," he said, "or some official notification of it, that I might announce it to him." [14]

By March 23, Mosby had been promoted to a captaincy in the Provisional Army of the Confederate States, and enjoined to proceed at once to organize a company, "with the understanding that it [was] to be placed on a footing with all troops of the line, and to be mustered unconditionally into the Confederate service." The instructions continued: "Though you are to be its captain, the men will have the privilege of electing the lieutenants. . . . When the requisite number of men are enrolled, an officer will be designated to muster the company into the service." [15]

Two days later Mosby received from Stuart an elaboration on these orders. "By all means," wrote Stuart, "ignore the term 'Partisan Ranger.' It is in bad repute. Call your command 'Mosby's Regulars,' and it will give it a tone of meaning and solid worth." He then offered his former scout some practical advice on recruiting:

> You will have to be very much on your guard against incorporating in your command deserters from other branches of the service. Insist upon the most unequivocal evidence of honorable discharge in all cases. Non-conscripts under and over age will be very advantageous. . . . As there is no time within which you are required to raise this command, you ought to be very fastidious in choosing your men, and make them always stand the test of battle and temptation to neglect duty before acceptance. . . . Your praise is on every lip, and the compliment the President has paid you is as marked as it is deserved.[16]

Things were finally falling into place for the lawyer-turned-soldier. He had at last attained status as an independent commander, and he now had his commission. He even had his family: in mid-March, Pauline and the children arrived in Fauquier, and were put up at James Hathaway's house.

Despite the presence of his family, Mosby did not remain idle after the capture of Stoughton. On St. Patrick's Day his local woodcutter-guide, John Underwood, led him through the pine forests along the Loudoun and Hampshire railroad, right to the rear of a new target—the Federal picket post at Herndon Station. It was his first attack in broad daylight. A Union dispatch tells what happened:

> On the 17th instant, at 1 P.M., the reserve picket post at Herndon Station, consisting of 25 men . . . , was surprised by Captain Mosby . . . and 21 of our men . . . captured. . . . The surprise was so complete that the men made but little or no resistance. The enemy . . . entered on foot by a bridle-path in rear of the post, capturing the vidette stationed on the road before he was able to give the alarm.[17]

Mosby lost not one of his forty men.

Prior to leaving the scene, the raiders noticed four officer's horses tethered outside the house of a known Union man, Nat

Hanna. A search of the house's lower floor revealed a finely laid table but nothing else of importance, except the strange absence of diners. As the Confederates harangued Mrs. Hanna about her friendship with Yankees, a group of searchers upstairs noticed a small door off the second floor, evidently the entry to a garret. Ames drew his revolver and kicked the door open. He then peeped carefully into the darkness, and called. Since there was no reply, he saw no harm in firing.

Now, magically, the room came alive with whispers. Three blue-coated officers advanced with their hands up, and just as they stooped to pass through the low doorway, a fourth man, as yet unseen, stepped on the plaster and plunged through the ceiling onto the Confederates below. With the lime dust and mortar brushed off, the unwilling acrobat was seen to be a major, and all—Yankees included—roared in approval of his spectacular entry.

Only one piece of business remained. "As we left the house," said Mosby, "the lunch disappeared with us."[18]

A week later the growing band struck again—near the Potomac, at Chantilly—but this time its retreat proved more devastating to the enemy than the attack had been. Mosby reported to Stuart:

> I did not succeed in gaining their rear . . . and only captured 4 or 5 videttes. It being late in the evening, and our horses very much jaded, I concluded to return. I had not gone over a mile back when we saw a large body of the enemy's cavalry, which, according to their own reports, numbered 200 men, rapidly pursuing. I feigned a retreat, desiring to draw them off from their camps. At a point where the enemy had blockaded the road with fallen trees I formed to receive them, for . . . I knew they would imagine themselves fallen into an ambuscade. When they had come within 100 yards of me, I ordered a charge, to which my men responded with a vim that swept everything before them. . . . It was more of a chase than a fight for 4 or 5 miles. . . . I did not have over 50 men with me.[19]

Mosby's ragtag band had for the first time routed a force four times its size, killing and wounding several. Without the loss of a single man it had taken thirty-five prisoners. The men were beginning to feel themselves unbeatable. "My success had been so uninterrupted," said Mosby, "that the men thought that victory was chained to my standard. Men who go into a fight under the influence of such feelings are next to invincible, and are generally victors before it begins."[20]

His intuition of the advantage of offensive action under almost any circumstance was being vindicated. "They had expected to see our backs," he said of this event, "and not our faces. It was a rule from which, during the war, I never departed, not to stand still and receive a charge, but always to act on the offensive."[21]

In this action Mosby had with him for the first time an English captain named Bradford Hoskins, already decorated for bravery in the Crimea and a veteran of Garibaldi's Sicilian campaign. Small and muscular, expert with the saber, Hoskins thoroughly enjoyed his introduction to service with Mosby, calling it "better than a fox chase."[22]

At the March 31 meeting at Rector's Cross Roads, Mosby was elated to see sixty-nine men, his largest contingent yet. What bothered him was that he knew no more than a dozen, and had no idea where the rest had come from. Despite his misgivings at operating with such a poorly organized and possibly uncontrollable mob, it was clear that he would have to use them if he meant to keep them. He therefore herded his crowd of hopefuls into the Fairfax forests, and with the help of Underwood, arrived without incident at a spot near Dranesville, westernmost of the Northern cavalry outposts.

Mosby had planned to strike the Yankee camp here, but was pleasantly surprised to see that his raids were already having the effect he'd predicted: the Yanks had dismantled the post and pulled it closer to Washington, behind the nearly uncrossable Difficult Run. The post at Herndon Station, he discovered, had also been moved back. Nothing could be done that day. Since it was late, and both men and horses were exhausted from forty miles of snow and mud, it was necessary to find forage for the animals and to put up for the night. By midnight, with horses fed and confined in a barnyard, the men were bedding down at Miskel's farm, a wedge of land formed by the juncture of Broad Run with the Potomac. Across the river in Maryland they could see Union campfires, but since neither these troops nor those on the Virginia side had been alerted to their presence—or so the men thought—all expected to pass the night safely.

As he knew almost no one in the group, Mosby was reluctant to command and did not order a guard set on the nearby Leesburg Pike. After a final check on the horses, all went to sleep.

At sunrise on April 1, Dick Moran, who had stayed with friends on the pike, came running pell-mell down the farm road, yelling in his foghorn voice: "The Yankees are coming! The Yankees are coming! Mount! Mount!" Mosby dashed from the farmhouse, buckling on his arms as he came, and sleepy men began tumbling from the hayloft and porches just in time to see 150 blue-clad troopers cantering down the long road from the turnpike, sabers unsheathed. They appeared to know exactly what they were there for.

The way to the pike was now blocked, deep streams lay on two sides of the farm, and nearly all the horses were without saddles or bridles. Mosby, not knowing whether anyone would listen, shouted to the men that they were to stand and fight, adding that they were to hold their fire for the moment and concentrate on getting as many horses bridled as possible. They were outnumbered by more than two to one, and trapped by the First Vermont Cavalry, under Capt. Henry C. Flint.

"As Capt. Flint dashed forward at the head of his squadron," wrote Mosby in later years, "their sabres flashing in the rays of the morning sun, I felt like my final hour had come. . . . In every sense, things looked rather blue for us."[23] Flint, confident of his game, divided the command, sending half around to the Confederates' rear, while half formed on their front. The soldiers in front, once through the farm gate, took care to lock it behind them, cutting off all escape to the pike. Troops on the Maryland side of the river began to cheer wildly at the lopsided affair they were about to witness. Flint took his time disposing his men. Mosby's party, only half of which was ready for a fight, continued feverishly to bridle horses in the barnyard.

"When I saw [him] divide his command," commented Mosby, "I knew that my chances had improved at least fifty percent. When he got to within fifty yards of the gate of the barnyard, I opened the gate and advanced, pistol in hand, on foot to meet him, and at the same time called to the men that had already got mounted to follow me."[24]

The men may have been new, but the effect was magical. "They responded with one of those demoniac yells," he continued, "which those who once heard never forgot and dashed forward . . . 'as reapers descend to the harvest of death.'" Harry Hatcher, one of Mosby's "regulars," leaped from a horse and threw Mosby up in his place. Suddenly a full-fledged rebel charge was on. "Unlike my adversaries," Mosby said, "I was trammelled with no tradition that required me to use an obsolete weapon." The revolvers proved devastating at close range. Flint was one of the first men killed, and the Federal troopers, armed largely with thin steel, started to fall back. A moment more and they wheeled, scrambling for the outer gate, which was, of course, locked. In the words of General Stahel: "They got wedged together, and a fearful state of confusion followed, while Mosby's men followed them up and poured into the crowd a severe fire. . . . In comparison to the number engaged, our loss was very heavy." Young Sam Chapman, a divinity student when he had answered Virginia's call to arms, had quickly emptied his two pistols. Saber in hand now, he was up in his stirrups and, as Mosby put it, "dealing [blows] right and left with . . . theological fervor." Other men, reins clenched in their teeth, were firing with both hands into the densely packed Yankees. When the gate finally fell, a great chase ensued. "I got pretty close to one," wrote Mosby, "who, seeing that he was bound to be shot or caught, jumped off his horse and sat down on the roadside. As I passed him he called out to me, 'You have played us a nice April fool, boys!'"[25]

Mosby, fifteen minutes earlier the outgunned and surprised underdog, had lost one man killed and three wounded. He took more than eighty prisoners, nearly a hundred fully equipped horses, and left two dozen dead or wounded Yankees strewn along several miles of slushy roadside. Stahel for his part was embarrassed, and chalked up the fiasco to "bad management on the part of the officers and the cowardice of the men."[26]

Three weeks later, when Mosby's account of this action was passed on to Secretary of War James A. Seddon, the Secretary scribbled across the bottom of the page: "Nominate as major if it has not been previously done."[27] Before April was out, Mosby had received his new commission.

The main attraction of service with Stuart's former scout was the opportunity of plunder—or at least of getting a horse—and once a man's cupidity had been satisfied he was likely to leave. Prior to forming his first company, Mosby never knew how many men were going to show up for a raid on a given date. The need to send escorts to Richmond with prisoners also cut into manpower. The men he attracted were an amalgam of soldiers home on furlough, deserters, discharged veterans, and wounded (some of whom arrived with crutches strapped to their saddles). Marylanders, not bound by laws affecting Confederate soldiers, made up a large part of Mosby's force; they braved Union pickets to swim the Potomac and find him. Both old men and boys came to him from their homes, as did infantrymen of all ages, anxious to try their hand at cavalry fighting.

Mosby needed these "conglomerates," as he called them, yet he held no illusions about their usual motivation or dependability. Of them he quipped, "They resemble the Democratic party at least in one particular, for they are held together by the cohesive power of public plunder."[28]

Despite Stuart's admonition about the type of man he ought to accept, Mosby generally took a practical view and didn't ask many questions, at least in the early days. Army commanders began to snipe at him for stealing their men, complaining to Lee and Stuart, and the broad margin of the partisan's life soon started to shrink. Mosby found this irritating, commenting later:

> Although a revolutionary government, none was ever so much under the domination of red tape as the one at Richmond. . . . When I received these complaints, which were sent through, but did not emanate from headquarters, I notified the men that they were forbidden any longer to assist me in destroying the enemy. . . . I always had a Confederate fire in my rear as well as that of the public enemy in my front.[29]

What made idealistic Confederate authorities most uncomfortable about permitting Mosby to operate was that, by so doing, they appeared to be sanctioning piracy. To Mosby, however—who seems never to have appropriated even a halter strap for himself—dangling the carrot of plunder was the only way he could hope to build manpower. He saw nothing reprehensible in this, or even illegal, since the Confederate Congress itself had, in the Partisan Ranger Act of April 1862, given its blessing to freebooting commands. Following his appointment as captain in March, and Stuart's warning to avoid partisan connotations, Mosby had snapped back: "The men who have joined me have done so under the impression that they are to be entitled to the privileges allowed in the Partisan Ranger Act. If they are to be denied them I cannot accept the appointment."[30]

Lee entered the discussion after Mosby had been appointed major, supporting Stuart. "No authority has been given to Major Mosby," he wrote, "to raise partisan troops. . . . He was commissioned . . . until he could organize companies that could be mustered regularly into the service."[31] Mosby was not satisfied with such a response, even from Lee. True to form, he took the matter to the top, in this case to the Secretary of War, who ruled that Major Mosby was in fact within his rights to recruit partisan troops.

Although objections were to be raised over and over during the war, Mosby stopped his ears. He had gotten the answer he wanted.

By the end of April, the 118,000-man Army of the Potomac, now under Maj. Gen. Joseph E. Hooker, was again in motion, and preparing to cross the Rappahannock—a small contingent below Fredericksburg this time, but the bulk of the army at the fords further upstream. By May 1 it had crossed and was locked in another titanic struggle with the much smaller forces of Lee and Jackson, awaiting it near a place called Chancellorsville.

On May 2, Stonewall Jackson, returning to his lines from a reconnaissance in the fading evening light, was felled with a single bullet fired by one of his own men. With his left arm amputated he could not command, and a few days later he contracted pneumonia and died. Into the breach stepped Stuart, taking command of Jackson's infantry and artillery in addition to his own cavalry. By May 5, the bungling Yankees had again been badly mauled.

Mosby, alerted in the waning days of April that Hooker was on the move, started toward the Rappahannock himself, planning to bite the enormous Union army in the rear with his eighty men. As the command hurried along the Fredericksburg Road from Warrenton shortly after daybreak on May 3, the roar of battle could be heard twenty miles off. But at this point an opportunity materialized closer at hand: a group of Yankee cavalrymen, evidently sent to guard the Orange and Alexandria railroad during the battle, could be seen relaxing around some houses not far from the tracks. They seemed unaware of the rebels' presence.

Instead of striking Hooker's rear, Mosby decided, he would attack this cavalry troop. The decision proved to be a mistake. "I committed a great error in allowing myself to be diverted by their presence from the purpose of my expedition," he later wrote.

They were perfectly harmless where they were, and could not help Hooker in the great battle then raging. I should, at least, have endeavored to avoid a fight by marching around them. If I had succeeded in destroying them all, it would hardly have been the equivalent of the damage I might have done to Hooker by appearing at United States ford during the agony of the fight. There all of his wagons were packed. It would be difficult to calculate the demoralizing effect of the news on his army that the enemy was in their rear, and their trains and rations were burning up.[32]

It was a bright, warm morning, and the Union troopers were stretched out on the grass, enjoying the sun. Their horses, haltered only, were grazing on the young spring clover. When Mosby's men cantered into the clearing, three hundred yards away, the Yankees scarcely looked up, taking the newcomers for Union cavalry—that is, until the rebel yell was raised and the horsemen began their charge. Many of the startled soldiers at once dove into a frame building nearby and opened fire on the approaching cavalry. Mosby ordered his men to charge the house and jumped into the thick of the attack himself. "I came up just in front of two windows by the chimney," he said, "from which a hot fire was poured that brought down several men by my side. But I paid them back with interest when I got to the window, into which I emptied two Colt's revolvers. The house was as densely packed as a sardine box; and it was almost impossible to fire into it without hitting somebody."[33]

Sam Chapman and others broke down the door, and all on the first floor threw down their arms and came out. The men on the second floor continued to blaze away, but they too surrendered shortly after Mosby ordered hay to be banked around the house and lighted. As the place threatened to become an inferno, white flags and heads of coughing men began to issue from the windows above. The remainder of the Yankees now stumbled out, choking from the thick smoke, their hands in the air, their feet slipping on the bloodied floor.

Here everything came unglued. A detachment of the Fifth New York Cavalry had heard gunfire, and was trotting over to investigate. Mosby's force, engaged in rounding up the Yankee horses and stray cavalrymen, was by this time scattered and in no condition to meet a threat. It became every man for himself, and the rebels took off in all directions. At this time, said Mosby, his command was "a mere aggregation of men casually gathered, belonging to many different regiments," who happened to be in those parts. "Of course," he explained, "such a body has none of the cohesion and discipline that springs from organization, no matter how brave the men may be individually."[34]

It was a rout—Mosby's first. He lost one man killed and twenty captured.

In the following days Mosby's chastened band occupied itself with burning railroad bridges on the Orange and Alexandria (again strongly guarded), and in other forms of harassment; but Mosby was beginning to feel that something new was needed. "I found out," he said,

> . . . the difficulty of making any impression with my small command on the force guarding the road. I could keep them

on the watch, and in a state of anxiety and alarm; but, while this might satisfy Stuart and Gen. Lee, the men on whom I had to depend to do the work would not be content with such results. In order to retain them, it was necessary for me to stimulate their enthusiasm with something more tangible. War to them was not an abstraction; it meant prisoners, arms, horses and sutler's stores; remote consequences were not much considered.[35]

On May 19 he sent Fount Beattie to Stuart with a request for a mountain howitzer.

As Lee, shadowed by Hooker, began his great arc west and northward that was to culminate in Gettysburg, Mosby made plans to offer Hooker some distraction by blowing a locomotive off the tracks behind his army.

By May 29 he had his gun: a light, bronze-barreled cannon with 2⅝-inch bore, Richmond-made, but captured from the Yanks the previous year at Ball's Bluff. After a day of target practice in Fauquier, he set out with the new weapon, fifteen rounds of grape and cannister shot, and about forty men, to penetrate Hooker's thick curtain of infantry and cavalry drawn up about the railroad between Manassas and Catlett's Station. Getting into these lines was to prove considerably easier than getting out.

Although Yankee camps were closely spaced along the railroad, the men succeeded in slipping between two of them, and spent the night of May 29 in the pines along the track. They intended to hit the first train out of Manassas in the morning. When dawn broke, a few men were sent into the open to cut the telegraph wire and pry a rail out, while Sam Chapman, an experienced artillerist, worked in the pines setting up the howitzer. The man who crouched by the railroad to warn of the approaching train had not long to wait. Scrambling up the embankment just before the target came puffing into view, he dashed into the pines and Chapman rammed home a charge.

The locomotive hit the loosened rail, veered off the track, and ground to a halt on the roadbed, wallowing helplessly. As the infantry guard piled out, firing on reflex into the woods, Chapman sent a charge of grape into the cars and Mosby ordered the men forward. The effect was electric: the infantrymen nearly trampled one another in an effort to reach the pines on the other side of the tracks. Chapman sent a shell through the engine's boiler now, and the escaping steam created a hellish din. In a moment the attackers had scattered hay bales about and set the train afire, taking off what they could in the process, including several small barrels of fresh shad destined for the front. A few U.S. Mail bags were thrown out of the burning cars, lashed hurriedly to the howitzer carriage, and with the gun made ready, the men now bent their efforts to escape.

"I have been criticized a good deal at the North," said Mosby of this event, "for capturing trains on railroads used for military purposes. . . . There was nobody but soldiers on this train, but," he continued, with his frequently surprising directness, "if there had been women and children, too, it would have been all the same to me. Those who travel on a road running through a military district must accept the risk of the accidents of war. It does not hurt people any more to be killed in a railroad wreck than having their heads knocked off by a cannon shot."[36]

As the raiders hurried through the woods, the howitzer bouncing along behind a careening team, a long drum roll was spreading through the surrounding Union camps and bugles were calling Yankee troopers to horse. The men very soon found their way barred by a contingent of the Fifth New York. Chapman responded by quickly unlimbering and lobbing a shell into the party, by luck killing the commanding officer's horse. The Yankees stampeded in their efforts to escape.

Mosby continued his retreat, which for the moment had all the character of an advance. "It would, of course, have been easy to save ourselves by scattering through the woods," he said, "but I was fighting on a point of honor. I wanted to save the howitzer, or, if I had to lose it, I was determined to exact all that it was worth in blood."[37]

The broken New York regiment quickly re-formed and pursued, emboldened now by the knowledge that they were facing a small force. Chapman dampened their zeal with another shell. Mosby then ordered Chapman to move on ahead through the woods with the gun. He himself, with six men,

would hang on the edge of the wood to slow up the pursuit.
After this the gun would be positioned for a stand.

Clouds of cavalry began to appear. As the small Confederate rearguard retreated along the woods road, the Yankee advance suddenly lunged forward. After a fierce hand-to-
hand the pursuers were driven back, but when the smoke had
cleared, Bradford Hoskins was discovered by the roadside in
a pool of blood. Since it was impossible either to stay with the
Englishman or to carry him off, Mosby ordered him left
where he was, and all galloped away.

Hoskins died at a nearby farmhouse two days later.

Mosby sent word to Chapman now to halt and unlimber at
the head of a narrow lane on a hillside ahead, a lane hemmed
in on both sides by high fences. It was a position approach-
able from only one direction. "I knew," he said, "we could
hold the position as long as the ammunition lasted for the
gun." By the time the Yankees again came into view, preparations were complete, and Chapman, Beattie, and R. P.
Montjoy had taken their places by the gun, waiting. "Their
faces beamed with what the Romans called the *gaudia cer-
taminis*," Mosby said, "and they had never looked so happy
in their lives. As for myself, realizing the desperate straits we
were in, I wished I was somewhere else."[38]

When the Federal cavalry came within two hundred yards,
they were again sent flying by Chapman. They re-formed and
came up once more, now in a tight, suicidal column, four
abreast between the fences. Chapman raked them with cannister and grape. As the Yankees fled to regroup, the rebels
charged them, then backed up to cover the gun again.

"At last," said Mosby, "the supreme moment came. Chapman had rammed home his last round . . . and a heavy column was again advancing. I sat on my horse just behind the
gun; when they got within 50 yards, it again belched with fire
and knocked down a number of men and horses in their
front."[39]

With the Yankees halted, Mosby again ordered a charge. It
seems, however, that his horse had had enough, for the animal drove headlong through the Federal cavalry totally out of
control. Speed, however, proved insufficient protection for its
rider. "As I passed by a big cavalryman," said Mosby, "he

struck me a blow with his sabre on the shoulder that nearly knocked me from my seat. At the same instant my pistol flashed, and he reeled from his saddle."[40]

All but the gun crew had left off protecting the now-useless gun, and the Yankees made a dash at it. Montjoy was captured at the gun, but only after having fired his last cartridge. Chapman, swinging the rammer like a madman, fell with a bullet through the thigh. The howitzer was taken, and it became every man for himself. Mosby, crashing through the woods with his aching shoulder, striving desperately to control his horse, was nearly knocked out of the saddle again by the tremendous blow of a tree limb that bloodied his face.

No further pursuit was made.

Stuart, when he heard of the affair, wrote Mosby that he might sell a gun for so high a price any time he wished.

The battalion returned to Fauquier to lick its wounds. After a brief foray into Fairfax, during Lee's and Hooker's adagio advance northward, Mosby spent a day or so with his wife and children at James Hathaway's house. On the night of June 8 he was nearly captured here by a detachment of the First New York, which crashed into his bedroom. Had the Yankees looked in the walnut tree whose branches reached the open bedroom window, they'd have saved themselves nearly two years of further headaches, but they did not. After a fruitless discussion with an indignant Pauline, up to her neck in bedcovers, they left, taking Hathaway and several stolen Yankee horses with them.

Since Mosby was forbidden to accept men subject to regular army conscription, it had taken him over two months to reach the legal minimum for a company: sixty men. By early June, however, he had the requisite number enrolled, and a headquarters officer arrived at Rector's Cross Roads to witness the company's swearing in and the election of officers. He had come to witness a charade. "In compliance with the law," wrote Mosby, "I had to go through the form of an election. But I really appointed the officers, and told the men to vote for them. This was my rule as long as I had a command, and with two or three exceptions their conduct vindicated my judgment."[41] What the headquarters man reported about these "elections" can only be conjectured.

With his newly formed Forty-third Battalion Partisan Rangers, Mosby headed now across the Potomac for a raid at Seneca Mills, Maryland. But it was an ill-starred day, for one of his brand-new lieutenants, George Whitescarver, was killed there.

Lee meanwhile continued northward, and Mosby recalled: "I had no positive knowledge of the intention of Gen. Lee to invade the North, but all signs pointed that way. First came the news of Milroy's rout by Ewell at Winchester. As I was looking for Stuart every day, I made no more raids that week, but held my men ready to do any work that he wanted."[42]

Lt. Gen. Richard S. Ewell, with an entire corps, was moving very fast. After capturing 4,000 to 5,000 of Robert Milroy's force at Winchester, he crossed the Potomac on June 15. Lee, with James Longstreet's and A. P. Hill's corps, followed more slowly down the Valley, halting for an entire week while Stuart got into position east of the Blue Ridge—Stuart's task being to keep Federal eyes away from the rebel operation. Hooker formed a third line, interposing himself between Stuart and Washington.

Lincoln was furious with Hooker for not forcing Lee to a stand. "If the head of Lee's army is at Martinsburg and the tail of it . . . between Fredericksburg and Chancellorsville," he remarked, "the animal must be very slim somewhere. Could you not break him?"[43] He reminded Hooker that Lee's army, not Richmond, was now his true objective.

As Ewell was crossing the Potomac, Stuart, with 5,000 men, was fording the Rappahannock, and by June 16 had arrived at Kitty Shacklett's house at Piedmont Station, Fauquier. Mosby met him there early on the morning of the seventeenth. After a warm reunion (they had not seen one another in three months), Mosby—noting that Stuart "was mounted on a very indifferent horse"—amused his commander by presenting him with a fine animal which he claimed to have recently acquired from a Michigan lieutenant.[44] He told Stuart what he knew of Hooker's movements and arranged to meet him again in Middleburg later that day.

In the afternoon, Blackford was with Stuart when Mosby appeared and recorded his impressions of a changed friend:

> Mosby by this time had become famous. I had not seen him for more than a year and the change in his appearance was striking. When he was a member of my company and afterwards when he became Adjutant of our regiment . . . he was careless about his dress and mount and presented anything but a soldierly appearance. As we were riding along the road at the head of the column one evening we saw a horseman, handsomely dressed, gallop across the field towards us and lift his horse lightly over the fence a short distance ahead, and approach us. I could scarcely believe my eyes when I recognized in this dashing looking officer my old friend and the now celebrated guerrilla chief, Mosby. He . . . was fully posted as to the movements of the enemy.[45]

After a short conference with Stuart at which he was forced to endure some *sotto voce* jibes about the appearance of his rough-looking followers, Mosby took three dozen of his toughest and headed into the middle of Hooker's army.

"My command," he wrote,

> was now . . . environed on all sides by the camps of [Hooker's] different corps. Along the pike a continuous stream of troops, with all the impedimenta of war, poured along. Taking three men with me . . . I rode out into the column of Union troops as they passed along. As it was dark, they had no suspicion who we were, although we were all dressed in full Confederate uniform. A man by the name of Birch lived in a house near the roadside, and I discovered three horses standing at his front gate, with a man holding them. . . . I was sure that he was an orderly, and that they were officers' horses. We rode up, and asked him to whom they belonged. He replied that they were Maj. Stirling's and Capt. Fisher's and that they were just from Gen. Hooker's headquarters.[46]

The four Confederates must have smiled in the dark.

Mosby called the orderly, an Irishman, over to him. Upon reaching his side, the man found himself seized roughly by the collar and heard the whispered message: "You are my prisoner. My name is Mosby." The Irishman did not immediately see the pistol in the dark, and may also have been a little hard of hearing, for he became indignant.

"My name is *not* Mosby, ye blitherin' idiot," he cried. "I'm as good a Union man as ye are!"

"You're the very sort I'm after," answered the man in the saddle, without relinquishing his hold. Just then the two officers left the house, chatting. Mosby at once saluted and engaged them in friendly conversation, while two of his men advanced, hands extended to accept the officers' sidearms. The officers, thinking the men were somehow acquaintances, offered their hands in return. When they saw the revolvers now leveled at them from all sides and realized what had happened, they burst out laughing.

"I asked them what they were laughing at," said Mosby. "They said they had laughed so much about their people being gobbled up by me that they were now enjoying the joke . . . on themselves."[47] With the pleasantries behind them, and the party disarmed and mounted, Mosby got around to asking about the dispatches he knew they carried. The papers were readily turned over. After stopping to read them, Mosby sent them off to Stuart with Norman Smith.

While Gen. Alfred Pleasonton, with a greatly improved Union cavalry, was pressing Stuart back against the Blue Ridge—Stuart resisting with the most inspired cavalry fighting of his career—Mosby traveled freely between Stuart's and Hooker's camps, disrupting Northern supply lines and soaking up intelligence. On the twenty-second he stumbled into a devastating ambush prepared by Gen. George Meade, who had acted on a tip about his comings and goings between the lines. Several men were wounded in the surprise attack: Montjoy had a finger shot off, Charlie Hall took a ball in the shoulder, and John Ballard lost a leg. Mosby himself was unhurt.

On the rainy afternoon of the twenty-third he was alone behind Hooker's lines, and, on his way out, happened upon two cherry-picking Yankee cavalrymen, easily captured. Tying the heads of the men's horses together, he led them off in the drizzle, intending to take the pike to Bull Run Mountain, where he would then slip into Confederate lines by a hidden path. When he reached the pike, however, he found it filled with a mile-long column of Union wagons, with strong cavalry guard. "I was anxious to get to Stuart that night," he said,

and knew that if I waited for the train to pass, it would be dark, and I could not find the mountain path. So I drew my pistol, held it under cover, and told my prisoners that if they spoke a word they would be dead men. I then rode, with them by my side, through a gap in the fence into the pike, right among the Union cavalry. We could not cross over at that point, as the fence on the other side of the road was too high for our horses to leap. We went along for 200 yards . . . through the wagon train and cavalry escort, until we got to a road leading away from the pike. Here we turned off. The gum cloth I had over my shoulders to protect me from the rain, as it did not cover one-third of my body, did not conceal the uniform I wore. I had ridden through the ranks of a column of Union cavalry in broad daylight, with two prisoners, and my elbow had actually struck against one as I passed. . . . Early the next morning I was again at Stuart's headquarters.[48]

By Sunday, the twenty-first, Pleasonton had succeeded in backing Stuart up against the Blue Ridge, and in finally getting a look at Lee's army, resting at Berryville. The fighting on this day had been especially fierce and destructive around Middleburg and Upperville, as indicated by the account of James Williamson, one of Mosby's rangers:

On the morning after the fight . . . , white men and negroes were engaged in burying the dead. One poor fellow lay in a fence corner, his brains spattered over the rails, while another had one-half of his head carried away by a shell. . . . In one field, . . . where Stuart made a desperate charge to save his train of wagons and ambulances, I counted 31 dead horses. The ground in many places was torn up in great holes and furrows by shot and shell. Roads through the fields in all directions, and big gaps in the stone fences, showed where the cavalry and artillery had ploughed through. The country around presented a scene of desolation; wheat fields trodden down and cornfields in many places looking as though they had never been planted. A poor horse that had had one of its hind legs shot away had grazed around in a circle. I thought it an act of mercy to put a ball through the head of the suffering creature.[49]

After observing Lee, Pleasonton retired to Aldie, taking no further offensive action.

Here began the chain of events that was to cloud Stuart's name forever, and to occupy Mosby's attention for many years. Stuart, who did not arrive at Gettysburg until after the battle had started, was blamed by many for the Southern defeat, and Mosby was to spend much of his life defending him against this charge—taking his defense, in the words of one critic, "beyond sound argument."[50]

Lee had written to Stuart on the twenty-third his preference that the cavalry cross into Maryland from the Shenandoah Valley, west of the Blue Ridge. But he had added:

> You will however be able to judge whether you can pass around their army without hinderance [*sic*], doing them all the damage you can, and cross the river east of the mountains. In either case, after crossing the river, you must move on and feel the right of Ewell's troops, collecting information, provisions, etc. . . . I think the sooner you cross into Maryland, after tomorrow, the better.[51]

Early on the morning of the twenty-fourth, Mosby arrived from Hooker's camps and reported to Stuart that the Yankees were not moving, and that it would therefore be an easy thing to pass through their camps *east* of the mountains and cross the Potomac ahead of them. Stuart immediately sent his reply to Lee. "I was at headquarters," noted Mosby,

> when Stuart wrote his last dispatch to Lee, informing him of the route he would go, and sat by him when he was writing it—in fact, I dictated a large part of it. I had just returned from a scout inside the enemy's lines and brought the intelligence that induced Stuart to undertake to pass through them. I remember that Fitz Lee and Hampton came into the room while we were writing.[52]

Stuart, planning to take three of his five brigades with him, arranged to meet Mosby behind Hooker's lines on the twenty-fifth, when Mosby would take command of his advance through the Northern camps and then into Maryland. The other two brigades would be detailed to hold the Blue Ridge passes until the main army had crossed the river, and thereafter be governed by Lee.

With Fitz Lee's, W. H. F. Lee's, and Hampton's brigades (some 2,000 men in all), Stuart started eastward in the morning darkness of June 25, expecting to rendezvous with Mosby, pass through Hooker's army, and cross the Potomac that night. No one—including Mosby—knew that Hooker's army would start moving that day.

What Stuart actually encountered was not an army in camp but Hancock's corps on the march northward, filling the road that he had to cross. After throwing some shells at the Northerners, he resigned himself to circling around behind them, then striking for the Potomac obliquely, heading almost directly southeast.

He did not reach Maryland till 3:00 A.M. on June 28, when Lee was already at Chambersburg; and he never connected with Mosby, who eventually crossed the river from the Shenandoah Valley.

For two days Stuart frolicked through the lush Maryland countryside, parading, pillaging, and generally throwing panic into the Federal government, which saw an attack upon Washington as a distinct possibility. During several days the government's communication with the Union army was cut, Washington was isolated, and Stuart's rambunctious column attracted more attention than Lee's army in the Cumberland Valley. Stuart at length arrived in Pennsylvania encumbered with hundreds of prisoners, 125 wagons, 900 mules, mountains of forage, bacon, hams, and sugar, and gallons of whiskey.

Mosby, with no hope of finding him in the confusion, crossed into Maryland on July 1 with a handful of men, and did his best to find Lee in southern Pennsylvania. Unsuccessful, he gathered up some fat Yankee livestock and returned to his Virginia haunts. He had no idea of the great tragedy being enacted at that moment on a field in Gettysburg.

It started to rain on July 4, and did not let up for ten days. Lee's macerated army began limping back to the rising Potomac fords, which they did not enter until the night of the thirteenth, near the height of the flooding. But Meade—who had now replaced Hooker—was following. At some risk, therefore, the tottering columns began to move across, some on pontoons at Falling Waters, others struggling, single file, through the swift, wide water at Williamsport, their hundreds of shiny musket barrels illuminated by great bonfires on the shore. Lee then withdrew slowly southward to the old Rappahannock line, with Meade shadowing him across Loudoun and Fauquier. Like Hooker, however, Meade lacked an instinct for the jugular, and by midsummer 1863 the Army of Northern Virginia lay safely behind the Rappahannock, with the Army of the Potomac entrenched along the Orange and Alexandria.

Nothing had changed, except for the 51,000 Americans killed, wounded, or captured at Gettysburg.

In the wake of Gettysburg, Mosby set up his command in the middle of Meade's army and entered into a period of pillaging and old-fashioned rustling that infuriated Northern commanders and mystified his own. Brig. Gen. George Armstrong Custer in late July got up a force of three hundred picked men to "capture Mosby or drive him out of the country."[53] Col. Charles R. Lowell, Jr., nephew of James Russell Lowell, scoured the sweltering countryside for him in July and August.

To cope with Mosby's depradations, Lowell proposed the establishment of a regular cavalry escort of thirty to fifty men for all sutlers' wagons moving between Alexandria and Centreville—"all sutlers and stray wagons to be halted and compelled to come with this escort"—and by August 20, Meade had ordered the plan put into effect.[54] In retaliation for Confederates' lack of respect for paroles, and for the "bushwhacking" that was keeping the Yankees close to their camps, Custer—his hands still bound by tradition—hinted at the need for reevaluation of traditional measures. "I can suppress bushwhacking," he told Pleasonton on August 13, "and render every man within the limits of my command practically loyal, if allowed to deal with them as I choose."[55]

Mosby's pillaging not only aroused Northern commanders; it displeased Lee as well. Bothered by the reports of wagon-stealing and by his suspicion that Mosby was starting to attract a near-criminal element, Lee scribbled on Mosby's August 4 report: "I greatly commend Major Mosby for his boldness and good management. I fear he exercises but little control over his men. . . . His attention has been more directed toward the capture of wagons than military damage to the enemy."[56] On the same day he continued in a critical vein to Stuart:

I have heard that [Mosby] has now with him a large number of men, yet his expeditions are undertaken with very few, and his attention seems more directed to the capture of sutlers' wagons, etc., than to the injury of the enemy's communications and outposts. The capture and destruction of wagon trains is advantageous, but the supply of the Federal Army is carried on by the railroad. If that should be injured, it would cause him to detach largely for its security, and thus weaken his main army. . . .

I do not know the cause for undertaking his expeditions with so few men, whether it is from policy or the difficulty of collecting them. I have heard of his men, among them officers, being in the rear of this army selling captured goods, sutlers' stores, etc. This had better be attended to. . . . It has also been reported to me that many deserters from this army have joined him. . . . If this is true, I am sure it must be without the knowledge of Major Mosby, but I desire you to call his attention to this matter, to prevent his being imposed on.[57]

A dispatch sent on the same day from Secretary of War James Seddon to the commandant at Charlottesville indicated broader suspicion that Mosby's men were taking advantage of their position. It quoted a newspaper article to the effect that Mosby's rangers had just earned a tidy $30,000 by the sale of Yankee plunder in Charlottesville. "You are requested to inquire whether such sale was made," wrote Seddon, "and to report the facts to the Department."[58]

It is not known what Mosby's immediate reaction to this criticism was, for a few days later, during an attempt to relieve the Thirteenth New York Cavalry of a drove of horses near Billy Gooding's tavern in Fairfax, he was shot. Lt. Thomas Turner took command as Mosby, wounded in the leg and side, was spirited away to his parents' home—Idle Wilde, near Lynchburg. Pauline, again pregnant, had left northern Virginia for Idle Wilde only days before, but by now had gone on to Kentucky. She did not return to her in-laws' until September 2.

Mosby thrived on being home. In a diary entry for August 31, his mother noted: "Jno doing very well and very cheerful. He laughs, talks, and eats all the time." On September 1: "Jno has been sitting in the passage listening to the music." And on September 6, after Pauline's arrival: "Jno is walking all about the yard, though his wounds are still quite sore. We all enjoy being together very much."[59] During his two weeks at home he convinced his mother to let his eighteen-year-old brother, Willie, join his command, and by late October—to Virginia Mosby's great sorrow—Willie, too, had left for northern Virginia.

Mosby wasted little time in convalescing. After a week in Richmond he returned to Fauquier, and was back in the saddle by September 20. A week later he slipped into Alexandria with half a dozen men and succeeded in kidnapping the aide to the Federal governor of Virginia, a Colonel Dulaney, who had made the simple mistake of answering his front door when Mosby knocked. Dulaney's son, French, was in Mosby's command at the time, and was part of this mission. After Dulaney senior had been escorted by Mosby himself to Richmond's Libby Prison, Mosby recounted the meeting between father and son in a letter to Pauline:

> It was quite an amusing scene, the interview between Colonel Dulaney and his son. Just as we were about leaving the Colonel sarcastically remarked to his son that he had an old pair of shoes he had better take, as he reckoned they were darned scarce in the Confederacy, whereupon the son, holding up his leg, which was encased in a fine pair of cavalry boots just captured from a sutler, asked the old man what he thought of that.[60]

On the way back to Fauquier his men found the time to splash turpentine over the railroad bridge spanning Cameron Run, and—directly under the guns of two forts—ignite it, leaving it a web of charcoal.

In his September report, Mosby took to the defense of his

methods, maintaining to Stuart: "The military value of the species of warfare I have waged is not measured by the number of prisoners and material of war captured from the enemy, but by the heavy detail it has already compelled him to make, and which I hope to make him increase, . . . to guard his communications, and to that extent diminishing his aggressive strength."[61] In endorsing the report, Stuart took up the cudgels for Mosby: "The capture of . . . prominent Union officials as well as the destruction of bridges, trains, etc., was the subject of special instructions which he is faithfully carrying out."[62]

Lee and Seddon seemed mollified. Mosby had spoken to both men on his trip to Richmond after the Dulaney capture, and he reported to Pauline that both were highly pleased with him.

If there had been some softening of Lee's feeling, sentiment among the Yankees was growing for concerted action—both against guerrillas and against the citizens who harbored them. Col. Horace B. Sargent, of the First Massachusetts Cavalry, complained to headquarters in early September:

> Tonight . . . there is not an armed rebel. . . . Tomorrow the woods may be full of them. A policy of extermination alone can achieve the end expected. Every man and horse must be sent within the lines, every house destroyed, every tree girdled and set on fire, before we can approach security against the secret combination of a sudden force within musket range of our outposts. Attila, King of the Huns, adopted the only method that can exterminate these citizen soldiers. . . . I can clear this country with fire and sword, and no mortal can do it in any other way. The attempt to discriminate nicely between the just and the unjust is fatal to our safety.[63]

On October 28, Maj. Gen. Henry Halleck, general-in-chief of Union armies, commented bitterly:

> Most of these difficulties are caused by the . . . pretended noncombatant inhabitants of the country. They pretend to act the part of neutrals, but do not. They give aid, shelter, and concealment to guerrilla and robber bands like that of Mosby, who are continually destroying our roads, burning our bridges,

and capturing wagon trains. . . . Men who act in this manner
. . . within our lines, have, under the laws of civilized war,
forfeited their lives.[64]

By early October Mosby had attracted enough of the type
men he needed to form a second company, and by December,
enough for a third. He had increasing difficulty in keeping out
unsavory types such as Lewis Powell, for example (known as
Lewis Payne when hanged for his part in the Lincoln assassination), who joined him during this period. He had to
work continually at weeding out this element, his usual remedy being to send the man directly to the regular army. He
made an effort to know the name, face, and general character
of every man in the command.

Although for the most part good fighting men, his rangers
were, in some ways, the "featherbed soldiers" they were accused of being. They were strangers to camp routine. They
slept not outdoors but in comfortable quarters provided by a
sympathetic populace. They seldom even made coffee for
themselves, let alone fried bacon, soaked hardtack, or washed
a shirt. Most couldn't pitch a tent and didn't know the first
thing about cavalry drill. "The truth is," said John Alexander,
a ranger himself, "we were an undisciplined lot. During . . .
my service I learned but four commands—fall in and count
off by fours, march, close up, and charge."[65]

"There was another movement," he added, "with which we
were not altogether unfamiliar, an order technically known as
the 'skedaddle,' but I never heard the command given. The
Rangers seemed to know instinctively when that movement
was appropriate, and never waited for the word."[66] In fact, it
was the rangers' very lack of regimentation that made them
successful; they were encouraged to think for themselves.

Boarding with local families made for as many obligations
as privileges. Off-duty rangers were, in the Southern tradition, expected to act as gentlemen, and their commander
made it clear that violations of this trust would receive his
personal attention. A man who broke into a Quaker milk-
house was sent immediately to the regular army, despite the
intercession of his astounded captain.

Mosby extended his rule from the military into the civil

sphere, playing judge and jury to an assortment of deserters, blockade runners, looters, cutthroats, and other disreputable characters who were blossoming in the absence of stable government. His men were instructed simply to shoot rustlers without debate, and strangers in "Mosby's Confederacy" were required to show evidence of legitimate business. He also rigidly enforced conscription for the regular army.

If the success of the Forty-third Battalion Partisan Rangers was founded ultimately upon the sympathy of the people, it was more immediately rooted in the men's expertise with firearms. With all ammunition supplied by the Federal government, target practice cost nothing but time, and most men became dead shots. A favorite exercise was to try to fire three bullets into a tree while riding past at full gallop. "This deadly aptness with the revolver," commented Alexander,

> not only reacted on our men and gave them nerve and self-confidence, but it increased their efficiency and formidability to a degree that one can scarcely appreciate. . . . It is one thing to shoot for the purpose of making smoke and noise, to shoot at random, or automatically in volleys; it is an awfully different thing to shoot to kill. Believe me, a calm, cool "dead-shot" behind a Colt's revolver or a Spencer repeating rifle has more moral force than a gatling gun. The average soldier has an unconquerable prejudice against a pistol which he knows is going to hit somebody when it goes off.[67]

Many of Mosby's soldiers were young—teenagers, or men just out of their teens. The older men in the command were for the most part veterans of regular service; a number of them were former officers, who preferred serving as a private under a man like Mosby to retaining a commission in a more bureaucratic setting. "Captains," said Alexander, "were about as plentiful in our command as colonels are . . . in civil life. . . . One can hardly estimate the benefits which the discipline and experience of this class of men brought to our band of amateur soldiers."[68]

All the professionalism at Mosby's disposal, however, was to prove insufficient in preventing a serious setback shortly after New Year's, 1864.

Despite the wave of cold air and succession of ice storms that

had trumpeted in the New Year, whip-tough Maryland cavalry under Maj. Henry A. Cole had stayed outdoors, looking
for guerrillas. On New Year's Day they'd cornered their
quarry at Rectortown, Fauquier County. Although outnum-
bering the rebels two to one, however, Cole had lost over half
his eighty-man force in the blazing gunfight that followed, and
the rest had been chased without dignity back to camp. The
force that had routed the Marylanders was commanded by
Mosby's right-hand man, veteran cavalry officer Capt. William R. Smith of Company B.

About a week after this event Mosby was approached by
Frank Stringfellow, one of Stuart's scouts, with a proposal
that he and Mosby team up to attack Cole's regiment in its
camp on a bluff near the juncture of the Shenandoah with the
Potomac. Stringfellow had been scouting the area, he said,
and the job looked easy. The camp could be approached from
the rear, near the Potomac, without disturbing the pickets,
who guarded only the road in front. The attack could be made
at night, when all were asleep.

Mosby said yes, and two nights later, in the cold starlight,
he took the lead of a hundred-man column of blanket-
swathed rebel horsemen, plodding northward along dimly
outlined roads toward Harpers Ferry. Stringfellow and his ten
men were to meet them close to the Yankee camp. The mer-
cury hovered near zero, and many rangers rode with reins
gripped between teeth and hands buried in clothing or beneath saddle blankets. Others had dismounted, to trot alongside the column until feeling returned to their feet. The horses
snorted hot vapor, and the sound of their hooves was muffled
by nearly a foot of powdery snow.

After a two-hour stop at Woodgrove, home of ranger
Henry Heaton, the riders continued, arriving at the Potomac
in the early hours of Sunday morning. The men had still not
been told the nature of their mission. Stringfellow materialized out of the trees now, and led them along the Potomac
to a path running up the steep side of Loudoun Heights. After
ordering his men to dismount and prepare to climb the
wooded cliff single file, Mosby informed them that the path
would bring them into the rear of a cavalry camp, and that
they were to wait on top until told what to do. Leading their

horses, the men began the climb, pulling themselves up the icy path by grasping at trees and bushes. Stringfellow and his few men disappeared as mysteriously as they had come, their mission to surround Cole's cabin and seize him before Mosby struck.

Mosby, on top now, told Smith to hurry the men along—all had to be in position before Stringfellow started. Montjoy was sent back with six men to take the pickets on the road, before they could rouse the garrison at Harpers Ferry, less than a mile away.

A squad of dismounted men began to spread out among the tents of the sleeping troopers, while the remainder labored up the cliff to take positions. Mosby was at the edge of the bluff, hurrying each man to his assignment as he arrived. Suddenly, with more than half the attackers still strung out on the cliffside, a terrific uproar was heard from the direction String-fellow had taken. In a moment mounted soldiers could be seen galloping through the dim light toward Mosby's men, firing and yelling. Smith and Turner, unable to identify the attackers in the dark, shouted: "Charge them, boys, charge them!" and all opened fire on the approaching horsemen, wounding several of what turned out to be Stringfellow's force.

The thirty men on top, thoroughly disconcerted, now began firing in every direction, riddling the Yankee tents with bullets. Smith was shouting: "Give the damned Yankees no quarter! Shoot every damned son of a bitch down and secure the horses!" Terrified soldiers within the tents rolled out of their cots screaming: "We surrender, we surrender! The camp is yours. Stop! Stop firing!"

When the firing began, the pickets had galloped off to Harpers Ferry to sound the alarm; Montjoy had not managed to reach them in time. In five minutes the road would be alive with Yankee infantry.

As the two hundred frightened troopers started to poke their heads out of the tents, they saw the size of the attacking force. Rallied by a young captain named Vernon, many grabbed their carbines and dashed from their tents, first in twos and threes, then in larger groups. They ran barefoot and half naked over the icy ground to take refuge behind a thick growth of frozen bushes higher up, from where they began to rake the attackers with a murderous fire.

So stiff had the resistance suddenly become that the men still on the mountainside refused even to enter the camp. With the signal cannon at Harpers Ferry booming now, Mosby called loudly for retreat. A blistering fire continued from the defenders, who were shooting from every corner of the camp—from behind tent flaps, through the doors and windows of an old cabin, out of small trees and bushes—shooting at anything that moved. Men all over were crumpling in black heaps upon the snow. Charlie Paxson fell, then Henry Edmunds and Lieutenant Turner. Shrieks issued from tents as bullets, whistling everywhere, found unintended marks. Balls threw up chunks of frozen earth in every direction. Men stood nearly toe to toe in the weak starlight, firing at one another, each calling for the other's surrender.

As the invaders inched backward to the edge of the camp, firing as they went, William Chapman (Sam's brother), Captain Smith, and one or two other mounted men were still careening around amid the tents. Smith, revolver in hand, rode past a soldier sprawled upon a patch of blood-darkened snow, paying no attention until he heard the cry: "Boys, for God's sake don't leave me here!" It was Paxson. Smith wheeled, tried to pull Paxson up onto his own horse, but without success, then sent another rider, John Tyler Grayson, for a horse. Chapman was nearby, and described the confusion that followed Grayson's departure:

A few seconds after he left there was a shot fired at us from a group not twenty steps distant. Capt. Smith and I returned the fire, and then a volley was fired at us. The flash from the volley for a moment blinded me and a feeling of thankfulness that we had escaped, possessed me, when suddenly Smith leaped upward from the saddle and fell on the right side of his horse, . . . both feet hung in the stirrups with his head on the snow. I sprung from my horse and asked him how he was shot, but he gave no reply. I endeavored to lift him into the saddle but he was too heavy for me. I . . . tried to unbutton his overcoat . . . but my hands had become so cold after removing my gloves to go into the fight that I could not unbutton a single button. I knocked his feet from the stirrups, mounted my horse and led his horse from the camp.[69]

Chapman soon discovered he was the last Confederate in camp, and hurried down the blood-stained path to escape before the arrival of reinforcements—the Thirty-fourth Massachusetts Infantry, coming at the double quick, Smith was dead, and Paxson left to die. The others, including Turner, who was bleeding heavily, had somehow been carried off the field.

Mosby was grief-stricken at the loss of Turner, who died that same day, and especially of Smith, who had been worshipped by the men. They had been his two best officers. At daybreak he sent Chapman and Montjoy back to Cole's camp under flag of truce to recover Smith's body, but the men were denied entry by a furious Cole. "You tell Mosby," Cole shouted, "that any member of this man's family, any citizen, can claim his body—but not Mosby."

"If Mosby wants this body so badly," concluded Cole, "let him try attacking this camp once more."

To a man, the battalion was so dispirited by this loss that they attempted nothing for nearly a month.

6

FIRESTORM

I cared nothing for the form of a thrust if it brought blood. I did not play with foils.

—John S. Mosby, *War Reminiscences*

ON MARCH 9, Lincoln's new commander arrived in Washington for his first meeting with the President. One week earlier, his appointment as lieutenant general had been confirmed by the Senate. Today he was to receive his commission, and in three days would officially take command of all armies of the United States.

Ulysses Grant's rise to power had been remarkable. Sturdiness and dependability as an infantry officer in the war against Mexico had been, prior to the Civil War, the only traits to recommend him. He had been graduated from West Point in the bottom half of his class; during a peacetime assignment in California, separated from wife and children, he'd fallen prey to periodic depression which he'd attempted to stave off with heavy doses of alcohol. In 1854 he had thrown off his commission and returned, a virtually penniless civilian, to his family in Illinois. If he had few resources he had even less luck, and came to fail successively in farming and real estate. He even tried his hand at clerking in a customshouse. In 1861, just three years before his elevation to the post of general-in-chief, Grant was working for his brothers, selling leather goods.

The war brought resurrection. He reenlisted, was quickly given a command, and soon began to forge the chain of impressive victories that brought him to the attention of the President: Fort Donelson, Shiloh, Chattanooga, and, most importantly, Vicksburg.

He was a plain man—as direct as most cigar-chompers—and he liked to be with plain people. His military philosophy was as direct as his personal manner: Find out where your enemy is, get at him as soon as you can, strike at him as hard as you can, and move on. He was exactly what the President had been looking for.

After his meeting with Lincoln, Grant hurried away to put the commands of the western armies in order, returning later in the month for a more protracted session at the White House. During this second talk Grant remained silent as Lincoln alternately complained of his past difficulties with commanders and expounded his own plan for the future. Grant in fact said so little that when he took his leave, Lincoln knew no more of his new commander's plan of campaign than he had known before.

The plan that Grant was keeping to himself was not complicated, and not entirely new. It was, however, a departure from previous strategies in that Richmond would no longer be the objective of Northern armies, and, for the first time, all U.S. armies would work in concert. Richmond and the Confederacy, Grant reasoned, would fall of their own weight if the South were dismembered, and this surgery could be performed only by a large-scale and coordinated movement. But the end could not be accomplished without the removal of the great roadblock in Virginia: the army of Robert E. Lee. The immediate objective in Virginia, therefore, would be not to assail Richmond, but to seek out and crush this army wherever it was found. With the South dismembered and Lee bled dry, the desired result would follow.

The new commander would direct the campaign, he announced, not from a desk in the War Department, but from a tent in the field, traveling with George Meade's fast-moving Army of the Potomac.

From the day Grant joined Meade's army in the field, the Confederacy had just over a year to live.

The defeat by Cole in January had proven to be only a foretaste of what Mosby would face in early 1864, as he met a series of setbacks from friend as well as foe. In February, a number of his men were captured through the treachery of one John Cornwell, a Southerner, and just before that his command had been struck a heavy blow by the Confederate army itself. It was only by some adroit string-pulling in Richmond that he managed to stay on his feet.

There had always been jealous as well as disinterested criticism among Confederate commanders on the subject of freebooting warriors. But in early January, young Brig. Gen. Thomas L. Rosser caught the attention of Lee with a well-prepared blast at partisans as "a nuisance and an evil to the service." Confederate partisans, an untamed lot by any standard, included at that time not only Mosby's troops but those of several other commanders such as Kincheloe, McNeill, O'Ferrall, and Gilmor. "Without discipline, order, or organization," wrote Rosser, "they roam broadcast over the country, a band of thieves. . . . They are a terror to the citizens and an injury to the cause. . . . [They] have engaged in this business for the sake of gain." [1]

Few of Mosby's men would have denied the latter charge, and Mosby himself was among the first to admit the difficulty of screening out common thieves.

Rosser pointed out that the effect of irregulars upon the service was bad, since the partisan life was more attractive than regular army service. Dissatisfaction was on the rise, he said, and, through desertions, available manpower was on the decline. Mosby's men, he added, were a prime example of what was wrong. They were "living at their ease and enjoying the comforts of home," while his own men were chafing for such a "soft place," and restive under the discipline of the ranks. [2]

"If it is necessary," Rosser continued, "for troops to operate within the lines of the enemy, then require the commanding officer to keep them in an organized condition, to rendezvous within our lines, and move upon the enemy when opportunity is offered." [3]

"Major Mosby," he wrote, "is of inestimable service to the Yankee army in keeping their men from straggling." He closed with a plea that the partisan system be corrected, and asked Lee to seek corroboration of its evils, if necessary, from Jubal Early or Fitz Lee. [4]

When Stuart saw the letter, one week later, he agreed that "such organizations, as a rule, [were] detrimental to the best interests of the army," but stated that Mosby's was an efficient band—the most efficient he knew of.[5]

Rosser's immediate goal, however, was soon gained, for on January 22, Lee wrote in a report endorsement: "I recommend that the law authorizing these partisan corps be abolished. The evils resulting from their organization more than counterbalance the good they accomplish." Although just one day earlier he had written to Seddon requesting Mosby's commission as lieutenant colonel "under the act approved April 21, 1862, authorizing the President to commission . . . officers . . . with authority to form bands of partisan rangers," by February both he and Seddon were pressing the Congress in Richmond to abolish this Partisan Ranger Act. By mid-month it was done, and a version was passed incorporating what Rosser and others had desired. Partisan commands, the new law declared, would hereafter be considered regular cavalry, not partisan rangers. They would be brought under the "general condition of the . . . army as to discipline, control, and movements."[6]

Significantly for Lieutenant Colonel Mosby, however, Section 3 of the new act gave the Secretary of War some latitude in exempting "such companies as [were] serving within the lines of the enemy," and Mosby made a flying trip to Richmond to ensure himself a place among the exempt.[7] The opportunity for plunder, he had always contended, was the glue that held his men together; without it he could do little.

In the end Rosser won nothing from Mosby but his future distrust. By April 1, Lee, repeating the Rosser arguments, was recommending that all partisan troops—except Mosby's—be disbanded under the law. Seddon, by April 21, had made the final pronouncement: Mosby's and McNeill's commands would retain ranger status, remaining, in effect, freebooters. All others were to be brought into general service.

With the arrival of warmer weather, the great armies crawling out of winter quarters like sleepy bears into the sunshine, Mosby—now the Confederacy's eyes and ears in northern Virginia—readied himself for a serious effort. He would have about one month to decipher Grant's spring offensive. First, however, there were some housekeeping chores.

He began by getting a number of men started on "corn detail." Regarded as a plum, this periodic task meant exacting tribute in the form of grain, horses, and mules (and occasionally apple pies) from the Union sympathizers—largely Quakers—of Loudoun County. A second, less pleasant task, but one that Mosby demanded be done at intervals, was the job of distillery destruction. Liquor, insisted the abstemious Mosby, not only had a demoralizing effect upon fighting men but contributed to the scarcity of grain in an area where every stalk and ear was needed for food or fodder. No stills were tolerated in "Mosby's Confederacy," and, needless to say, drinking among his own men was frowned upon.

A third item of business was the formation of Company D, done at Paris on April 1. Amid the usual murmuring about his "elections," Mosby ordered an officer to read the names of those for whom votes were to be cast: R. P. Montjoy, of Mississippi, captain; Alfred Glascock, of Fauquier, first lieutenant; Charles Grogan and William Trunnell, both of Maryland, second and third lieutenants, respectively. No other candidates.

The reading of names was greeted by a stony silence. Mosby filled the void by announcing that any man not wishing to participate in this election or not willing to serve under these officers was to fall out, stand to be disarmed, and be sent under guard to the regular army at once. Only Marylanders would be exempt.

There were no takers. Mosby then stepped aside as, one by one, the new men came forward to cast their ballots in the customary unanimous election.

He was plagued throughout the war by problems of manpower—problems more of quality than of numbers. Rosser had, after all, been on the mark in many of his charges. Less than a week before this election Mosby had written to Stuart:

> Please grant no papers to any man coming to join my command unless he can furnish evidence of having been recruited by an agent of mine. The enrolling officer in Richmond has assumed to enlist men for me and I have had the trouble of sending them back. . . . You can very readily understand how necessary it is for success in my operations to have none but first-rate men.[8]

With foragers sent out and administrative chores taken care of, Mosby himself now began a month of hard riding, ranging from eastern Maryland to Culpeper to Harpers Ferry to Fredericksburg, funneling a steady stream of intelligence to Stuart. In late March he had reported that the Winchester and Potomac railroad (linking Winchester with Harpers Ferry) was being surveyed, and that a movement in the Valley therefore seemed likely. On April 11 he reported that troops were being pulled away from the defenses of Washington, the Veteran Invalid Corps substituted, and that troops from the West and from Meade's army were going to Butler's department, via Annapolis.

Clearly, for the first time in the war, a unified movement of many armies seemed to be in the works. Infantry, artillery, and even wagons were moving by flatcar in every direction. Grant was shoring up supply lines, positioning new depots, weeding out deadwood and sending it to the rear, adding sinew to his armies by putting the best men on the line. Reserves were swelling: Lincoln in February had called for 200,000 men, and in March for another 200,000. In July he would call for half a million.

By April 28, Mosby had reported that all but convalescent troops had left Annapolis two days earlier and that the local people were convinced something was in the wind on the Peninsula. "Something serious" was also expected in the Valley, he said. Next day he reported that despite what Northern papers were saying about Burnside's having gone to Fortress Monroe, he himself had seen Burnside's regiments at Bristoe, near Manassas. About 1,500 black troops were being left to guard the Orange and Alexandria, and the balance of Burnside's forces had been moved forward.

Grant's vision was approaching fruition; the firestorm was about to break. A war machine of half a million men in twenty-one corps was lurching forward, simultaneously, from the Atlantic to the Rio Grande: Banks in Texas, Sherman in Tennessee, Butler on the Peninsula, Meade on the Rappahannock, Crook in West Virginia, and Sigel in the Valley, leaving Burnside to hover over Washington and the vital railroad. The arms and legs of the Confederacy were about to be hacked away, and Lee's army cracked between Butler and

Meade. By midsummer the Confederacy would have been forcibly dismantled, and before year's end the work of reconstruction begun.

Or so Grant thought.

In the waning hours of April, Franz Sigel began his advance up the Valley, and just after midnight on May 4, Grant and the 118,000-man Army of the Potomac splashed into Germanna Ford on the Rapidan. Butler was already in motion up the Peninsula. Once across, Meade's army began moving southward, but did not get far. Almost as soon as the army had left the river, Lee's waiting veterans struck it in the tangled wood known as The Wilderness. For two days the Yankees hammered back with twice Lee's forces, both sides suffering frightful casualties. Much of the combat was at close quarters and hand to hand in a jungle of thickets that soon became an inferno. "The woods were set on fire by the bursting shells," wrote Grant, "and the conflagration raged. The wounded who had not strength to move themselves were either suffocated or burned to death."[9]

Checked with unexpected harshness, the Army of the Potomac disengaged to slip further along Lee's flank, only to find the rebels waiting again, this time astride the Richmond Road at Spotsylvania Court House. In a ten-day series of engagements here, great trees were cut down by murderous musket fire, yet Lee, despite his more than 9,000 casualties, held again. As they would soon do at Cold Harbor, doomed Northern soldiers pinned nametags to their sleeves before being hurled in waves against the entrenched Confederates. The slaughter did not stop until, in Blackford's words, "the ground in our front was piled so with the slain that in those hot days of May the stench became so intolerable that [Grant] had to desist."[10] The Federal Army had sustained nearly 20,000 casualties before its commander decided he must slip further south.

While Union forces were moving upon Spotsylvania Court House, the Army of the Potomac's new chief of cavalry, feisty little Philip H. Sheridan, had been sent around Lee's left flank with a huge force of 12,000 troopers, one of his objects being to draw out Stuart's cavalry for a fight. He succeeded in doing much more. In a sharp engagement near Richmond at a place called Yellow Tavern, Stuart himself was seriously wounded, and on May 12 he died. Stuart, always in the thickest of the fighting, had been killed by the first bullet ever to touch him.

Mosby was crushed by the news. Lee could not accept it. "Stuart, Stuart," he cried. "I can scarcely think of him without weeping."[11]

Grant, seeing that little could be done against the resilient and battle-hardened Southerners, slipped away again, hoping by a series of night marches to flank Lee, then to strike Richmond from the Peninsula (where Butler had already been bottled up by a small Confederate force). But when, on June 1, he arrived at Cold Harbor—eight miles northeast of Richmond—Lee was there also, between him and the city. In the finale of a series of assaults that has become almost symbolic of bloody futility, Grant, in a matter of minutes, sacrificed 7,000 men.

Since the crossing of the Rapidan one month earlier, Grant had lost a total of 55,000 men, a number about equal to Lee's entire army. Northern wives and mothers were appalled, and Northern papers began to refer to him as "The Butcher," but the sad-eyed man in the White House nodded in understanding. He wrote to Grant after Cold Harbor: "I have just received your dispatch. . . . I begin to see it: you will succeed. God bless you all."[12]

"In all the contests between Grant and Lee," noted Blackford,

> one is reminded of a fight between some powerful, awkward giant and a light, active and expert swordsman. But Grant was a man of strong common sense. . . . He knew that our resources were weakening and that he could afford to sacrifice three men to deprive us of one, and he did it. Grant took command of the army when it had been thoroughly disciplined by long service and was at its maximum of efficiency, with unbounded resources to keep it up to that point, while our army was just beginning to feel the effect of the exhaustion of our resources by constant and persistent bad management on the part of the government.

"How differently Lincoln managed!" he concluded. "But

he, fortunately for his side, had not been educated at West Point."[13]

By mid-June Grant had disengaged once again. Unable to get at Lee's army, he was forced now to pursue the dog-eared strategy of moving upon Richmond itself—this time by an assault upon the rail center of Petersburg, twenty-three miles south of the capital. Control of the railroad here would bring control of Richmond and the starvation of Lee's army.

Again Grant was to be disillusioned, for at Petersburg he was met by a small force under Pierre G. T. Beauregard, which stood him off until the arrival of Lee.

On June 15, Grant launched a four-day series of attacks on the entrenched Confederates that left him with 10,000 casualties and still no closer to victory. He was to sit in front of Petersburg for the next ten months.

In these six weeks of bitter fighting Grant had accomplished one important thing, although at great cost: the Southern rapier, Lee's once dangerous Army of Northern Virginia, had been broken and could never again be used as more than a home guard. As a threat to the North, it was dead.

Mosby, his command still growing, nipped at Sigel and Grant at the same time. Sending Adolphus ("Dolly") Richards and William Chapman to operate in the Valley, he himself set out in the second week of May with forty men to break Grant's supply line. Detaching squads along the way to burn railroad bridges, he arrived with a handful of men at Belle Plain, between Fredericksburg and the Potomac, and on May 17 struck a wagon train there, forcing the future assignment of heavy cavalry escorts in the area. His men in the Valley were dealing with Sigel's trains in like manner, with similar response.

By mid-May, the Shenandoah Valley was the scene of an active and earnest war. In the first pitched battle of the new campaign, a rebel force under John C. Breckinridge—fleshed out by the fuzz-cheeked cadets of the Virginia Military Institute—defeated Sigel at New Market and drove him back down the Valley to Strasburg. Sigel was immediately replaced by David Hunter, who, in a new offensive, was met head on at Lynchburg by Jubal Early, and the Yankee army again driven back. Early, however, succeeded in doing something extra: he leapfrogged Hunter, and by July 4 had dashed across the Potomac into Maryland.

To assist Early in his lightning offensive northward, Mosby—using artillery and dismounted sharpshooters—forced a crossing of the Potomac under heavy fire at Point of Rocks, then cut off rail and telegraph contact between Harpers Ferry and Washington for two days, gathered heaps of Federal goods, and slipped back into Virginia. Before returning to Maryland, however, he received distracting news: a body of Union cavalry was poking about Leesburg, asking questions about his command. The 150-man force, he found out, was made up of the Second Massachusetts and Thirteenth New York, and was led by none other than Maj. William H. Forbes, a Boston patrician with a fighter's reputation.

Taking on Forbes was a tempting prospect. Although Mosby had sent many of his men home with their Maryland plunder, he had retained enough to make the match about equal. He resolved to do it. After inquiring about the Yankees' present location and destination, he led his men down a back road to wait for them at Mount Zion Church, along their route home to Fairfax.

When the Federal regiments came in sight, Mosby's men opened, somewhat cautiously, with carbines and a twelve-pound Napoleon, then dashed forward to meet the seasoned Union troopers at close quarters. Revolvers cracked and blazed, and sabers flashed in the noonday sun as the two bodies of cavalry ran headlong at one another, colliding in a vicious, grunting hand-to-hand. Mosby and Forbes sought one another out. Forbes, who was later to become one of Mosby's most intimate friends, made a powerful thrust at his opponent, driving his saber through the Confederate's coat, and was subdued only when his horse fell upon him, shot dead.

It was a particularly savage encounter, with dead or disabled men and horses littering acres of ground. Mosby finally took off fifty-seven prisoners, including Forbes. He also took 100 horses and left more than fifty Yankees incapacitated or dead. If further proof were needed of the superiority of revolver over saber, his own losses were one killed and six lightly wounded.

Following this victory, he moved again to the assistance of

Early, whose progress had been slowed for a day by stiff resistance near Frederick. But it soon became evident that Early had bitten off too much, and there was little the rangers could do to help. By the time Early's small force arrived on the outskirts of Washington, the men were played out and virtually incapable of fighting. Easily driven off, they fell back at once toward Virginia, recrossing the Potomac on July 14.

Washington had been spared. But when the danger had passed, Lincoln demanded a new commander in the Shenandoah Valley.

On August 7, it was Philip Sheridan, the Army of the Potomac's thirty-three-year-old cavalry chief, who took command of the Army of the Shenandoah. Young Sheridan's appointment raised some official eyebrows, but Grant knew his man and pushed to get him. His orders to the new Valley commander were simple: Move upon Early, and do not stop until you have destroyed his army or driven him from the Shenandoah.

Three days later Sheridan set to work, marching up the Valley in force, pushing Early steadily backward toward his line of earthworks between Strasburg and Cedar Creek. Much was riding on Sheridan's shoulders. The President's election campaign was in full swing, and all knew that a victory at the polls would not be assisted by a defeat in the Valley. The newcomer was expected to do his job.

Mosby, if he was unable to hand Sheridan a defeat, strove at least to make him feel unwelcome. In the early morning blackness of August 13, a portion of a 525-wagon train carrying supplies to Sheridan's army around Winchester had parked near Berryville to water mules and stock. Many of the mules had been unhitched and slipped out of harness, and their drivers stretched out to sleep. As the night faded, a number of figures materialized slowly out of the fog and began to unlimber two small cannon—ostensibly for target practice. Those who noticed paid little attention, until the cannon were brought to bear on the train, and opened.

One of the first shots took off a mule's head; the rest was bedlam. More shells landed amid the wagons, and in a moment swarms of gray-clad, rebel-yelling riders broke from the mist, firing as they came. Horses and mules reared and dashed about wildly, upsetting wagons, some of which had by now been set afire by the horde of attackers. Mules still hitched ran in terror from flames that licked them from their own wagons. Some fell exhausted; others smashed their loads into trees or fences.

Defense was impossible amid the confusion, even if the train guard had lingered long enough to attempt it. When the clouds of dust and smoke finally settled, Mosby's force of three hundred held nearly its own number in prisoners, in addition to some seven hundred horses and mules and well over two hundred fat cattle—bound now for Lee's hungry army. They had burned or seized 75 fully loaded wagons: five days' rations for over 2,200 Yankee soldiers.

It was the most massive attack Mosby had ever mounted, and the opening act to several months of bare-knuckled warfare between his rangers and Sheridan's Army of the Shenandoah. Two days later Sheridan began retreating to Halltown, from which he had set out on the tenth, explaining his move as being due to reinforcements reportedly en route to Early.

By August 16, Grant, at his headquarters near Petersburg, had been told about Sheridan's guerrilla problem, and he wired the Valley commander a reminder: "The families of most of Mosby's men are known, and can be collected."[14]

"I think," he continued, "they should be taken and kept at Fort McHenry, or some secure place, as hostages for the good conduct of Mosby and his men." Then, in a sentence that was to bear bitter fruit: "Where any of Mosby's men are caught hang them without trial."[15]

Two hours later Grant had an afterthought. "If you can possibly spare a division of cavalry," he told Sheridan, "send them through Loudoun County, to destroy and carry off the crops, animals, negroes, and all men under fifty years of age capable of bearing arms. In this way you will get many of Mosby's men. All male citizens under fifty can fairly be held as prisoners of war."[16]

By August 18 the directive was being executed. From headquarters, Department of Washington, Maj. John M. Waite was ordered to take the Maryland-based Eighth Illinois Cavalry on a "thorough scout" through Loudoun County. The special object of his mission would be "to break up and exterminate any bands . . . of Mosby's . . . or other guerrillas which may be met." Waite, commanding what Mosby's men regarded as the finest cavalry regiment they ever faced, was ordered to move "with the utmost caution," due to "the nature of the country and . . . disposition of the inhabitants."[17]

The following day, Sheridan reminded Maj. Gen. Christopher C. Augur, commanding Department of Washington, of Grant's instruction of August 16 in dealing with Loudoun County. "All persons arrested," he said, "you will confine as prisoners of war . . . at such points . . . as you may deem best, or I will authorize the transfer of them to Fort McHenry."[18]

On August 20, with Waite's 650-man column heading across the Potomac, Sheridan informed Augur that he had a hundred men of his own who would "take the contract to clean out Mosby's gang." All that was wanted was a hundred Spencer repeaters for them. "Send them to me," he said, "if they can be found in Washington."[19]

By August 24, the Eighth Illinois had returned to barracks carrying sixty-two "rebel sympathizers," but admittedly having seen "no signs of the enemy, except small squads of Mosby's men."[20] Waite was to be sent out again as soon as his horses could be shod, "to destroy . . . the sources from which Mosby draws men, horses, and support."[21] His mandate included the hauling away or destruction of all hay, oats, corn, and wheat that could be found. Sheridan, for his part, informed Augur that he would shortly be commencing cavalry operations himself, and planned to do for the Shenandoah what he hoped Waite had done for Loudoun.

When Sheridan began again to move south, in the first week of September, it was with Grant's admonition to drive through to the Virginia Central railroad if possible. "Give the enemy no rest . . . ," Grant had said. "Do all the damage to railroads and crops you can. Carry off stock of all descriptions, and negroes, so as to prevent further planting. If the war is to last another year, we want the Shenandoah Valley to remain a barren waste."[22]

In mid-September, Mosby was again seriously wounded. He

and two of his men—Tom Love and Guy Broadwater—had unexpectedly run into a party of five troopers of the Thirteenth New York, near Aldie, on September 14. Once the initial shock of the encounter had passed, both sides began firing at a range of only a few yards. Two Yankee horses fell dead upon their riders, then a ball shattered the handle of Mosby's pistol and a second penetrated his groin. As their commander slumped forward in the saddle, Love and Broadwater drove off the three mounted Yanks, leaving the other two pinned beneath their horses. They then commandeered a light wagon and drove Mosby as rapidly as possible to White Plains, from where he was later sent to his parents' home.

On September 22, with Mosby recuperating at home, a 120-man squadron led by Sam Chapman also stumbled into some Yankees—in this case an entire brigade, south of Front Royal—and was forced to cut its way out in a desperate ride. In the melee, Chapman's men rode down and riddled with bullets a young lieutenant named McMasters who had just gotten to his feet and, it was later alleged, was in the act of surrendering. Through sheer boldness all finally made their escape—all but six. Five of these were quickly disarmed and taken into Front Royal under heavy guard; the sixth, seventeen-year-old Henry Rhodes, was subdued only after being run down in a streambed. He was dragged into Front Royal behind a pair of scampering cavalry horses.

There was no question what was about to happen. Too many had heard about McMasters.

Three of the prisoners—Thomas Anderson, Lucian Love, and David Jones—were given little chance to explain. They were pushed against a wall behind the courthouse by a mob of soldiers, and, while Federal commanders looked the other way, were shot to death. William Thomas Overby and a man named Carter were for some time held apart in a wagon lot. After being questioned by Sheridan's chief of cavalry, Maj. Gen. Alfred T. A. Torbert, about the location of "Mosby's camp," they were led out of town and drawn, struggling, up by their necks into the branches of a walnut tree. A sign affixed to one of the bodies read: "Such is the fate of all Mosby's men."[23]

While the two had been held in the wagon lot, Custer and

his staff had ridden past. Custer was occupied, in the words of an eyewitness, with "a large branch of damsons, which he picked and ate as he rode along."[24]

Young Henry Rhodes, the only one of the six from Front Royal, had never before ridden with Mosby's rangers, but had gone along this time on the chance of getting a horse. More dead than alive, the boy was dragged bleeding through the streets, his distraught mother trailing behind. The woman was eventually restrained by grim Union soldiers and Rhodes taken alone to the edge of town, where, with few preliminaries, someone volunteered to kill him. As the crowd drew away from the pair, the man ordered Rhodes to his feet, and then, while the battered prisoner did his best to comply, emptied a pistol into his face. What remained of Henry Rhodes was left at his mother's door in a wheelbarrow, covered by a sheet.

Four days later, in an apparently unrelated incident, Mosby's "headquarters" near Piedmont Station was burned to the ground.

By the time Mosby, hobbling on crutches, returned to his disheartened command at the end of September, Jubal Early had been defeated once at Winchester and again at Fisher's Hill. Grant, moreover, was pressing Sheridan to finish the job so as to close off forever the Confederates' covered way into Maryland and Pennsylvania, and to free up Sheridan's Sixth and Nineteenth Corps for duty at Petersburg. Sheridan, with a better feel for the vulnerability of Washington and the stubborn unpredictability of Early's skeleton army, demurred. More time, he said, would be needed to blunt Early's edge, and for now he wished to hold onto his troops.

Then, said Grant, press southward to strike the Central railroad, and you will cause the fall of Richmond.

"It will be exceedingly difficult for me to carry the infantry over the mountains and strike at the Central road," answered Sheridan from Harrisonburg. "I . . . think it best to take some position near Front Royal and operate with cavalry and infantry."[25] He had already pleaded the difficulty of supplying an army so far from base; even his messengers—to say nothing of his trains—were being forced to travel with heavy cavalry escort as protection against guerrillas. On September 21 he had asked Augur for 4,000 to 5,000 new troops to relieve men left to guard his communications.

Reluctantly, Grant acquiesced. "You may take up such position . . . as you think can and ought to be held," he answered, "and send all the force not required for this immediately here."[26]

To ease Sheridan's supply problem and to get his reinforcements as quickly as possible, Grant directed that the little Manassas Gap railroad, sixty miles of track joining Front Royal and Strasburg in the Valley with the Orange and Alexandria at Manassas, be refurbished. With this road reopened, Sheridan would no longer have to depend for supplies on the B & O at far-off Harpers Ferry, but could be provisioned directly from Alexandria, via the O & A and the Manassas Gap.

From Manassas to Piedmont Station only minor repairs would be necessary—three days' work. From Piedmont to Strasburg, however, bridges had been destroyed and even the rails taken up by Stonewall Jackson's army. Repairs to this section would take two to three weeks. Halleck and Sheridan saw the difficulty of the job before Grant did. Halleck wired Grant on October 4 that entrenched garrisons as well as cavalry pickets would be required to protect this road; that all rebel inhabitants north of it would have to be moved out of the area; and that "Mosby's gang of robbers who [had] so long infested that district" would also have to be cleaned out.[27]

I respectfully suggest," he added, "that Sheridan's cavalry should be required to accomplish this object before it is sent elsewhere. The two small regiments under General Augur have been so often cut up by Mosby's band that they are cowed and useless for that purpose."[28]

Sheridan, in his own message to Grant, commented, "I would have preferred sending troops to you by the Baltimore and Ohio Road," and warned that "the keeping open of the road to Front Royal [would] require large guards to protect it against a very small number of partisan troops."[29]

The work was already in motion despite their warnings. On October 3 the construction train working on the Orange and

Alexandria near the Rappahannock was ordered back to Manassas, and from there sent into Fauquier, the heart of "Mosby's Confederacy." The nervous workmen, protected only by a small guard, moved quickly, replacing ties and rails as necessary, strengthening bridges, rooting out thick growths of grass and weeds, and restringing or patching telegraph wire.

On October 4, as the construction train neared Thoroughfare Gap, the still-crippled Mosby and two hundred men fired into it, then melted quickly into the countryside to regroup before the expected arrival of reinforcements. By next day the road was blue with troops: three companies of Pennsylvania infantry had arrived at Manassas and three more at Gainesville; two others were at Thoroughfare Gap, and eight at White Plains. One battalion of the Fifth Pennsylvania Heavy Artillery had advanced to Salem, another to Rectortown, and one lay in between. In addition, a cavalry company was clattering off the cars from Alexandria, charged with the risky task of providing courier service through to Sheridan's headquarters in the Valley. Over 2,000 infantry, cavalry, and artillery had poured in overnight to ensure completion of the road, and more were on the way.

Mosby struck them on October 5. Bursting from a wood near Salem with dismounted sharpshooters, two fieldpieces, and 250 horsemen, he attacked the Pennsylvanians in their camps, driving them without ceremony from their cooking fires and up the road to Rectortown, four miles north. The Yankees soon checked the rebel pursuit, but were forced to pass an uneasy and rainy night dug in beside the troops already in Rectortown to guard the construction train. Mosby hauled his two howitzers up to Rectortown next day, and on the following day had two more pieces in place.

For two days he attempted to blast the Yanks out, but without success—the guns could not be depressed sufficiently. In the meantime his men began tearing up track between Rectortown and Salem. In addition to harassing the construction train, they blocked further traffic into the area, on October 6 driving a train back to the Plains which had attempted to force passage under escort of six hundred bayonets.

In Washington, Augur scrambled to assemble a large force,

which he planned to lead in the field himself. While Mosby
was bombarding Rectortown, Augur was wiring the indefatigable Major Waite: "Collect all your cavalry as soon as
possible . . . and proceed with it to Middleburg and thence to
Rectortown . . . where I will meet you. It is possible you may
have to fight Mosby on the road about Middleburg. Be prepared for him. Be in haste."[30]

By seven the following morning, Augur was in White
Plains, and by noon, seven companies of Waite's Eighth Illinois Cavalry were moving to the southwest on the double.
Augur himself had had a difficult passage, since on the previous day advance parties of Mosby's battalion had thrown
the huge Federal engine "Grapeshot" off the track at Thoroughfare Gap, along with twelve cars of construction material, leaving the road perfectly blocked. In a day or so it was
cleared. Now under the eye of the coolly professional Eighth
Illinois, the track was relaid to Piedmont Station.

On the very day that construction was completed to Piedmont, what had been done came undone. Alfred Glascock
and a few of his company slipped between two picket posts
just west of the Plains, pried up a rail, and threw another
train down an embankment. The damage this time was significant: workers picking through the wreckage found the mangled bodies of several men, including the railroad's assistant
superintendent, M. J. McCrickett.

On October 11, Mosby and the Union cavalry locked horns
again, and Mosby—only recently returned to the saddle—was
left with a badly swollen and discolored ankle when his mount
was shot out from under him and his foot trampled upon by a
galloping Yankee cavalry horse. While resting next day with
sock and cane, he wrote to Pauline about the mishap, display-
ing a remarkably sanguine view of the future: "I don't think
the Yankees will be here long. I will bring you all over . . .
soon."[31]

Mosby was to prove correct in his assessment of the Yankee
staying power, but there was little reason at this time for him
to hold such a view. Augur, as a shield against guerrilla attacks, had commenced putting local residents aboard military
trains, a move guaranteed to cause even further sectional bitterness. Under cloudy circumstances, one such hostage—an

old man—was shot in the head by a Union train guard and died in an Alexandria hospital.

Even more ominous measures were in the wind. Halleck, on October 12, had ordered every house within five miles of the railroad "not occupied by persons known to be friendly" to be destroyed. He had also dictated that all males suspected of involvement with Mosby be sent to the Old Capitol prison, and that all forage, animals, and grain in the area be confiscated. "All timber and brush within musketry fire of the road," he decreed, "will be cut down and destroyed. . . . Any citizens found within five miles of the road hereafter will be considered as robbers and bushwhackers, and be treated accordingly. . . . For any further hostilities committed on this road . . . an additional strip of ten miles on each side will be laid waste, and that section of country entirely depopulated."[32]

With the Federal presence along the Manassas Gap road taking on suffocating proportions, Mosby determined to offer the Yankees some distraction: a strike at Sheridan's "secure" line, the Baltimore and Ohio. On the clear, frosty night of October 13, with a Federal railroad timetable tucked in his pocket, he took eighty-four men and hurried northward to the Potomac. By 2:00 A.M. of the fourteenth, the hard-riding cavalrymen had slipped between the pickets near Duffield's, just west of Harpers Ferry. Their arrival had been timed to coincide with the passage of the westbound passenger express out of Baltimore.

Once a few men had slid down the embankment to loosen a rail (within a roadcut, to cause minimal passenger injury), the exhausted riders took up stations; all, Mosby included, fell asleep.

"We did not hear the train coming," he recalled, "until it got up in the cut, and I was aroused and astounded by an explosion and a crash. As we had displaced a rail, the engine had run off the track, the boiler burst, and the air was filled with red-hot cinders and escaping steam. A good description of the scene can be found in Dante's 'Inferno.'"[33]

As little groups of frightened men and screaming women with children were being pulled out of the crippled train,

Mosby—still with cane and sock but now very much alert—stood on the embankment shouting directions above the din. Unknown to him, and contrary to his orders, his men were "going through" the passengers, relieving them of watches, rings, other jewelry, and cash. Being pulled out into the cold starlight by "the guerrilla chief, Jack Mosby" unnerved many, but left one group quite unmoved. A carload of non–English-speaking German immigrants refused to budge, guerrillas or no. "Set fire to the car," shouted Mosby, "and burn the Dutch, if they won't come out."[34]

"They had through tickets," he later wrote, "and thought they had a right to keep their seats."[35]

Piles of *New York Herald*s intended for Sheridan's army were rapidly scattered among the stolid immigrants and ignited. "Suddenly," said Mosby, "there was a grand illumination. The Germans now took in the situation and came tumbling, all in a pile, out of the flames."[36]

As the crackling fire illuminated the night, Mosby sat steady on his horse, rocklike amid the noise and confusion, conversing with the distraught passengers. "General Stevenson will not guard the railroad," he told one, his eyes riveted upon the flames, "and I am determined to make him perform his duty."[37] A hysterical woman dispatched Monroe Heiskell to Mosby with a desperate message: Tell him, please, that my husband is a Mason. "Tell her I can't help that," was Mosby's curt response.

With everything of value packed into gunny sacks or strapped across their saddles, including a chest containing over $170,000 worth of Federal payroll, the Confederates mounted up and rode hurriedly away, leaving the forlorn travelers alongside the smoldering wreckage. The few Yankee soldiers who had been aboard were carried off with them.

"Among the latter," wrote Mosby,

was a young German lieutenant who . . . was on his way to join his regiment in Sheridan's army. I was attracted by his personal appearance, struck up a conversation with him, and rode by him for several miles. He was dressed in a fine beavercloth overcoat; high boots, and a new hat with gilt cord and tassel. After we were pretty well acquainted, I said to him, "We have done you no harm. Why did you come over here to fight us?" "Oh," he said, "I only come to learn de art of war." I then left him and rode to the head of the column, as the enemy were about, and there was a prospect of a fight. It was not long before the German came trotting up to join me. There had been such a metamorphosis that I scarcely recognized him. One of my men had exchanged his old clothes with him for his new ones, and he complained about it. I asked him if he had not told me that he came to Virginia to learn the art of war. "Yes," he replied. "Very well," I said, "this is your first lesson." [38]

Loss of the payroll was stunning to Sheridan's army, where a wider plot was feared. A number of paymasters at Martinsburg were immediately confined to quarters and their funds put under guard. Fears of a plot were heightened when the B & O was struck again that day by William Chapman. During succeeding days Mosby compounded the confusion by making a quick, surgical thrust into Fairfax, fifty miles to the east. The Eighth Illinois, sent in pursuit, ended only by chasing its tail. "They did what I was maneuvering to make them do," concluded a smug Mosby, "—spend their time and waste their strength in pursuit of a Jack-o'-lantern." [39]

By the third week of October, Early had been whipped again—this time at Cedar Creek—and Federal control of the Valley as well as Lincoln's reelection were virtually assured. But because of guerrillas, the Manassas Gap railroad effort was failing, stalled cold at Piedmont Station.

Before month's end, Grant had yielded to Sheridan: the Manassas Gap plan would be scotched. Rails and telegraph lines were ordered taken up immediately, back to Manassas. The better-protected Winchester and Potomac line would instead be opened northward to the B & O at Harpers Ferry. Mosby ever afterward regarded his blocking of the Manassas Gap road as his greatest wartime feat, maintaining that his men tied up so many troops and caused so much uncertainty in the Valley that Grant was unable to marshal sufficient force to crush Petersburg before spring. With some justification he made the claim that his men had provided Richmond and the Confederacy with six extra months of life. [40]

The day before Mosby had struck the B & O, one of his men, young Ab Willis, was en route back to the command, having just escorted a group of prisoners to Richmond. In Rappahannock County, however, his trip was cut short: he fell into the hands of some angry Yankees, disturbed over the recent murder of a U.S. soldier. Once Willis had been identified as a Mosby man, his troubles became unmanageable. Hauled out to a lonely spot, his arms were tied behind him, a sapling was forced over double, and his neck fixed by a noose to the top of it. Willis and the sapling were then released, and Willis shot skyward, left to a brief struggle amid a riot of colorful foliage.

While greatly relieved Federal construction crews were tearing up railroad track as quickly as possible, Mosby turned his attention to the killings of his men. He had lost seven men in a month to executions. With families being hounded from their homes, their lands burned over, and old men forced at gunpoint to ride as hostages aboard Federal trains, the Federal effort in northern Virginia seemed to be increasing in barbarism. On October 29, therefore, he sent his brother Willie to Lee with a letter proposing retaliation. Speaking of his own seven losses, which he blamed directly on Custer (not on Grant or Sheridan), he told Lee: "It is my purpose to hang an equal number of Custer's men whenever I capture them." [41]

Both Lee and Seddon gave their cordial approval, and by November 6, on a cool fall Sunday morning, twenty-seven of Custer's men were lined up in a sunny hollow near Goose Creek, at Rectortown, waiting to draw lots to be hanged. Many of the rangers found the matter distasteful, but none more so than their commander. Ordering his lieutenants to supervise the drawing, Mosby withdrew, refusing to witness the scene.

Twenty-seven scraps of paper were cut up, seven were numbered, then all were folded and thrown into a brown felt hat. One man took the hat and moved along the line, ordering each to draw a scrap. As the prisoners drew their scraps, some wept softly; others stared in disbelief. Some broke down like children and begged for their lives.

There were, in fact, children present. The prisoners included a Federal newsboy and a drummer boy. The newsboy, captured several times before and always released, was let go this time as well. Not so the other lad. Unaware until he was put into line that he was to draw lots for his life, he lapsed into virtual shock. His shock deepened considerably when he drew the seventh number.

Guy Broadwater moved off to tell Mosby about the boy, and returned with Mosby's order to release him. The remaining prisoners would draw again for his number.

With the drawing finished, the seven devastated men were segregated, hoisted upon horses, and led off toward Sheridan's lines with a small guard. Mosby had ordered them hanged as closely as possible to the Union camps. Two of them were to receive an immediate reprieve: Montjoy, returning from the Valley with a second batch of prisoners, recognized the two as fellow Masons, and ordered their release, substituting two of his own prisoners. Mosby was furious when he heard of the substitution. "Remember, Captain, in the future," he shouted, "that this command is not a Masonic lodge!"

By the time the party had arrived near Berryville—having stopped at several houses along the way to collect bed cords—it was raining and getting dark, and one of the prisoners had escaped. The jittery Confederates decided to move no closer to the Federal lines, but to get the job done then and there. One of the substituted men, Sgt. Charles Marvin of the Second New York Cavalry, recalled what happened next:

> The first man was gotten up, his hands tied behind him, a bed-cord doubled and tied around his neck; he was marched to a large tree beside the road, from which a limb projected. He was lifted in the air, the rope taken by one of the men on horseback and tied to the limb, and there he was left dangling. Two more were treated in the same manner.
>
> It took some considerable time and our executioners were becoming uneasy, . . . and they decided . . . to shoot the balance of us, as "this hanging is too damned slow work." [42]

With the first three bodies now twisting softly about the bed cords, the remaining three men were lined up, a revolver pointed at each and the command given to fire. Revolvers exploded on either side of Marvin, but the one directed at him only clicked. Coming to his senses more quickly than his captor, he struck the man as hard as he could and ran off into the night. He left his two companions not dead, but terribly wounded—one with a shattered elbow, the other with an eye and part of his head blown away. Both lived.

When on the following morning the three hanged men were discovered, one body was seen to bear a note. It had evidently been prepared beforehand: "These men have been hung in retaliation for an equal number of Colonel Mosby's men hung by order of General Custer, at Front Royal. Measure for measure."[43]

Mosby's purpose in carrying out the executions, he was to maintain all his life, had not been revenge. "Three or four got away in a rainstorm that night," he said. "If my motive had been *revenge* I would have ordered others to be executed in their place. I did not. I was really glad they got away as they carried the story to Sheridan's army which was the best way to stop the business."[44]

"My object," he wrote, "was to prevent the war from degenerating into a massacre." But he had also meant the executions as a warning. "I wanted Sheridan's soldiers to know," he said, "that, if they desired to fight under the black flag, I would meet them."[45]

He sent a letter through the lines directly to Sheridan, acknowledging responsibility for the executions, and explaining that any prisoners falling into his hands in the future would be treated "with the kindness due to their condition," unless "some new act of barbarity" should compel him "reluctantly to adopt a course of policy repulsive to humanity."[46] No further executions occurred on either side, but Mosby, never at ease with this memory, grew testy whenever the subject was brought up.

Sheridan had gotten the hundred Spencer repeaters he had requested in August, and had at once distributed them to a company of hard-boiled deadeyes commanded by former Indian fighter Richard Blazer. No sooner had he been issued the rifles than Blazer went to work: Before long his guerrillas had struck one of Mosby's squadrons in the Valley, cutting it up badly and taking several prisoners. Mosby's derision of the men who escaped was cruel and persistent. "You let those Yankees whip you?" he sneered. "Why I ought to get hoop skirts for you! I'll send you all into the first regiment we come across . . ."

By mid-November he had decided that Blazer would have to go. He ordered Richards to take not just any squadron, but the same squadron that Blazer had whipped, and finish him. On November 18, in what Mosby regarded as the most brilliant military action yet seen in the Shenandoah Valley, Richards lured Blazer into a diabolical ambush in which twenty-four Yankees, a quarter of Blazer's force, were killed and nearly every survivor either wounded or captured. In a single, quick, savage engagement, the entire "hundred rifles" had been eliminated. The humane and decent Blazer was himself run down and unhorsed by a pistol crack on the head before being taken prisoner. One of the four who ran him down was "the terrible Powell," who, as Lewis Payne, was to swing from a gallows in Washington the following summer.

The action had been vicious, an orgy of killing almost out of proportion to its significance. A young ranger named Puryear had been captured earlier by Blazer's men and during interrogation had been twice hoisted off the ground by his neck. He was still a prisoner when his captors fell into ambush. Almost with the first Confederate volley, he clubbed his guard, got hold of a pistol, and took off after his former interrogator, a Lieutenant Cole. He spotted Cole, already wounded and with his hands in the air, being disarmed at gunpoint by John Alexander. In a hot sweat Puryear reined up alongside the two horsemen, and with a face distorted by rage, leveled his cocked pistol at Cole's forehead.

"Don't shoot this man," shouted Alexander. "He's surrendered."

"This son of a bitch tried to hang me this morning!" shrieked Puryear, all but out of control.

"Is that true?" asked Alexander, looking at Cole.

Puryear restrained himself a moment longer, awaiting Cole's reply. He then squeezed the trigger, driving the unarmed man's body back against Alexander in a spray of blood and bone before it rolled out of the saddle to the ground.

Charles McDonough, another overwrought boy, pushed his

mount to the limit to catch a man who had just shot him—a deserter from his former regiment. Unable to get close, he fired his final ball into the fugitive's horse, dropping the animal upon its rider and pinning him to the ground. McDonough, bleeding, leaped off his own horse, begged a loaded pistol from another ranger, and nearly choking with rage ("God damn you, Harrell, I'm going to kill you!"), snapped the gun twice in the prostrate man's face before it finally exploded, blowing the crown of his victim's head off.

McDonough's end came a few months later. Hounded down by a pack of Federal troopers, with no chance of escape, he cupped his mouth around a pistol muzzle and blew his own head apart.

In the continuing discussion among Grant, Halleck, and Sheridan about sending reinforcements to Petersburg from the Valley, Grant was weakening. By the end of November he had told Halleck that Sheridan could keep the Sixth Corps if he still needed it. When Halleck wired this news to Sheridan, he added the reminder that "before any cavalry is sent away Mosby's band should be broken up."[47] Sheridan, however, did not have to be told that the time had come to deal with Mosby, who had for too long been operating successfully on two fronts.

"I will soon commence work on Mosby," he replied.

> Heretofore I have made no attempt to break him up, as I would have employed ten men to his one. . . . I will soon commence on Loudoun County, and let them know there is a God in Israel. . . . The people are beginning to see that [Mosby] . . . causes a loss to them of all that they have spent their lives in accumulating. . . . Those who live at home, in peace and plenty, want the duello part of this war to go on; but when they have to bear their burden by loss of property and comforts they will cry for peace.[48]

By next day the anti-guerrilla campaign was on. Sheridan issued orders to Bvt. Maj. Gen. Wesley Merritt to bring two brigades through Ashby's Gap, provisioned for four days, and, in Loudoun and northern Fauquier counties, to "consume and destroy all forage and subsistence, burn all barns and mills and their contents, and drive off all stock." The only restraint counseled was in the area of burning dwellings or offering personal violence to civilians. "The ultimate results," continued the order, "of the guerrilla system of warfare is the total destruction of all private rights in the country occupied by such parties. This destruction may as well commence at once, and the responsibility of it must rest upon the authorities at Richmond, who have acknowledged the legitimacy of guerrilla bands."[49]

On November 28, Sheridan telegraphed Gen. John D. Stevenson at Harpers Ferry: "Merritt's division of cavalry crossed the Blue Ridge this morning. . . . Should complaints come in from the citizens of Loudoun County tell them that they have furnished too many meals to guerrillas to expect much sympathy."[50]

Two days later Sheridan's chief of staff wired Stevenson a Sheridan afterthought: "You will direct and order all newspaper correspondents in your district that from and after this morning, Nov. 30, they will not publish any accounts of the movements of troops to or from this army."[51]

By December 3, Merritt's division had returned, reporting the mission a complete success—except that almost no guerrillas had been seen. "The money value of damage done," said the report, "may be estimated by millions. . . . The destruction . . . was most complete."[52]

Merritt's work in Loudoun had been nearly comparable to what Sherman was doing across Georgia. Almost every barn, stable, and hay rick had been burned. Five to six thousand head of cattle had been destroyed or driven off, and over five hundred horses taken. Hams had been chopped off cooling hog carcasses with axes, and the remainder thrown onto bonfires or trampled into the mud. Homes were looted, if not burned. Pillars of dense black smoke rose for days on every horizon, and dull fires flickered lazily on all sides, whipped from time to time by a fresh breeze. Before Merritt had left, smoke and the smell of burning flesh had settled over Loudoun Valley in a thick blanket. Mosby's men attacked small parties when they could, but mostly avoided engagement, concentrating instead on saving the stock. The animals were driven into already-burned areas or into hiding places.

The destruction of Mosby's breadbasket now made possible a move that Sheridan had been unable to carry out all fall. By the time Merritt had turned in his report, most of the Sixth Corps was on its way to Petersburg.

Mosby, too, headed for Petersburg at this time—to speak to Robert E. Lee.

Aristides Monteiro was a surgeon in the Twenty-sixth Virginia, Wise's brigade, stationed at Petersburg. While returning to barracks from Richmond in early December he was accosted on a station platform by a wild-looking but strangely familiar man. "There was something," wrote Monteiro, "about this officer's appearance that would attract the attention of the most indifferent observer. . . . He wore a rough, unkempt beard that imparted a wild yet care-worn expression to his otherwise animated and somewhat fierce physiognomy."[53] He was thrilled to discover that the striking-looking officer was his old classmate, the now-famous Mosby, whom he'd last seen in the Albemarle jail.

After a warm reunion during which Monteiro learned that Mosby was en route to Petersburg to speak to Lee, Mosby asked the doctor what he thought about joining a band of partisans. He said that his present surgeon, Will Dunn, was too fond of fighting, and he was looking for a doctor more interested in curing than killing. Monteiro was delighted at the opportunity. But, he warned, Mosby would first have to get through the forest of red tape involved in such a reassignment.

On arrival at the hospital in Petersburg, Monteiro arranged for an extra horse, and the old friends rode together to Lee's headquarters. After introducing his friend to Lee, Mosby told the commander—"in his usual curt and snappish manner," according to Monteiro—that he wanted the doctor assigned to his own command.[54] The haggard Lee said that Mosby would have to see the army's medical director, Dr. Lafayette Guild, about such a request; he himself could do nothing. The two men then took their leave, rode across the pontoon bridge spanning the Appomattox, and drew up before the medical director's tent.

Monteiro took the liberty of awakening his superior, who

had been napping, and Mosby bluntly stated the object of
their visit. Guild, still half asleep and not realizing who his
visitor was, muttered only that such a change would be impossible and made again for his cot.

Mosby exploded. "This *infamous* red tape!" he cried. "It's
the halter of stupidity and indolence that's strangled Lee and
starved the Southern armies. I *won't* submit to it. You do
what I ask, sir, or you will have an order to that effect by
tomorrow morning from the Secretary of War!"

At this the doctor came fully to his senses and asked the
identity of Monteiro's impudent friend. When informed, he
turned a shade paler, apologized, and reached for Mosby's
hand. Mosby, after a "ghastly grin" at the doctor, thanked
him for at last adopting the proper way of getting important
business done and galloped off, promising to contact Monteiro in the morning.[55]

Monteiro was assured that his transfer would be arranged at
once.

On December 20, Mosby returned to Fauquier to enter
upon what would be for him the last stage of the war. While
in Petersburg and Richmond, he had spoken with both Lee
and Seddon about a division of his command into two bat-
talions, with William Chapman commanding one and Dolly
Richards the other. His plea was that since his scope of duties
was broader than that of equivalent officers in the regular service, he had little time to attend to details of organization and
discipline, which would be better handled under a new arrangement.

The reorganization was approved, and Mosby was promised
immediate appointment as a full colonel. At the same time
William Chapman was commissioned lieutenant colonel, to
take command of the less experienced companies C, E, F,
and the most recently organized G; Dolly Richards was made
a major, with command of the veteran companies A and B, as
well as D.

Mid-December 1864 marked the beginning of a period of
sleet, wet snow, and ice—common winter fare in northern
Virginia. On December 10, Sheridan had advised Grant that
the Valley was under seven inches of snow, and on the

twelfth, that they were in the grip of new snowstorms and intense cold. The bad weather let up for a few days, but had returned by the twentieth, when Mosby arrived from Richmond.

Despite the weather there was to be a "frolic," the occasion being the wedding of the battalion's ordnance sergeant, Jake Lavender. The commander himself planned to be there, if only to show off a wardrobe befitting a full colonel. He arrived for the reception at Joe Blackwell's attired in the latest and best in blockade goods: drab hat with ostrich plume, gold cord and star; heavy black beavercloth overcoat; cape lined with English scarlet; gray cloak, also lined with scarlet. Beneath all this he wore a gray sack coat—still with only two stars on the collar—gray trousers with yellow cord down the seam, and long, shiny cavalry boots. With his "unkempt brown beard" and "somewhat fierce physiognomy," he was easily the most conspicuous of a striking assemblage.

As evening fell and the assortment of grizzled guests began to arrive, a horseman pounded up the icy path and called out for Colonel Mosby. A large Federal column had just been spotted, he said, heading out of Salem toward Rectortown. Mosby pulled on his scarlet-lined cloak and slipped out with Tom Love. The two mounted and headed quickly toward the Rectortown Road to have a look. After an unexpected encounter with a pair of Federal flankers, during which shots were fired by the Yankees, the two men retired to a windswept hilltop to observe the column in safety. What they saw moving on the road was half a thousand-man Federal force sent out the day before from Fairfax to clean out livestock missed by Merritt three weeks earlier.

Smoke was soon observed curling out of the railroad cut in Rectortown, and Mosby decided that the troopers must be staying the night. He and Love first headed to a nearby farmhouse, where they left word with a ranger that Chapman and Richards were to attack the camp at dawn. They then rode toward Rector's Cross Roads to collect more men.

By this time night had fallen, and with it came a freezing rain. The road was slick with ice, a thick sheath of which was building up around the trees. Passing the house of Ludwell Lake, father of a ranger, the two riders saw the candlelit windows and remembered they'd not had dinner. They tethered their mounts and entered just as the table was being laid. Fat old Lake was there, in company with his daughter, recently returned from a visit to her husband in the Federal prison at Point Lookout. Both father and daughter began bustling about at once to make room for the unexpected and honored guests.

Mosby and Love had left their sidearms thrown over their saddles.

"We were enjoying our supper," wrote Mosby, "and her account of the trip . . . when suddenly we heard the tramp of horses around the house. One door of the dining room opened toward the back yard, and on opening it, I discovered several cavalrymen."[56]

It was the advance of the Thirteenth and Sixteenth New York, attracted by the sight of the two military horses tied at the front door. The Yankees, it turned out, had stopped in Rectortown only to warm themselves, and at the moment more than three hundred troopers were nearing the front gate.

"Hastily shutting the door," continued Mosby,

I turned . . . but just then a number of Northern officers and soldiers walked into the room. . . . As the Northerners entered the room, I placed my hands on my coat collar to conceal my stars, and a few words passed between us. The situation seemed desperate. . . . I knew that if they discovered my rank, to say nothing of my name, they would guard me . . . carefully. . . .

But a few seconds elapsed before firing began in the back yard. One of the bullets passed through the window, making a round hole in the glass and striking me in the stomach. . . . My self-possession in concealing the stars on my collar saved me from being carried off a prisoner, dead or alive. The officers had not detected the strategem, when I exclaimed, "I am shot!" . . . My exclamation was not because I felt hurt, but to get up a panic in order that I might escape. It had the desired effect. Old man Lake and his daughter waltzed around the room, the cavalrymen on the outside kept up their fire, and this created a stampede of the officers in the room with me. In the confusion to get out of the way there was a sort of hurdle race, in which the supper table was knocked over, and the tallow lights put out. In a few seconds I was left in the room with no one but Love, Lake, and his daughter. . . .

By this time the terrible wound was having its effect; I was bleeding profusely and getting faint. There was a door which opened from the dining room into an adjoining bedroom, and I determined to play the part of a dying man. I walked into the room, pulled off my coat, on which were the insignia of my rank, tucked it away under the bureau so that no one could see it, and then lay down with my head towards the bureau. After several minutes the panic subsided, and the Northerners returned. . . . They found my old friend Lake dancing a hornpipe. . . . Having heard me fall on the floor, he thought I was dead—the truth was he was almost as near dead as I was. The daughter was screaming, the room in which I lay was dark, and it was some minutes before the soldiers collected their senses sufficiently to strike a light.[57]

Love was quickly taken prisoner, and Lake and his daughter were questioned about the wounded man's identity. To Mosby's immense relief, they swore never to have seen him before. Maj. Douglas Frazar, commanding the New York cavalry, approached the prostrate Mosby with a lighted candle. "I . . . found a man lying on the floor," reported Frazar,

apparently in great agony. I asked him his name; he answered, Lieutenant Johnston, Sixth Virginia Cavalry. He was in his shirtsleeves—light blue cotton shirt—no hat, no boots, and no insignia of rank; nothing to denote in the slightest degree that he was not what he pretended to be. I told him I must see his wound to see whether to bring him or not. I opened . . . his pants, and found that a pistol bullet had entered the abdomen about two inches below and to the left of the navel; a wound that I felt assured was mortal. I therefore ordered all from the room, remarking, he will die in twenty-four hours.[58]

"I only gasped a few words," said Mosby, "and affected to be dying. They left the room hurriedly, after stripping me of my . . . trousers, evidently supposing that a dead man would have no use for them. The only sensible man among them was an Irishman, who said, as he took a last look at me, 'He is worth several dead men yet.' . . . Fortunately they never saw my coat."[59]

Mosby lay still for five or ten minutes, until certain that the Northerners had gone. Lake and his daughter, convinced they had just seen the guerrilla chief shot to death in their house, sat staring into the fire.

"I rose from the pool of blood in which I was lying," continued Mosby, "and walked into the room. . . . They were as much astonished to see me as if I had risen from the tomb. . . . We examined the wound. . . . Shortly I became sick and faint. My own belief was that the wound was mortal."[60]

As soon as Lake recovered from his shock, he called out excitedly to two black boys to hitch up an oxcart. Mosby wanted to be taken to Aquilla Glascock's farm nearby, before the Federals discovered their mistake and returned.

"After a while," he recalled, "the ox-cart was announced, and I was rolled up in quilts and blankets and put into it. It was an awful night—a howling storm of snow, rain, and sleet. I was lying on my back in the cart—we had to go two miles . . . over a frozen road cut into deep ruts. . . . I was almost perfectly stiff with cold, and my hair was a clotted mass of ice."[61]

The wedding party dissolved when word reached Blackwell's, and before daybreak a number of rangers had arrived at the small cabin in Glascock's woods. Others fanned out through the area to watch the Yankees and to discourage snooping. Will Dunn and another surgeon were summoned, and early in the morning Mosby was chloroformed and the ball removed. After a week of rest in various safe houses in Fauquier, he was taken by a devious route to his father's home.

Several rangers had been picked up in the cavalry sweep, and despite their vehement denials that the man shot had even been a member of Mosby's battalion—let alone Mosby himself—the truth began to dawn on the Yankees: they had actually had Mosby in hand and let him get away. Frazar, known to have been half-drunk during the incident, came in for severe criticism. Col. William Gamble, commanding First Separate Cavalry Brigade at Fairfax, wrote in his December 27 report: "Major Frazar did not search the officer for papers, nor inquire who he was from the people in the house; neither did he search the house; and, although two ambulances and a medical officer were with the command, the wounded rebel officer was not examined or brought in."[62] On January 1 he noted on Frazar's own report: "I exceedingly regret that such a blunder was made. I have given directions that all wounded officers and men of the enemy be hereafter brought in, although I thought any officer ought to have brains and common sense enough to do so without an order."[63]

Even as Mosby was being carried to his parents' home, heavy forces from Sheridan's Valley army and Augur's Washington defenses were scouring Loudoun and Fauquier counties in search of him. Some civilians who had seen his ambulance pass reported to Federal troopers that he was spitting blood and appeared close to death.

Actually, soon after arriving home he started to mend, as Monteiro, newly released from duty at Petersburg and hurrying to his bedside, found out. "Monteiro was a great wit," wrote Mosby, "and had been with me only a few minutes when he got me to laughing. This produced a hemorrhage from my wound, and it took all his surgical skill to repair the damage his talk had done."[64]

On December 31, Sheridan wired Bvt. Maj. Gen. William H. Emory from Winchester: "How are you getting along? This storm is unfortunate. I have no news today, except the death of Mosby. He died from his wounds at Charlottesville."[65]

7

SURVIVOR

Major Parsons can return . . . now that Booth has been
caught. The general wishes you to try and hunt up Mosby.
—C. H. Morgan to Alfred T.
A. Torbert, April 28, 1865

O
N THE NIGHT of Sunday, April 2, under cover of
darkness, Lee's army began to slip away from the
trenches at Petersburg.

It was all but finished. On the previous day,
Sheridan, recently arrived from a victorious Valley campaign,
had cracked the Confederate right and taken more than 3,000
prisoners at Five Forks, 17 miles to the southwest. Union artillery had then played upon the Petersburg works throughout
the night, softening them for the final assault, and on Sunday
morning, in a thick ground fog, Grant had begun to storm in.
By noon of this glorious spring day he had almost succeeded
in taking the prize that had eluded him for nearly a year.

With the armor of Confederate trenches at Petersburg torn
apart, Richmond's belly was bare. At 10:00 A.M., therefore,
Lee telegraphed President Davis that the capital ought to be
evacuated that night, and preparations for the flight of the
Confederate government were set in motion at once.

As darkness fell over the crumbling Petersburg defenses,
horsemen and men on foot began running about, shouting the
latest orders: burn all pontoon bridges immediately, and all
units drive westward for regrouping at Amelia Court House.
An attempt was then to be made to link up with Johnston's
army, fighting Sherman in North Carolina. Petersburg and the
capital were being left to the enemy.

At the same moment a tide of humanity was washing into
the westward roads out of Richmond. William Blackford was
caught up in it and described the scene:

[There] came a perfect army of bureau clerks, quartermasters, commissaries, and ordnance officers—all dressed in fine clothes and uniforms, with white faces, scared half to death, fellows who had for the most part been in these bomb-proof offices ever since the war began and who did not relish the prospect of smelling powder now, nor of having to rough it a bit like ordinary mortals in the field. Then there were . . . politicians, members of Congress, prominent citizens, almost all on foot, but sometimes there were wagons and carriages loaded with them.

Fat old naval commodores limped along, he said, puffing and blowing, and "cursing everything black and blue." Women, too, were fleeing with their families, and, he noted, "Generally they were calmer than the men."[1]

The women seem to have provided the evacuation's only scrap of dignity.

Lee had wanted to give up Richmond several days earlier, but Davis had resisted. By holding onto Richmond until Grant was practically at the gates, however, he lost all hope of a controlled retreat and condemned his army to fly before Grant and Sheridan with little order and almost no provisions.

"Why Jeff. Davis should have preferred to be kicked out of Richmond to evacuating it in a dignified manner," complained Blackford, "I suppose he himself does not know. It was the egotistical, bull-headed obstinacy of the man, no doubt. He was sitting in church in Richmond when Grant broke our line. I suppose he thought praying would help him out of the scrape his folly had placed him in."[2]

In the confusion and panic the lower part of the town was burned—site of huge tobacco warehouses, filled to the brim.

"Millions and millions of dollars worth of property was destroyed," continued Blackford in a vein reminiscent of his remarks on Manassas. "Here went up in smoke tobacco enough to have made things easy in the whole state. Many and many a family had put their all in tobacco, stored in the warehouses there and then burned. Burned by nothing else in the world than Davis' obstinacy in not retiring sooner so that order could have been secured."[3]

By 3:00 A.M. on the third, the Yankees realized that Petersburg was defenseless. Within an hour they were in possession of the city, and five hours later their columns were marching into a still-smoldering Richmond.

Grant did not bother to harass the rear of the fleeing army, but struck without hesitation for its head. In combination with Sheridan's troops, now, he raced to cut off Lee's escape, the two Federal armies pouring on a deadly skirmish fire from the flank with sixteen-shot repeating rifles. Lack of adequate food began to take its toll on the Southerners as great numbers of soldiers, forced to march daily on scraps of bacon and crackers, started to collapse and fall out of the ranks. The life of the tattered Confederacy was quickly becoming measurable in hours.

On the seventh, after punishing the Confederate remnant for most of a week, Grant sent a team through rebel lines under flag of truce. When Lee's orderlies came forward to meet the Federal officers, one of them was handed a note suggesting the immediate surrender of the Army of Northern Virginia.

Merritt's raid in early December had devastated Loudoun and upper Fauquier, making it now indistinguishable from the rest of northern Virginia. The constant crisscrossing of warring armies had long since turned the land between Alexandria and Brandy Station into a wasteland; across the Blue Ridge, Sheridan had charred the fecund Shenandoah Valley beyond recognition, burning barns, slaughtering and seizing stock, destroying and carrying off crops. Now all over these once beautiful northern counties, smoke-blackened chimneys stood stark against the winter sky, marking the homesites of a former age. In "Mosby's Confederacy," raiding and burning went on sporadically into the new year, as pressure continued both from Sheridan and Augur.

The destruction had its desired effect: not enough food was left in the Loudoun Valley to sustain Mosby's seven companies, and popular support was eroding. Immediately after New Year's, therefore, William Chapman took his four companies to winter in the relatively untouched Northern Neck—that part of tidewater Virginia bounded by the Potomac in the north and the Rappahannock to the south.

Richards remained behind with his three companies, and despite constant harassment by Sheridan and Augur, continued scaled-down operations both in the Valley and in Fairfax. In late January he derailed and burned another train on the B & O, and in a February action that again showed him to be the equal of Mosby as a guerrilla commander, he dealt very harshly with the Fourteenth Pennsylvania Cavalry near Ashby's Gap.

On the day that Chapman was packing up to head for the Northern Neck, the wounded Mosby was arriving home, accompanied by his brother and a surgeon, and soon to be joined by Monteiro. He recovered quickly. By mid-month he was seen, lean and drawn, walking in downtown Lynchburg; by early February, Richmond papers were reporting his appearance in the capital. He came as a hero. On January 30, still gaunt from his ordeal, he was escorted to a privileged chair on the floor of the Confederate House of Delegates. On February 1 he was, in his words, "paid . . . a singular compliment" by the Senate. As he wrote to Pauline on February 3:

> I have had every mark of respect and attention shown me in Richmond. . . . I reckon you would have been very much amused at my awkwardness when going through the embarrassing ceremony of being introduced to the legislature. Old Lud Lake wasn't half as much frightened when the Yankees were shooting all around him. But the worst part was when the ladies' turn came. If there had been any decent way of doing so I would have backed clean out.[4]

He took good advantage of the respite. The artist Edward Caledon Bruce—presently engaged in painting General Lee—was also working on a portrait of him, he told Pauline, as was the French artist, Guillaume.

On Thursday, February 2, after his appearance at the legislature, Mosby drove to Petersburg for a talk with Lee. In reference probably to a gift he had once made to the general, he reported to Pauline that "on his writing table was a small tobacco box to which he pointed," asking if his guest recognized it, "at the same time remarking that 'he was very proud of it, and showed it to everyone who came to see him.'"[5]

Lee always seemed to have time for Mosby, perhaps due

partly to the fact that his own father had been a partisan fighter against the British. He invited the visiting convalescent to share his meager dinner—a sorry-looking leg of mutton which, Lee said, "some of his staff officers must have stolen."[6] After dinner, candles flickering between the two men, Lee spoke to him freely, criticizing Johnston for having retired to Richmond instead of threatening Washington in the spring of 1862 and for not having made a stand afterward with his full army at Williamsburg when falling back from Yorktown.

As Mosby took his leave, Lee encouraged him to get some of his men together when he felt up to it, and give the Yankees around Petersburg a taste of what he'd been dealing out further north.

"Lee," commented Mosby, "was the most aggressive man I met in the war."[7]

The Sunday after his dinner with Lee, Mosby accepted an invitation from Col. Robert Ould, Confederate commissioner of prisoner exchange, to join him on the steamer *Mary Allison,* scheduled that day to take several hundred Yankee prisoners down the James for exchange. Since his public appearances in Richmond, Mosby had acquired an entourage of female admirers who also found a way to get onto the *Mary Allison.* A subsequent article in the *Washington Evening Star* noted their presence with him on the exchange boat, and Mosby's overall conviviality. "He seems to be quite friendly with some of our officers," stated the article, "but the majority of them did not notice him. He looks quite thin."[8]

What the *Star* did not report was that when the sallow Confederate stepped on deck, chatting with his new acquaintances, a blue-coated boy burst from the throng of prisoners and flung his arms about him. He was a drummer named Jimmie Daly, on his way to be exchanged. Mosby, embarrassed, had now to explain to his companions how he had once saved the lad from hanging at a place called Rectortown.

By mid-month Mosby had come home to spend a few days with his wife, three children, and parents before returning to his command in Fauquier. But the South was crumbling around them. Sherman was cutting a swath of destruction through the Carolinas, and men were deserting Lee's army in droves as Lee struggled with his government for a soldier's simple right to sufficient food. Gen. John B. Gordon told how he'd been accosted during these terrible days by a hungry private with the tongue-in-cheek question: "I say, General, can't you give us a little fodder?"[9]

But even proper rations could not have held the South together at this point. By early March, with Mosby returned to his command and preparing to engage in new battles, Early had been finally swept from the Shenandoah Valley, and Sheridan was pushing his trains and cannon through axle-deep mud in grim-faced advance upon Charlottesville and Petersburg.

Sunday, April 9, dawned clear and bright, and the smell of apple and peach blossom gave substance to the air. In the Confederate camps, now pitched around Appomattox Court House, soldiers who seldom had time to notice light, color, or smell were savoring a day that promised to be different. The sun had rolled up over the horizon, was beginning already to cast shortening shadows, and still the expectant army had received no marching orders. With only some desultory cannon and musket fire in the distance, weary men began to settle around their cooking fires in the waxing sunshine, pull out well-worn pipes, and speculate.

Blackford was dumbstruck when a Union officer rode boldly into this scene and asked to speak to General Gordon. He was further astonished when this "short, heavily built, coarse-looking man" introduced himself as Gen. Philip Sheridan.[10] While Sheridan and Gordon conferred, a rattling skirmish fire broke out nearby; but all over, Confederate batteries were becoming gradually silent, limbering up, and moving, ghostlike, to the rear.

Lee, impeccable in full dress uniform, with sword and sash, had ridden over that morning to meet a mud-spattered Grant in the nearby McLean farmhouse, signing articles of surrender there. Lee and his staff then moved back to their bivouac in an apple orchard, where they spent the remainder of the day. Blackford, assigned to the cordon surrounding the Southern commander, observed that Lee was like a caged lion—"in one of his savage moods."[11] Bothered by a steady stream of visitors on this, the blackest day of his life, he did little more than stand at attention and glare at all comers. Although shown great deference by everyone, he refused either to touch his hat or to shake hands with any, regardless of rank. He was curt, and saw to it that all interviews were kept as short and as unpleasant as possible.

Toward sundown, with Federal commissary wagons now distributing rations to the half-starved Confederates, Lee mounted his dapple-gray, Traveller, and moved off to his headquarters in the rear. As he passed through the ranks, his men cheered wildly, threw their hats into the air, shouted his name, and wept without shame.

Hat in hand now, and head bowed, Lee too wept.

In the days to come, the several thousand Confederates who would give their word not to bear arms against the United States during the course of the war would return to a land that was not the land they had left. It was in many places blackened and death-stricken, peopled by marauding bands of both whites and blacks who preyed upon returning soldier and civilian alike. The murderers and thieves were outnumbered only by the homeless, the crippled, the orphans, and the beggars. Railroad service had come to a halt, and commerce was nonexistent. Scarcity of goods and outrageous inflation made the beginning of a new life nearly hopeless. Civil authority was no more, and military authority had not yet come to be.

Civilization in the South would clearly have to be built again from the beginning.

On April 12, Mosby received an envelope, left at a letter drop in the Valley the day before, from headquarters, Middle Military Division, United States Army. The envelope contained a printed circular signed by Sheridan's successor in the Valley, Maj. Gen. Winfield Scott Hancock, which disclosed details of Lee's surrender and the parole of his troops, promised the destruction of "marauding bands," prohibited citizens from sheltering them, and contained the statement: "The guerrilla chief Mosby is not included in the parole."[12] Around the same time a circular with a similar statement about Mosby was received from Augur's department.

Curiously, in the envelope with Hancock's circular was a personal letter from the new commander's chief of staff, Bvt.

Brig. Gen. C. H. Morgan, calling on Mosby to surrender, and promising the same terms as had been extended to Lee, should Mosby "conclude to be governed by [Lee's] example."[13]

The circulars branded Mosby an outlaw, while Morgan's letter offered to deal with him as a gentleman. Confused, Mosby did not immediately respond. But by April 14, with guerrilla activities continuing unabated, Hancock decided he had waited long enough, and ordered a large-scale anti-guerrilla sweep of Loudoun and Fauquier counties with his own and Augur's troops. It was only the shooting at Ford's Theater that evening that prevented the joint action.

By Saturday, April 15, Mosby had framed a reply. William Chapman, just returned from his winter in the Northern Neck, was ordered to carry the letter into the Union camps, accompanied by Monteiro, Willie Mosby, and Walter Frankland. The letter stated that although "the emergency [had not] yet arisen which would justify the surrender of [his] command," Mosby would agree to a truce—a truce long enough to enable him to verify the facts about Lee's surrender.[14] He would then decide his own course. "I am ready to meet any person you may designate," he concluded, "to arrange the terms of an armistice."[15]

The four Confederates took the envelope, swam their horses across the rain-swollen Shenandoah, and under flag of truce, cantered into the Union lines at Winchester.

Despite suspicion at the highest levels of Mosby's complicity in the President's assassination, Hancock received Chapman and Monteiro cordially, even relaying to them a dinner invitation from his cavalry chief, General Torbert. After dictating a reply to Mosby's letter and chatting a while, Hancock escorted the two men to the door. He was smiling. "It is rumored," he said, "that Colonel Mosby is here. Observe the curiosity of the army to see your leader."

A press of troops, all craning their necks to see the two men, made exit impossible, so Hancock led them to the back door. But they were discovered there as well. Monteiro, with his gift for description, recorded the scene that followed.[16]

"Which is Mosby? Which is Mosby?" the soldiers asked one another. Chapman pointed to Monteiro and Monteiro at

Chapman. Then, as the two Confederates began to force their way through the sea of jostling blue coats, the comments became more colorful.

Some expressed surprise that "such an ornery man should have made sich a fuss in the wore." One said that "he must hav' bin an ugly cuss frum the way he behaved heself, but he wuz really wuss lookin' than we had spozen he wuz." Another: "Lor! what a hard-lookin' feller! No wonder he fout so, frum his looks. He looks like a foutin' man, he do."

"I ain't never seen no wuss lookin' man, I ain't. He don't look like he tame yet, he don't."

"He dang'rous feller to turn lose now, you bet."

"He don't look like a bad man. He ugly though."

"I wouldn't like to trus' him now, if he *has* gin it up, I woulden."

"No wonder we coulden ketch him befo'. He look like a fox, he do."

"Thank God he done gin it up, I say."

"I didn't think he look like that, I didn't."

"As the various reflections fell equally upon myself and my comrade," concluded Monteiro, " . . . we divided the doubtful compliments between us the best we could."[17]

At dinner Monteiro found the gaunt and moustachioed Torbert a "pleasant fellow, but excessively polite, and a little vain."[18] After some parting formalities the men collected their two companions—by now struggling manfully to empty a keg of Ohio whiskey with a tentful of Yankees—and headed back to Mosby with Hancock's favorable response. Hancock had agreed to an armistice. He regarded it, in fact, as already in effect, and had offered to send a representative to meet with Mosby at Millwood three days hence for the purpose of discussing the colonel's plans. The armistice would last until noon of the proposed meeting day—the following Tuesday.

The reply left Mosby unmoved. "One of Mosby's peculiarities," remarked the doctor,

> when engaged in profound meditation was the habit of picking his teeth with a wooden toothpick, gazing at nothing with great intensity, then deliberately chewing the toothpick until it was entirely destroyed. Until this process was ended it was

useless to address him, as he was never known to make a reply, even to the most important question, while any of the
toothpick remained. . . . On this occasion . . . he consumed
three or four toothpicks, and said not a word until the last
vestige of wood had disappeared. It was his custom when re-
covering from one of these protracted reveries to speak of
some subject entirely foreign to whatever theme furnished the
topic of his last conversation. After thinking . . . for a long
time he turned to me with a vacant expression and a most
unmeaning grin and asked me, with the air of a sick man . . . ,
"Doctor, what do you think of the widow." [19]

Mosby had a lady friend—a "grass widow"—whose husband
had been away for years in the California gold fields. She was
lately nursing an active interest in the doctor, abetted by
Mosby, who had represented Monteiro to her as quite a
catch.

"Confound the widow!" roared Monteiro. "What on earth
does the widow have to do with the serious business before us
now? How can you talk about something so frivolous as the
widow at a time like this?"

"I don't know," said Mosby absently. "The widow don't
seem so frivolous to me. I believe you're afraid of her."

When the subject had been finally exhausted, Mosby left a
spluttering Monteiro and went off by himself. The ominous
thought of a board of military justice had crossed his mind,
and he had no wish to be murdered by such a tribunal on the
basis of hearsay or newspaper evidence. On the other hand,
there could be no harm in talking. He would go to Millwood.

As noon of Tuesday the eighteenth approached, a large
number of Yankees were gathering at Millwood to witness the
expected surrender of the legendary Mosby; but the morning
went by and they grew progressively disappointed. He had
not come. Then, shortly before noon, at the very hour at
which the truce was to expire, the Confederate delegation
thundered into the little Valley town and dismounted hurriedly in front of its only "hotel," site of the proposed discussions.

Mosby was there, as were several of his officers and men.
Hancock's representative, a bespectacled brigadier named
George Chapman, was friendly, but expressed his regret that

Colonel Mosby had arrived so late; it would be difficult, he said, to arrange the terms of surrender in the half hour remaining before truce's end. Mosby, probably breathing a sigh of relief, proposed a further truce of forty-eight hours, and, conditional upon the approval of Hancock, a ten-day truce beyond that. He insisted upon a need to communicate with his government—despite General Chapman's gentle insistence that his "government" was no more—and hinted that he would probably not surrender the battalion under any circumstances but would instead disband, allowing his men to choose their own course.

"He informed me," reported Chapman later, "he had already advised his command that those who chose to do so could come and give their parole. For himself he said he had no favors to ask, being quite willing to stand by his acts, all of which he believed to be justifiable, and in the course of my conversation with him he remarked that he did not expect to remain in the country."[20]

They agreed to meet again at Millwood on the twentieth.

The brief meeting had been carried out with good feeling on both sides, and the Confederates had been particularly careful to express their regret over the death of the President.

When Hancock telegraphed Grant on the matter of a ten-day truce with Mosby, however, he was answered by a resounding no, which he attempted to relay at once to the Virginian.[21] The truce would end at noon on the twentieth, wrote Hancock, and if Mosby had not surrendered his battalion by then, no further terms could be offered. The message did not reach Mosby before his second arrival in Millwood.

As the Confederate officers stepped for the second time onto the hotel porch and strode into the parlor—late again—the eyes of dozens of silent Yankees followed them. General Chapman and his aides waited within. Almost as soon as he had sat down, Mosby was handed the envelope from Hancock.

This second meeting promised right away to be less pleasant than the first, for when Mosby had finished reading Hancock's negative reply, he was given a stern verbal warning as well: if he did not surrender his command at once, Hancock's

40,000 men—with nothing else at present to distract them—
would proceed immediately to dismantle "Mosby's Confederacy" and turn it into a desert. The choice was his.

The threat rocked him; his stunned response was only:
"Tell General Hancock he is able to do it."[22]

He determined to disband at once.

As if the moment were not fragile enough, it was made
more so by an irrepressible Louisiana lad named Hearn, a
ranger who had accompanied Mosby's party without invitation. Hearn was, in Monteiro's words, "a rough diamond,"
and no diplomat.[23] He fell in with some Yankees as soon as
Mosby and his twenty officers had entered the hotel, and in a
moment was engaged in heated discussion about the relative
merits of his and some of the Yankee horses he had seen tethered around town. Before long a race had been arranged.
Monteiro described what followed:

> [Hearn] had a vague suspicion that the Yankees had planned
> this meeting for the purpose of capturing Mosby and his of-
> ficers. . . . In the race with his Yankee competitor an event
> occurred that ripened his suspicion into a certainty. . . . Hern
> [*sic*] and his rival turfman, after testing the speed of their
> horses nearly a mile, ran into the solid ranks of a Federal
> brigade. . . . His suspicion of foul play became a fixed
> conviction. He abandoned the race and returned with . . . ear-
> nestness and speed. . . . Just as the [Yankee general] an-
> nounced to Mosby . . . "The truce has ended . . . "—at this
> moment Hern rushed into the room. . . . "Colonel, Colonel,"
> he exclaimed, "the infernal devils have sot a trap for you; I jist
> now run out about a mile and I found a thousand uv um a
> hidin' in the bushes! They're in ambush! Less fight um, Colo-
> nel; darn um! It's a trick; it's a trick to capture us, by G_d, it
> is!"[24]

Chairs were overturned throughout the room as jittery
Confederates sprang to their feet. Mosby, one hand moving
toward his revolver, rose quickly and looked around the
room. His men were ready, fanning out, watching. General
Chapman came cautiously to his feet and said something, attempting to defuse the situation.

"Sir," Mosby snapped at him, "if we are no longer under

the protection of our truce we are of course at the mercy of your men. We shall protect ourselves."[25]

In a few quick strides he was at the door, followed by his officers. All then stormed across the porch, mounted, and lashed their animals mercilessly in a dead run to the Shenandoah, and safety. Hancock later reported only that Mosby had become "very much agitated" upon learning that no further truce would be offered, and made immediate plans to run the rebel command to the ground.[26]

On the following morning, Friday, the remnant of Mosby's 800-man command (some had already surrendered) headed to a final gathering at Salem. The men drifted in from all directions to join the companies forming up on a green near the edge of town. They were dressed impeccably for the occasion. All wore clean gray uniforms, shiny cavalry boots, and soft hats topped with waving plumes. They were mounted and armed with the best the Yankee cavalry had been able to supply.

The April air was damp and raw, relic of an early morning rain and of a thick ground fog that still hung over the country. As the men filed in, Mosby paced up and down the muddy street, occasionally talking to a lady or stopping a soldier for a moment of conversation. At noon the order was given to mount, and the several hundred riders formed up in a double line across the green. Mosby waited, and then, as nervous horses tossed their heads, rode slowly along the silent ranks of moist-eyed men in final inspection. He returned to his place and looked on as his brother and the two battalion commanders each stepped forward with a piece of paper, to declaim together his farewell address:

> Soldiers! I have summoned you to gather for the last time. The vision we have cherished of a free and independent country has vanished, and that country is now the spoil of a conqueror. I disband your organization in preference to surrendering it to our enemies. I am now no longer your commander. After an association of more than two eventful years, I part from you with a just pride in the fame of your achievements and grateful recollections of your generous kindness to myself. And now at this moment of bidding you a final adieu, accept the assurance of my unchanging confidence and regard. Farewell![27]

After a long moment, three resounding cheers were raised, and ranks were broken forever.

On Saturday, April 22, William Chapman and two hundred of Mosby's now-storied rangers rode into the Union lines around Winchester to sign their paroles. Others would head elsewhere to surrender. Many of the men with Chapman, expecting their horses to be confiscated, had been careful to leave their own mounts at home and instead had procured old farm animals that had long ago been turned out to pasture, some lame, others blind, and most suffering from some form of crippling affliction. The Yankees could not help but notice.

"These ain't the nags you boys been chasin' us up and down the Valley with, is they?" asked one mock-incredulous Yank.

Another: "Say, Johnnie, when was you boys paid off last anyway?"

"Not since we run that paymaster's train offen the B & O," was the quick rejoinder to this one.

Meanwhile Mosby, with a few diehards, headed south to join Johnston's army. But on his arrival at the outskirts of Richmond, he learned that that army was no more. Johnston had surrendered. There was no longer anyone to fight with and nothing to fight for. He urged the rest of his men to surrender.

In early May—with a $5,000 price now upon his head and some of his own men out to claim it—Mosby set out alone for Lynchburg and home. By a combination of boldness and furtiveness, he dodged Federal troops across Virginia for the following month, visiting Richmond, Charlottesville, and Lynchburg. His family, meanwhile, was pressing Lee through intermediaries to find out what the Yankees had in store for him if he were to turn himself in.

After several weeks of outlaw life, sleeping in barns, woods, and fields across the Virginia wasteland, staying with relatives and friends, Mosby received word that his parole would be accepted if he would come in to sign. On June 12 he came home, and next day borrowed a buggy from a neighbor to drive into Lynchburg with Willie. Both brothers were armed, and Mosby, despite the war's having ended two months before, was in full Confederate uniform.

The two men proceeded cautiously in the Yankee-occupied town, going first to the relative safety of a cousin's law office until they could verify the Federal commandant's intentions. Mosby's worst fears were realized when word was brought of a change in plans: something had gone wrong, and the current orders from Washington were to arrest him on sight.

He began to pace furiously. "I had brought my pistols in my holsters with me—they were lying on the floor," he recalled. "I took the pistols from the holsters and laid them on the table by me and remarked, 'I am *ultimus Romanorum*—I will not submit to arrest. I will kill the first man who attempts it.'"[28]

A man was sent flying to warn the commandant, General Gregg, that the partisan leader was planning to cut his way out of town. Mosby continued:

I threw my holsters with my pistols across my shoulder and with my brother walked down to the street. A great crowd of citizens and soldiers had collected but there was no hostile demonstration. Just then Capt. Charles Blackford came up and told me that several gentlemen of Lynchburg had authorized him to say to me that if I wished to leave the country they would furnish me all the money I needed. I declined the offer. . . . I [was not] willing by flight to confess that I had been guilty of any act that should make me an exception from other Confederate officers.[29]

Gregg, aware that Mosby had come in good faith, ordered his troops not to touch the Confederate while he was in town. The following day, however, fifty cavalrymen stormed into the front yard at Idle Wilde, and although their quarry had flown, they succeeded in badly frightening Mosby's mother.

Two days later word was received that the arrest order had been somehow rescinded, and that an approach would again be welcome.

On June 17 the two brothers, tired but more wary than ever, again climbed into the buggy for the drive into town. This time, however, all went well. On this day the renowned partisan leader and last Confederate officer to surrender signed the piece of paper which meant that for him the struggle was finally over.

At least that was what he thought it meant.

PEACE

Mosby in his first postwar photo as a civilian, his favorite photograph of himself. *Credit: Cook Collection, Valentine Museum*

8

PARIAH

The South has imitated Saturn in devouring his own children.
                            —John S. Mosby to B. L.
                            Fletcher, July 20, 1880

I T MIGHT HAVE BEEN an awkward moment, but it proved not to be: the two soldiers, formerly enemies, took to each other instantly. Mosby had seen Grant before—once in a box at the National Theater with General Sherman, and once at the inauguration in 1869—but this was the first time he had come actually face to face with the man who, seven years before, had battered Lee and the South into submission. The meeting had been arranged by friends, chiefly by Virginia's Senator John F. Lewis, to bring together two men who might be of service to one another. It was 1872, and Grant was gearing up for a second run at the presidency. Mosby, some felt, could be the man to help him through the difficult "Southern question," the solution of which had so far eluded him. Grant, thought Mosby, might be the man to save the South from itself.

The meeting was a coup of sorts for each. Reporters crowded about the north portico of the White House in the warm May sunshine to glean what they could from the unusual get-together. "In his personal appearance," noted the *Washington Star* that evening,

Colonel M. hardly comes up to the popular idea of a guerrilla chief. . . . He is a little below the medium height. His face is smooth shaved, and he is apparently about 35 years of age. He is a pleasant spoken and mild mannered man, and to converse with him one could scarce bring himself to believe that he is really the man who harassed the rear of our armies in Virginia during the rebellion.[1]

With the initial pleasantries behind them, Grant, Mosby,

159

and the remainder of the party adjourned to the second floor
to talk business. Among those present were Senator Lewis,
Philadelphia journalist John W. Forney, Mississippi carpetbag
senator Adelbert Ames, and Mosby's twelve-year-old son
Beverly.[2]

The President, settling down in a favorite leather chair, fin-
gered a particularly vile-looking cigar, and allowed Forney to
break the ice.

"Colonel Mosby," Forney began with a smile, "I have
heard of you before."

The Virginia man flashed a weaker smile and answered,
somewhat gravely, "Yes, and I've heard of you, sir—through
your paper. I used to get it nearly every day through the lines.
Seems to me I've read some pretty sharp things in it about
myself."

"Had I known you were such a good-looking young man,"
replied the unflappable Forney, "I would not have been so
hard upon you."

The ice went out in a gush of laughter, and Grant shifted in
his chair.

Colonel Mosby, said the President, had once nearly changed
the course of the war, although probably even now didn't realize it. Mosby's ears pricked up, and all attention moved to
President Grant.

"In the spring of 1864," he began in his low-pitched but
marvelously distinct and musical voice, "just after I had taken
command of the army, I was returning by rail from Washington to Culpeper, where my headquarters were at the time. I'd
just come from seeing Mr. Lincoln—my last meeting with him
before our great offensive began. The train was coming up to
Warrenton Junction, and we all noticed a heavy cloud of dust
east of the road—the sort of cloud that might be made by a
body of cavalry on a charge."

He paused to savor his listeners' attentive silence, then
went on:

"I ordered the train stopped at the Junction, and sent
someone to inquire about the cause of the dust. The man at
the station, a trifle excited, replied that Colonel Mosby
here"—the President inclined his head toward his guest—

"had crossed the road only a few moments, in full pursuit of some Federal cavalry."

"I breathed a sigh of relief when I heard it," continued the President. "I've no doubt that, had he seen us coming, he would have preferred seizing a Yankee railroad train to whatever he was up to at the moment—and surely he would have been pleased to find me among the passengers." He smiled faintly at Mosby as he lit a fresh cigar, and in the midst of a venomous smoke cloud, shook out the match.

"I was on a special train, as I recall—with no guard."

During the murmur of approval following Grant's story, Mosby made a lame attempt at humor. "Well," he said, "if I had got hold of that particular train, maybe I'd be President now and General Grant here would be calling on me." Polite laughter followed.

After further reminiscing, the meeting came to the point: How did Mosby think the "Southrons" in general, and Virginia in particular, would vote in November if the choice were between Grant and Greeley? Horace Greeley—long-time editor of the *New York Tribune,* political activist, maverick philosopher, a man increasingly regarded as a simple crackpot and thoroughly detested in the South—had just been nominated by the burgeoning Liberal splinter of Grant's own Radical Republican party to run against the President in November. It was believed that the Democrats, unable to field a stronger candidate, would also endorse Greeley at their convention in July.

"I think," answered Mosby slowly, "that the South this time will not vote for a party, but for a man. Southerners will vote for whoever will be most generous to them, regardless of party. Lord knows they can't expect much of old Horace. But they surrendered to you, sir, and you have nothing to lose by liberality. If Southerners can *see* that, they'll vote for you."

Grant, who had so far seen precious little evidence that the South would support him against anybody, replied somewhat defensively that he'd always been well-disposed toward the Southern people; that if anything he'd done in the South seemed harsh, it was simply the result of his upholding laws he was sworn to uphold.

"Why, right after the war," he said, leaning forward in his chair, "I had the greatest difficulty in persuading Johnson to be lenient to your people. He was bent especially on arresting General Lee and other prominent Confederates—wanted them tried for treason. He was forever sending to me, asking when their trials were going to get under way. My reply was invariably, 'Not until they violate their oaths.'"

"Although the South does not seem to know it," concluded the President, sitting back again, "I've frequently been sympathetic to its problems."

The point struck a responsive chord in Mosby. He'd been harassed continually after the war, he said, despite his parole. Several times he'd been arrested on petty or trumped-up charges. "To put a stop to this," he explained, looking around the group, "my wife went to see old Andy himself. Now Johnson and my wife's daddy had served together in the House before the war, and Johnson had always been a friend of my wife's family—so she expected a good result from the visit."

"Well," he continued, "Johnson had a reputation in the North for being soft on Southrons, but he was not soft on all of them. He was downright rude to Pauline—told her that if he had his way all the damn rebel leaders like her husband would be stretching hemp, and that she'd do him a great favor by clearing out of his office."

He looked at the President. "You remember, General, that she went to see you then?" Grant nodded.

"You gave her the piece of paper I needed—in your own handwriting: exemption from arrest, and permission to travel anywhere in the United States. No one ever bothered me again, I can tell you."

Slipping his arm around his son's shoulder, he drew the boy close as he continued: "Li'l Reverdy here was with her that day—six years old he was. When he knelt down that night in the Metropolitan Hotel to say his prayers with his ma he said, 'Ma, may I pray to god to send old Johnson to the devil?'" The boy's ears went scarlet in the laughter that followed.

"There are a good many," agreed the President, smiling, "who would have joined gratefully in Bev's prayer."

At this moment Secretary of State Hamilton Fish entered for a private word with the President. When he had left,

Grant returned to the point: What about Greeley and the South?

Mosby warmed to the subject. The election of Greeley, he said, would open a Pandora's box of evils upon Southerners. The men surrounding Greeley could be expected to be worse even than those who had wormed their way into Grant's own administration. The President winced.

"If the South has to undergo further humiliation," continued Mosby, "I for one don't want it to be at the hands of that fanatical old philosopher. But that's *my* stand—I can't say yet how Virginia or the South would go. Some of my acquaintance would not vote for Horace—but others would. In my own district, now, Lewis McKenzie's come out for Greeley. Mack is very popular with the Negroes—he may well carry them over with him for Horace." A smile played over Mosby's thin lips as he concluded: "But let him do it, general. Let him take the Negroes, and you take the white folks."

"Yes," remarked Grant, harumphing a little, "yes, well, I think there's not so much difference between Greeley and myself politically. The issue between us is purely personal."

Mosby agreed, pointing out that Greeley had actually advocated or attempted to justify nearly all of Grant's policies. "But," he added in allusion to the heavy-handed militarism of Radical reconstruction, "if I am to be ruled by isms, general, I prefer a military despotism to the despotism of isms that Horace would supply." Grant was coming to appreciate his outspoken guest.

If the Democrats at their July convention should put up anyone but Greeley, concluded Mosby, he personally would have to vote with his party. He could not support the President. On the other hand, if Greeley were the nominee, he would not only vote for Grant but would "stomp the state" in his behalf. If a proper movement could be gotten under way, he added, Grant had a fair chance of winning Virginia.

As the President escorted his guests to the door, Mosby determined to put Grant's professed goodwill toward the South to the test.

"There are many men in the South, Mr. President—as you well know—who are still under political disabilities," he began. "They can't hold political office, or even vote. They're still not full-fledged citizens. Mind you, I'm not in that position myself, but I know many who are. You just can't imagine the humiliation this is to a Southern man, in addition to being plain unfair."

"Now I know, General," he continued, facing the attentive President squarely, "that you're in favor of relieving Southerners of these disabilities, and it's men like Sumner who've made it impossible to get a new amnesty bill through the Senate. But if you could try again—I mean really try—I believe it would be very well received in the South."

"It would be a real olive branch," concluded Mosby, "and I believe it would at least buy you Virginia."

The President, after a moment's further silence, reached for Mosby's hand. "I'll see if something can be done," he said.

Interviewed in his hotel room after the meeting, Mosby was asked to sum up his impressions of President Grant. "Oh," he answered, "he is very plain; one don't feel small in his presence. You don't have that awe or reverence one had when ushered into the presence of Gen. Lee. I was very much pleased with Grant and my reception."[3]

A few days after the White House meeting, Massachusetts congressman Benjamin Butler (known below the Mason-Dixon line as "Beast" Butler) inexplicably introduced to the House floor a new amnesty measure for Southerners. The bill was rushed through the House under a suppression of rules, and then, in a night session on the same day, pushed through the Senate while Senator Sumner was napping. The President signed it at once.

At a stroke of Grant's pen, scores more of the South's leading men were freed of restrictions placed upon their citizenship by the Fourteenth Amendment. Many Confederates previously excluded from public office geared up at once for congressional and other political races, including even the former vice president of the Confederacy, Alexander H. Stephens, who was seated in the United States Congress the following year.

If life had been bad in the South during the war, it had in some ways become worse over the past seven years of peace. Great adjustments had been required of Southern whites to assimilate nearly 4 million freedmen, to say nothing of the pressures created by Northerners streaming southward out of every motive imaginable.

In the aftermath of war, people moved in all directions in search of a better life. But it was the abrupt mobilization of the former slaves that gave the times their unique stamp, and that was the most unpredictable factor of all. In the summer of 1865, more than 20,000 blacks flocked into Washington; even greater numbers crowded into Charleston, New Orleans, Memphis, and other Southern cities. Most were not slow to appreciate their new position and showed little eagerness for employment by former masters. Pilferage grew as hungry blacks strove to feed themselves. Potato patches were raided; cupboards were swept clean by departing slaves; horses, mules, and cattle were stolen. Blacks collected in towns to while away the hours, content to watch the white man scurry about to get a black's work done.

Even the most liberal of slaveholders found emancipation a choking pill.

A generation of white veterans—crippled in one way or another by the war, and as aimless as the blacks—added to the simmering social cauldron. Social agencies in the South did their best to cope with these enormous problems, and for some time the Freedmen's Bureau, at least, was highly successful. But the war had destroyed most existing social agencies, and educational institutions were only beginning to dig themselves out of the ashes.

The land was at peace, but not far removed from violence. Blue-coated troopers kept order until civilian governments could be set up, but many soldiers were not as broad-minded about secessionists as Lincoln and Grant had been. Former Confederates had to tread carefully.

Mosby was particularly vulnerable in the months following Appomattox. He had become a legend in the North: a predator, dangerous and seldom-sighted. Now that he lived in their midst, tamed flesh and blood, ordinary, he became an object of curiosity and distrust.

Two months after signing his parole, in August 1865, Mosby stepped off a train in Alexandria and found himself at the center of a large, rubbernecking crowd of both blacks and whites, who moved along the street with him and followed him into a store, eventually blocking the sidewalk and spilling out into the street. Obstruction of traffic seemed reason enough to arrest a man like Mosby, and it was done. Authorities detained him in Alexandria for two days. "The Yankees," he later noted, "seemed to look upon me as a sort of menagerie and I had to pay the penalty of their inordinate curiosity."[4]

By the following month, he had rented living quarters and hung out his lawyer's shingle in Warrenton, Fauquier County, heartland of his former "Confederacy." He was well known here, generally liked, and had decided that an office in Warrenton would ensure him a profitable place in the great sea of litigation certain to follow the war. In addition to a rebirth of business in Warrenton, a rudimentary social life was also reasserting itself. In fact he noted in a breezy, gossipy letter to Monteiro in September that Fauquier had been "quite gay" that summer, with "tournaments . . . the order of the day." He reported further that "Miss Sophie and Col. Welby" seemed to be "near the jumping off place," and he was sure the doctor would want to know that "Miss Margaret" still flourished "like a green bay tree."[5]

By November, he'd extended his law practice into neighboring Fairfax and Prince William counties. In December, the *Washington Star* noted drily that Mosby, who had "probably done more mule-stealing than any man living," was presently helping to prosecute the internal revenue collector of Prince William County for mule-stealing.[6]

During January 1866 he was arrested again—this time in Leesburg—and it was in the following month that a disgusted Pauline went to see first Johnson and then Grant, with the result that he was relieved of Federal attention in the future. The year was seriously marred for him by the death of his sister, Victoria, in October. On the brighter side, he had seen the birth of a second daughter, Virginia Stuart, and the growth of his renewed law practice. As he told Monteiro in December, if the "infernal Yanks" would leave Southerners alone, he thought he could make a living.[7]

In 1867, apart from a brief public controversy with Thomas

Rosser and a private one with Jubal Early ("that old fraud," in Mosby's words, "in a moral sense a hog"), he did his best to keep a low profile.[8] But he couldn't avoid attracting attention. In October of that year the *Star,* noting his presence at a public meeting in Leesburg, reported a general "turning of heads" when he was discovered at the rear of the hall, and the word "Mosby" buzzing through the crowd. "In personal appearance," remarked the *Star,*

> he looks the lawyer even less than the warrior. Dressed in careless, easy Virginia style, with white slouch hat, a dust-stained bob-tail coat, milk and molasses colored pants and vest (the latter minus two or three buttons), a badly adjusted false front tooth, a figure of medium size, close shaven, sunburnt youthful face, slouched shoulders, quiet, taciturn, undemonstrative in manner, it was not quite easy to believe that he was the individual whose name and daredevil achievements figured in the papers almost daily during the war.[9]

A month later, on a visit to New York City in which he sat for Mathew Brady and purchased two engravings for a home he had just bought, a greater sensation was caused by his appearance at a meeting of the Gold Board—during the war one of the busiest of New York's new financial exchanges. According to the *New York Post,* his presence generated "considerable excitement," culminating in a written request to the presiding officer for his immediate ejection. The message was read aloud, and Mosby rose to leave. The meeting, however, quickly broke up as a few renegade members pressed forward to shake his hand, while others stood apart and continued the clamor for his dismissal. "He was . . . loudly hissed," said the *Post,* and the excitement continued until long after the Board's enforced adjournment.[10]

"My friends say," he wrote to Pauline next day, "that my breaking up the Gold Board is my greatest exploit."[11]

There were two reconstruction periods in the South: a brief one following the war, in which the South was given the opportunity to reconstruct itself under the patronage of a relatively benign but increasingly impotent President; and a longer, darker one, imposed by a vindictive Congress, a Congress so powerful that it came close to casting the President from office.

By the close of 1865, Southern state governments were busy putting their houses in order as quickly as possible, thankful for the spirit of Appomattox that seemed still to radiate from Washington. They hurried to do all the right things: repudiate the Confederate debt, abjure secession as a state's right, and outlaw slavery within their borders. President Johnson had already issued a declaration of amnesty, and even those who had been excepted from it had been urged to make personal application to him. He seemed bent not on destroying, but merely on humiliating the planter class.

The South as a section, however, retained its pride, or, more accurately, refused to demonstrate the proper humility, and to the North it seemed that Southerners were planning to take up life where it had been left off. "Black Codes" were being passed by unrepentant Southern legislatures, giving black men certain rights but circumscribing them so tightly as to make the condition of freedmen almost indistinguishable from slavery. Efforts by Northerners to educate the Negro or to teach him the responsibilities of citizenship were being met with force, rapidly becoming terrorism. Unpardoned and impenitent Confederates were being elected to statehouses and even to congressional seats by large pluralities of voters who seemed unconscious of the Congress's rising temperature.

Congress, aroused at the sight of a process that promised to be the undoing of Appomattox, girded itself for battle.

By the end of 1866, enough new Republican sinew had been incorporated into the congressional body for it to begin the taming of the President and the real reconstruction of the South. In March of the following year, while pressure was being applied to the President in a variety of ways, a stunned South was slapped under martial law by the First Reconstruction Act, and ratification of the once dead but arbitrarily revived Fourteenth Amendment—protecting the Negro and punishing the white Southern ruling class—was announced as part of the new price of readmission to union.

Blacks were converted to Republican capital as hastily as possible through huge voter registration drives among freedmen. A number of these new voters were groomed for even greater things: blacks who had a short time before been chopping cotton or waiting on table found themselves stuffed into starched shirts and planted behind tiny desks in state legislatures. To cap off this insult to the white South, a flood of carpetbaggers poured down to assist in the rehabilitation of their poor or misguided brethren.

Conquered in war, the South reacted strongly to being reconquered in peace. Terrorist organizations coalesced almost spontaneously. Groups like the Ku Klux Klan and the Knights of the White Camellia arose to ensure that the hapless blacks remembered who they were and where they lived, and to discourage "white-cravatted gentlemen from Andover" from meddling in Southern affairs. For several years these groups, hooded or otherwise incognito, roamed the South, flogging, terrorizing, or killing blacks and their supporters, burning homes and black schools, assaulting reconstruction officials, and perpetrating any form of violence likely to guarantee the maintenance of white supremacy in the South.

Despite this white Southern backlash of the late sixties, Southern states—under the supervision of unblinking Union generals—were put through the paces of voter registration and the rewriting of state constitutions along lines made plain by the Radical Congress. White voters were required to take the "ironclad oath," which at this time included swearing not only to future loyalty but, preposterously, to past loyalty. By July 1868, most Southern states, carpetbag governments well in place, had been readmitted to statehood.

Once the Republican Congress had succeeded in breaking Johnson and had gotten off on what it considered to be the right foot in the South, it began to cast about for a man of its own stripe to install in the White House. It did not have to look far. The Conqueror himself, Ulysses S. Grant, was eminently available. He seemed a pliant man, with no strong political allegiances and no known ambitions. Having prosecuted a successful war in a most impressive manner, he could be expected to show administrative ability. He was a man of overshadowing fame.

Grant allowed himself to be courted, and at the Republican Convention in May was nominated on the first ballot. The campaign that followed—against Horatio Seymour, New

York Democrat—was nearly as bloody as the war. The Republicans "waved the bloody shirt" with vigor, resuscitating as many war ghosts as possible. "Vote as you fought!" the country was urged. The Democrats were characterized as a "sewer," a "loathsome receptacle" for every element of treason, inhumanity, and barbarism. They were pilloried as the standardbearers of rebellion and Negro repression. Union League organizers in the South intensified their efforts at the political education of the Negro, making sure along the way that the former slaves understood clearly to which party they owed their freedom.

Thanks in great measure to the freedmen's vote, Grant won. But his popular edge was slim. Once he'd been installed in office, his party took steps to ensure a thicker margin next time: those blacks who had been prevented from voting by strongarm tactics were given the protection of the new Fifteenth Amendment, and in 1870 and 1871 the Enforcement Acts and the draconian Ku Klux Act were passed, just to erase any lingering Southern doubts about the new amendment's meaning.

Grant's view of a chief executive was, at minimum, one who was sworn to uphold the Constitution, and he upheld it especially well in the South. The Amnesty Act of May 1872, passed ultimately at Mosby's prodding, was indeed to be the first olive branch the South would see from U. S. Grant after Appomattox.

Grant was borne into the White House on a "tidal wave of expectation," in Henry Adams's phrase.[12] The country, suspicious in certain sectors, was nevertheless willing to extend to him whatever goodwill it had, and was encouraged by the caution with which he approached some of the thornier problems of his early presidency.

The nation was soon disappointed, however, at how he surrounded himself with mediocrity. With the exception of New York's Hamilton Fish, his able Secretary of State, Ohio's Jacob D. Cox at Interior, and the Bay State's Ebenezer Hoar in the Attorney General's office, his cabinet was notable only for obscurity and lack of talent. His "kitchen cabinet" of unsworn advisers was top-heavy with uniforms and shot through with cronies. By the end of his first term, as the scandals began to seep out, his administration was being called "the great barbecue," and the tidal wave of expectation had broken upon the shoals. Cox and Hoar soon gave way to more malleable individuals—only Fish managed to ride it out—and men like Orville Babcock, the general's military aide during the war, gained an ascendancy hitherto unknown in mere presidential secretaries.

The intelligentsia, unable to fathom Grant, were especially cruel to him. As the antithetical nature of his personality began to surface, he became the great national enigma, and only the most astute could resist facile generalization. Adams reported that his friend, Adam Badeau—long-time Grant intimate—viewed the President as "an intermittent energy, immensely powerful when awake, but passive and plastic in repose."[13] In Adams's own opinion, "Grant's simplicity was more disconcerting than the complexity of a Talleyrand."[14]

Although the President was capable of acting with great energy and determination, his mind, according to Badeau, "for stretches of time . . . seemed torpid." Grant's aides, he continued, "could never measure his character or be sure when he would act. They could never follow a mental process in his thought. They were not sure that he did think."[15]

Anyone could come into his presence, but only a few were admitted to his thought. Grant "would sit *and listen and listen,*" said one observer. Another who knew him noted, "He could be granite—by the Lord, he could be granite."[16]

The new President was so retiring in manner as almost to give the appearance of shyness, and seemed incapable of light talk or banter. He was devoid of subtlety; if a man but showed loyalty, he would go through fire for him. Intellectuals and reformers he distrusted, preferring the "boys," oblivious of their motives. When he gave his friendship, he gave it without reserve. Cured of his drinking by this time, he clung to one vice: the consumption in immense quantities of black, rank, and poisonous cigars.

Mosby, an outsider and hardly an intellectual, was to find himself welcomed with the "boys." Grant was a kindred spirit, a soldier. Mosby took no notice of the President's taciturnity, which mirrored his own, and which certainly befitted

a warrior. "He was the best listener I ever saw," he said of
the President, "and one of the quickest to see the core of a
question."[17] Mosby never spoke of Grant's personal distance,
on which so many others remarked. Either Grant did not
keep this distance from him, or Mosby was not seeking great
intimacy from the most famous of living soldiers and the highest elected official of the land.

If Northern intellectuals used delicate scalpels in their eager
dissection of the President, the common Southerner used
hammer and saw. An editorial in the *Missouri Vindicator* just
prior to Grant's nomination began: "Of all the empty pig-
bladders that the war blew up to elephantine proportions,
none was, none is, none could be more utterly contemptible,
unworthy and despicable than the drunken creature whose
name [has been] raised for the presidency." The piece went
on to call him the "butcher of The Wilderness," and characterized him as "stupid [and] smoke-enveloped," a "reeling,
hiccuping, whiskey soaked jig dancer," concluding that he
was "despicable, and bestial."[18] An ex-Confederate officer
once referred to him in a public speech as "the dummy who
drives his horse along the Jersey beach."[19]

But Adams took the knife deeper than any. "[Grant] had
no right to exist," he said. "He should have been extinct for
ages. . . . The progress of evolution from President Washington to President Grant, was alone evidence enough to upset
Darwin."[20]

Mosby saw none of this, and was to fix himself as firmly to
Grant as a barnacle to a ship.

At Grant's first inaugural, Mosby had melted into the crowd,
one of thousands caught up in the "tidal wave of expectation." If he was not a neutral observer, he was not necessarily
a hostile one. "In common with most Southern soldiers," he
later wrote, "I had a very kindly feeling towards General
Grant, not only on account of his magnanimous conduct at
Appomattox, but also for his treatment of me at the close of
hostilities."[21] By now he knew that the parole finally offered
him had been offered at the insistence of Grant.

Despite certain feelings of gratitude, however, he was in no
hurry to meet his benefactor. "I had never called on him . . . ,"

he said. "If I had done so, and if he had received me even politely, we should both have been subjected to severe criticism, so bitter was the feeling between the sections at the time."[22]

As the "great barbecue" got under way, Mosby kept his nose buried in his profession, intending to avoid politics and giving little thought to Republicanism. "As we had all been opposed to the Republican party before the war," he said, "it was a point of honor to keep on voting that way." But there were even stronger reasons for such opposition now. "Like most Southern men," he declared, "I . . . was sore and very restive under military government." (Mosby had in fact told a Philadelphia paper at the time that the administration of affairs in Virginia was in the hands of "a lot of bounty jumpers and jailbirds," whose only qualification was that they could take the ironclad oath, but who "generally [took] anything else they [could] lay their hands on.")[23]

His impatience surfaced briefly in the fall of 1869 when he traded some hot words with the Fauquier County sheriff, William H. Boyd. There is evidence that it was Boyd, formerly of the First New York Cavalry, who had crashed into Mosby's bedroom on a June night a few years earlier and forced him up a walnut tree. Apart from this, however, Mosby questioned Boyd's very right to hold his office. The short-fused Virginian tried to goad the Northerner into a duel, but Boyd hedged, and the matter was eventually dropped. A month later Boyd sold out his office and left.

Despite Mosby's intention to keep out of politics, he had begun at least to flirt with it that summer, during Virginia's first postwar gubernatorial campaign. Virginia, not yet readmitted to union, had finally succeeded in hammering together an acceptable constitution, and by executive order, elections were scheduled for July 6. Claws were bared throughout the state as the Radicals prepared to seize the Virginia statehouse, and the growing Conservative party (a coalition of Democrats and old-line Whigs united in the belief that white made right) prepared to challenge. The Rads planned on installing as governor Gen. Henry H. Wells, of Rochester, New York, presently serving as appointed provisional governor. The first announced Conservative candidate, Dr. Robert E.

Withers, a stern white supremacist, had been cast aside by the
party in favor of a Northerner, but a Northerner as conservative as the most blue-blooded Virginian. He was Gilbert
C. Walker, of Binghamton, New York.

Mosby, regarding the election as "a contest between civilization and barbarism," came out publicly for the Conservative Walker. When it was announced that Walker was to
speak at Warrenton on a certain day in June, locals who were
put off by Walker's "Northernness" insisted that attendance
at a wedding in Upperville that day was more important than
hearing a carpetbagger speak—even a white supremacist carpetbagger. Mosby, also invited to the wedding, instead stayed
in Warrenton to meet Walker and to introduce him to the few
who had remained in town for his speech. "I hoped," he said,
"that my example might have some influence to induce them
to vote for him in spite of their prejudices. I remember saying
then that I would as soon have thought of riding to the rear
when I ordered my men to charge as to leave Warrenton that
day." [24]

The man for whom Mosby had skipped a wedding in fact
became next governor of Virginia, with the largest majority
yet seen in a Virginia gubernatorial election. When Virginia
was readmitted to statehood the following January, therefore,
it was with a strong counter-reconstructionary government
well in place.

And Mosby had cut his political teeth, very visibly, as a
twenty-four-carat Virginia Conservative.

In March 1870 he was in Richmond, awaiting word of the
nomination of fellow Warrenton attorney and state legislator
James Keith to the bench of the Eleventh Virginia Circuit.
While walking near the Capitol, he was startled to see a ca-
daverous Robert E. Lee—now president of Washington College in Lexington—strolling slowly with his daughter Agnes.
He had seen Lee several times since the war, but today the
general's haggard look disturbed him. He was not, said
Mosby, "the Apollo" he had known in the army.[25] After a
few moments of small talk with the former Confederate
leader, Mosby walked on, promising to drop in on him later
at his hotel.

In Lee's room a short while afterward, he found conversation difficult. "I felt oppressed," he said, "by the great memories that his presence revived, and while both of us were thinking about the war, neither of us referred to it."[26] The brief conversation turned upon current events only.

Bothered by his meeting with Lee, Mosby left the hotel only to run into another Confederate luminary, but one whose light had dimmed considerably: Gen. George E. Pickett, known best for the desperate charge made by his division at Gettysburg. Pickett seemed interested in the fact that Lee was in town, and asked Mosby to return with him to Lee's room. Mosby did not immediately understand Pickett's need for company on such a visit, but Pickett made it plain that he did not wish to be alone with Lee. He reluctantly agreed, and with Pickett, retraced his steps to Lee's hotel.

Mosby was now the unwilling witness to a stranger reunion than even his own had been. It did not last five minutes, but was notable as much for its coldness as for its brevity.

He was annoyed at having to be part of such an embarrassment. Mosby had heard of an estrangement between Lee and Pickett, but knew little about it. In addition to the rumor that Pickett had not even been part of "Pickett's charge," it was known that in the waning days of the war, Pickett, Rosser, and Fitz Lee—all well fortified with Madeira—had been behind the lines at a shad bake while Sheridan was flanking their army at Five Forks. It was not, however, until years later that Mosby was to learn the depths of Lee's disgust over this event. Lee, it developed, had gone into a rage when he heard of Pickett's absence at Five Forks, and ordered his immediate arrest. A few days later, noticing Pickett still among his troops on the retreat from Petersburg, he was heard to exclaim with great bitterness, "Is that man still with this army?"

As Pickett and Mosby left the hotel, Pickett, affected as deeply as his companion, began to abuse Lee, calling him "that old man," and muttering about how he'd had his division massacred at Gettysburg. Mosby was at his boiling point. "Well," he snapped, "it made you immortal," and walked away.[27]

"You know," wrote Mosby to Keith in later years, "that I have a high but a rational admiration for General Lee; I am not a blind idolator. To me he is not infallible. . . . I think, with all due reverence, that General Lee should be judged by the same measure that other men are."[28] And on another occasion: "I am aware that in Virginia there is a sentiment that tolerates only one side of a question that concerns General Lee. . . . For General Lee I have always had a deep affection, but . . . the fashionable cult that exalts him above mortality and makes him incapable of error is . . . irrational."[29]

Grant himself felt something similar about Lee. "A large part of the National army . . . ," he was to note in his *Memoirs*, "and most of the press of the country, clothed General Lee with [almost superhuman abilities], but I had known him personally, and knew that he was mortal."[30]

Mosby was to see Lee once more in Alexandria the following summer, but by that October the Apollo of the South would be dead.

John Mosby was a devoted family man. By the opening of the new decade, at thirty-six, he was the father of five children ranging in age from eleven to infancy. One of his biographers, privy to firsthand information from Mosby's children, relates that he was a doting parent and liked to have his children with him whenever possible, even on business trips.[31] His wartime letters to Pauline invariably closed with a tender expression of affection for his children. He was an educational-minded father, and as the children grew, he encouraged them to read by the practical device of paying them a fee for every book completed, explaining that if he wanted them to pick up the reading habit, it made more sense to pay them directly to read than to pay a tutor to teach them. He sent May, at least, to the best Catholic schools in Washington, and in the early seventies both she and Bev were sent to a convent school in Montreal, the result of his daughter's pleas that they be allowed to study where some of their wealthier playmates studied.

He had only one known vice: he consumed coffee much as Grant consumed cigars. Hard liquor held no magic for him, but he welcomed an occasional lager or glass of claret. He did not smoke. While he liked music, especially the piano entertainments provided by his several sisters, he played no instrument himself and had trouble carrying a tune. He despised games, considering cards a waste of time and boasting in his old age that he had yet to see a baseball game. He kept a few fast horses, and enjoyed watching them race.

As he passed into his forties, he grew a trifle absent-minded. Beverly recalled that, as a child, he once had had to inform his father that the reason the office key he was fumbling with would not open the door was that the door belonged to the Warren-Green Hotel. His office was across the street.

Death struck the family again in late 1870, this time taking his sister Ada, in her late teens or early twenties. Summoned to her bedside at Idle Wilde in December, he arrived with his two boys, aged ten and seven, only to find Ada in a delirium. Within a short time she died. On the day of the funeral he wrote a touching letter to Pauline, kept home by a sixth pregnancy:

I took Bev and Johnnie in the room where she was lying this morning. . . . They both kissed her just before she was laid in the coffin. . . . Just before she died she made Florie bring her a picture—the Sacred Heart of Jesus. . . . She always said during her illness that she had no desire to recover and would tell Ma every day how she would pray for us all when she got to heaven. O! I never knew before the depths of my love for her, but yet I do not feel the bitterness of grief I otherwise would have done if she had gone unprepared. I know that her soul without the stain of sin now lives in heaven. It is a source of great consolation to me that you and I did all we could to make her comfortable in her sickness. . . . Bev and Johnnie do everything they can to comfort Ma and Pa. They sit by them all the time with their arms around their necks, caressing them.[32]

A few months later Pauline gave birth to a baby girl. She named the child Ada.

The influence of Pauline's Catholicism upon the Scots-Welsh Protestantism of Mosby and his family was remarkable. Mosby himself, of course, came most strongly under her sway, but was agnostic enough and ornery enough to avoid formal entanglement. His sisters were another story. Some of them, at least, became not merely Catholics but rabid Catholics, writing letters to each other filled with talk of Benediction and scapulars. His sons served Mass at the local parish church, and his youngest sister, Florie, became a Sister of Charity. Little by little this scion of a hoary Protestantism found his life and home filling up with medals, rosaries, and saints.

Mosby was excited as he packed his things in the hotel after his first meeting with Grant. He hurried to the wharves and hopped onto the Aquia Creek boat, planning to debark at Alexandria for a rail connection home. He was so enthused, however, and so full of the possibilities apparently opening up for the South, that he made the mistake of bubbling over in front of a fellow passenger, the stone-faced South Carolina aristocrat Wade Hampton, and missed his stop.

"I was so intense in my feelings," he wrote, "and so absorbed in the subject that I was unconscious of the boat's stopping at Alexandria, and did not discover it until the bell tolled when we were passing Mount Vernon."[33] Mount Vernon is a good ten miles beyond Alexandria; it is not recorded how he got home.

By early June, Mosby was demonstrating the truth of what the secessionist editor, J. Austin Sperry, had said of him earlier—that his politics was as irregular as his fighting. Having recently helped elect a Conservative to the governor's chair, he was now throwing himself enthusiastically behind the Northern Radical Grant.

On June 1 he wrote to a cohort, Judge James Lyons of Richmond, "If we start this movement we ought to exert ourselves to make it a success."[34] Further demonstrating his affinity for the irregular, he next turned to the man who had locked him in the Albemarle jail for shooting Turpin: William J. Robertson, previously on the bench of the Virginia Supreme Court of Appeals and presently practicing law in Charlottesville. Robertson, however, more interested in making money in corporate law than entering the thicket of Virginia politics, declined to come out strongly for Grant.

Writing to Judge Lyons again on June 6, Mosby said, "I

think it best . . . to work in a quiet way to consolidate opposition to Greeley until the Baltimore Convention meets. After that we can then meet if Greeley is nominated to organize against him."[35] He attempted to snare former governor Henry A. Wise into his group, and in July contacted Alexander H. Stephens, former vice president of the Confederacy, now relieved of political disabilities by Grant's recent amnesty proclamation and making his own bid for one of Georgia's congressional seats.

Alexander Hamilton Stephens—"Little Ellick" to his fellow Georgians—was, in 1872, a sixty-year-old arthritic Southern maverick, with sallow complexion, cracked-falsetto voice, and not more than 100 pounds on his frame. To his contemporaries he appeared "small, sick, and sorrowful," a "queer-looking bundle."[36] He'd been the conscience of the Confederacy, frequently finding himself in opposition to Confederate government policies. Immediately following the war, during the "Confederate phase" of reconstruction, he'd been sent to Congress, but—still among the unpardoned—had not been seated. In 1871 he'd bought an interest in Atlanta's *Southern Sun,* and was by now filling its editorial pages with endless arguments against the marriage of Democrats with Liberal Republicans in support of Greeley.

In his first letter to the great man, Mosby felt constrained to introduce himself. "You may perhaps have heard of me," he wrote, somewhat timidly, "as a partisan officer."[37] Stephens answered him at once, assuring Mosby that they were in total accord in judging the Democratic platform, but pleading serious infirmities as his reason for not entering an active pro-Grant campaign.

Mosby saw at least that he had a friend, another irregular who could offer moral support if nothing else. Later on, when the campaign had become white-hot and Southerners were beginning to treat Mosby as a leper, he was to confess to Stephens, "It is but seldom now that I receive a word of cheer from a Southern source and the last few months have been to me like a passage through 'the Valley of the Shadow of Death' so great has become the intolerance of our poor infatuated people."[38]

By late July, Greeley had been nominated by the Democrats and Mosby had come out for Grant. He was so enthusiastic that he offered to debate the issues publicly with anyone the local Democrats cared to send against him. He would be waiting, he said, at Salem, on August 3.

The opposition took it as a joke and announced they'd send John B. Withers to take up the cudgels for Greeley. Withers, mayor of Warrenton, was a novice at stump speaking, and the implication was that no better man would be needed. Predictably, Mosby took offense, and let it be known that if Withers dared to show up, he and all his Democrat-Conservative cronies could expect to be publicly denounced. Withers, reacting as an affronted gentleman, announced that he was ready to meet Mosby not just on the rostrum but on *any* field. This implication, too, was clear.

"The well-known character of both parties for playing with the trigger," chuckled the *Star,* "made the timid judge at Warrenton very nervous."[39] The "timid judge at Warrenton" was, of course, Mosby's friend, James Keith, who quickly locked up both men until feathers could be smoothed.

The argument was somehow buried in time, and the debate went on as scheduled, in a grove, before a festive Saturday afternoon crowd. The Democrats ultimately put up not Withers, but Mosby's close friend, Gen. Eppa Hunton, fellow Warrenton attorney. Hunton, also freed of political disabilities by Grant's recent declaration, was in the midst of his own race for a congressional seat. He was better equipped than Withers to expound the Democratic viewpoint, even if embarrassed by representing Greeley before a Southern crowd.

The Salem debate was regarded as the opening of the presidential campaign in Virginia, and as it turned out, the Democrats would have fared badly had they not sent their best. The *Star*'s comment afterward was, "[Mosby] speaks as fiercely as he fights. Take him all in all, he is an ugly customer to tackle, either in the field or on the rostrum."[40] Both men, however, were greatly liked in upper Fauquier at this time, and interest was high as the gabbling crowd pressed around the speakers' platform.

Hunton spoke first, turning his remarks less into a defense of Greeley—indefensible in the South—than into an attack upon Grant for having so zealously enforced the Ku Klux law. He spoke at length on this theme, laying before the sympathetic crowd several cases of Confederates jailed, in his opinion, prejudicially. His remarks were warmly received by a crowd well in tune with his sentiments.

Then Mosby rose to speak: one of the last Confederates to surrender, about to explain why his people should follow him into the camp of the despised Northern Republicans. The crowd fell silent.

In the no-holds-barred style of the day, Mosby launched his speech by characterizing the Liberal Republican splinter—led by such outstanding men as Carl Schurz, Charles Francis Adams, and William Cullen Bryant—as a band of "plunderers, bummers, foragers and dead beats." (Adams was later to become a Mosby friend.) He scorned their platform, he said—in fact he scorned everybody's platform. He was supporting Grant as a man, not as the head of a party. Grant, he maintained, was by far the lesser of the two evils for the South.

Picking up on a Hunton remark that Greeley wanted to make peace, wanted to "shake hands across the bloody chasm," Mosby shouted that he'd like to see a candidate who *wouldn't* shake hands—even across a "bloody chasm"—if it meant getting a vote. (Laughter and applause.) Greeley he characterized as an "old political rake, a constitutional, lifelong growler." He himself had just returned from the Democratic Convention, said Mosby. The men there, he bawled, had no principles; all they had was constituents. In this they differed from the Liberal Republicans, he added, who had plenty of principles but no constituents. (Laughter.) So the two parties fused, he declared, the Republicans supplying the principles (applause), and the Democrats the voters (more applause and laughter). The Democrats, he continued, "were the meanest, oddest lot of bummers and shysters . . . ever got together." It was enough to remind one of Barnum's family. (Laughter.) Horace Greeley, he shouted, now pounding the rostrum, was a tool of Tammany, and the "scarecrow of both continents."[41]

Greeley's chief claim to distinction, he said, was "his intolerant hate of the South, the wearing of a white hat, and walking down Broadway with one leg of his breeches stuck in his boot." (Laughter and applause.) He himself, Mosby avowed more gravely now, preferred a soldier to a fanatic. He supported Grant on his record, "the best platform a man can have." Grant was sure to win, Mosby predicted. "In fact," he shouted, "Greeley never could be a President unless he went to Liberia, and there his election would be doubtful." (Applause.)[42]

In reply to Hunton's excoriation of the President for his administration's imprisonment of Confederates under the Ku Klux law, Mosby emphasized that he was sure of one thing: Hunton and the South could never achieve the release of such men by abusing Grant. "Having been a Confederate soldier," he cried, "[gives] no immunity from punishment for crime, and . . . Confederate soldiers [are now] in the Virginia penitentiary."[43] He closed by urging his listeners to vote for Grant, and sat down to the generous applause of an appreciative audience.

As further evidence of Mosby's almost obsessive "irregularity," it might be noted that side by side with his Grant campaign he helped run a second one on behalf of Democrat Hunton. He in fact exerted himself strenuously throughout Hunton's race to ensure that Grant's party in Virginia put up no one against his friend. The Radical-backed independent who was expected to run, said the *Alexandria Gazette,* "was persuaded not to do so by Mosby."[44]

To no one's surprise, Hunton won in November. To the astonishment of many, however, Grant took Virginia in his own landslide victory, a feat made possible largely by Mosby.[45] He was jubilant. On November 7 he telegraphed the President: "Virginia casts her vote for Grant, peace, and reconciliation."[46]

Later that fall, when Hunton had gotten settled in his new congressional seat, Mosby asked him about a particular prisoner he'd mentioned most pathetically in his speech at Salem. What was his name, and what exactly were the charges against him? Hunton knew the name, he said—it was Randolph Shotwell—but of the charges he knew nothing. He admitted to having used the case to demonstrate a point without being familiar with the details. No matter, said Mosby. He wished to demonstrate a point now to Hunton: namely, the greater attractive power of honey over vinegar. He would, he said—through friendship with Grant—procure Shotwell's pardon. He at once wrote to the President and urged him, "as an act of mercy, as well as of public policy," to free the prisoner Shotwell.[47] It was immediately done.

As a demonstration of the potency of Mosby's strategy it was impressive; but this particular effort was ill-conceived. Shotwell turned out to have been guilty of serious crimes, including that of stripping and flogging a man nearly to death for the simple offense of holding a Republican seat in the North Carolina legislature. As if this revelation were not reason enough for Mosby's chagrin, Shotwell, a journalist, soon returned to his trade, and one of his editorial targets over the next several years became the "renegade Confederate" John Mosby. Shotwell apparently had no idea how he'd been freed.

Mosby met Grant shortly after the election, and by the end of the year it was rumored that the President had offered him the payoff he believed was expected—in this case the U.S. attorneyship for the Eastern District of Virginia. Mosby turned it down, explaining to the press that if he had accepted it, his motives might be misconstrued.

By this one stroke he won himself admission to Grant's inner circle; he had become one of the "boys."

On solid ground now as the President's semi-official expert on the Southern question, Mosby was able to dig out payoff after payoff for Virginians. Appointments in the patronage-heavy postal service began to flow to Mosby-recommended candidates, and it was not long before even two consular posts were being filled by Mosby people.

But as the summer of 1873 approached and Virginia geared up for its second postwar gubernatorial race, the newly minted "Republican" found himself increasingly uncomfortable with the Radical candidate, Col. Robert W. Hughes, who had been all over the lot politically. He decided to throw his support to Gen. James L. Kemper, the Conservative, and to put himself in opposition to Grant's party.

Judge Lyons was appalled at what seemed a cavalier disregard of the President. Mosby replied to him in July:

I have never concealed from Genl. Grant or anyone else that I intended to support the Conservative Candidate. . . . In every speech I made for Genl. Grant I disclaimed any purpose to affiliate with the Radicals in Va. I don't care whether Genl. Grant complains of me or not. . . . Because I supported him I am under no sort of obligation to support all the scoundrels in Va. who profess to be his friends. . . . As to what may be the effect of my course on Genl. Grant I don't know and I don't care. He certainly hasn't power enough to make me either support a Radical or even to be neutral in such a contest.[48]

He made it clear to Lyons that, for him, the point at issue was whether Virginia was going to be ruled by blacks and carpet-baggers or continue to be run by white Virginians. His support of Grant had nothing to do with this.

He began now a vigorous campaign for Kemper, taking the time at the end of August to explain his motives to the President. Speaking to Grant of appointments made at his request, he declared:

I sought [them] . . . for the purpose of vindicating your Administration from the charge that Southern men were proscribed by you. . . . I did express an earnest desire to bring our people around from a position of antagonism to one of accord with your Administration, but I never deemed it practicable to do so through the Radical organization of Virginia. In every public speech I made in the late presidential canvass, I repelled the idea that I intended to identify myself with the Negro party of Virginia, for I could not do so without social degradation. . . . If . . . you think that any appointments made at my request created an obligation on my part to support Mr. Hughes . . . , you can easily relieve me of such obligation by dismissing all of these appointees and filling their places with Mr. Hughes's friends.[49]

Despite an effort by some of Grant's party to do just that, none of Mosby's appointees was removed.

In September, prior to the election, the great financial empire of Jay Cooke and Co. split apart, bringing consternation into money circles and ringing in a years-long depression. The headlines were for weeks so overpowering that it went almost unnoticed that James Lawson Kemper had been elected thirty-fourth governor of Virginia.

Mosby became hopeful now of consolidating his gains by bringing his two prize exhibits—the Radical Grant and the Conservative Kemper—into the same political bed. Since Kemper disclaimed any association with the Democratic party but maintained that his only interest was retention of white control over the state, Mosby felt his task would not be difficult, and that the prospect was excellent for a fruitful Richmond-Washington relationship.

More importantly, Kemper was willing. Through Culpeper attorney James Barbour, Kemper asked for Mosby's input to his forthcoming inaugural address. He wanted to send the right signals to Washington, he said, without setting his party's teeth on edge.

Mosby hurried to Richmond, where Kemper outlined his broader plan. He wanted Mosby, he said, to see Grant at once and set up a meeting with him. He told Mosby also that as a pledge of Grant's goodwill he wanted the controversial Civil Rights bill, currently under discussion in the House, killed in its tracks. For obvious reasons, said the governor-elect, Mosby's purpose in going to Washington must be kept secret.

Mosby went straightway to the White House, where he laid Kemper's proposal before the President. As usual, Grant was cooperative: he would meet with Kemper, he said, and would take care of the Civil Rights bill at once.

"After I had seen Grant," related Mosby,

> he sent his brother-in-law, Casey . . . , with a letter to Ben Butler, who had charge of the [Civil Rights] bill, asking him not to put the bill on its passage. When the time came for taking a vote Butler moved to send the bill back to the committee. It slept there over a year. I returned to Richmond and reported to Kemper. He was delighted. I had arranged for him to visit Grant. The prospect for an alliance between Grant's administration and the Virginia people looked bright. If consummated it meant the death-knell to Negro government and carpet-baggery.[50]

But the scheme fell apart when Kemper "took the back track." At the last minute he backed out of the meeting with Grant. "On the day after my return to Richmond," explained

Mosby, "Kemper came to the hotel to see me. He was all broken up. The secret of my mission to Washington had got out, and a lot of politicians had called on him and frightened him. I was very mad at the way I had been duped and never spoke to him again."[51]

Mosby was embarrassed but his stock north of the Potomac, at least, was proving durable. At a time when Southern politicians were becoming wary of association with him, Mosby remained a favorite of Grant who, in the words of the *Star* the following April, "[found] in his former troublesome foe a kindred spirit and valuable supporter."[52]

Mosby at this time decided to enter a political contest himself, opposing Eppa Hunton for the Eighth District's congressional seat—not as a Radical but, of course, as an independent. He was in fact already campaigning in April in his "peculiarly active, energetic and dashing style," as the *Star* said, proposing to run on his "well-known platform of placing the conservative party of Virginia in accord with the Administration."[53]

"With all the influence of Grant's administration on my side," he had written a bit too confidently to a friend the previous month, "nobody could carry the bulk of the Radicals against me, and if a Rad runs to defeat me he makes Grant his enemy."[54]

By midsummer, however, it was becoming evident, even to him, that the name Mosby no longer worked magic in Virginia and that he could not win. His short temper was also hurting him. In early June he'd gotten into a "discussion" with an ex-state senator named Rixey that degenerated to the point where, as the *Star* noted, "a cane and a carriage whip were freely used."[55]

Shortly afterward, in spite of Mosby's warnings of dire consequences, the Radicals went on to nominate their own candidate and the sky refused to fall on them. Mosby, less than a decade after virtually ruling in his personal "Confederacy," now could not win an election there, and knew it. He dropped out of the race, but only after cajoling his Culpeper attorney friend, Barbour, into taking his place.

Grant gave Barbour what help he could, turning out the Warrenton postmaster for not supporting the candidate; but the district appeared to want Hunton again, despite the wide-spread admission, noted in the *Virginia Sentinel* that September, that over the past two years Mosby had represented the district better than its congressman. In the month of September alone Mosby had gotten Federal appointments for six Virginians, not to mention the legions of special mail agents, postal car clerks, postmasters, internal revenue collectors and clerks, and clerks in the Patent Office, Navy Department, and Departments of Interior, Treasury, and State whose appointments he'd already secured.

But the issue was personal. Mosby was no longer wanted. He was seen as a turncoat, and if no one dared call him a scalawag openly, the word hovered in the air around him.

Two emotional events contributed to the upsetting of his political applecart that summer. The first was the death of his eleven-month-old son, George, in mid-July—cause unknown—and the second was an eruption with Capt. Alexander D. Payne of Warrenton. Payne had said or done something construed by Mosby as an accusation of deceit in the conduct of his congressional race, and Mosby exploded, sending the inevitable challenge. Barbour agreed to be his second. The challenge made, Mosby hopped a train to Alexandria (a freight, to elude authorities), and made his way to Washington, expecting, he said, to meet Payne next day in Maryland and thereby avoid the penalties of Virginia's anti-dueling law. He had automatically credited Payne with a similar desire to fight outside Virginia, but this turned out not to be Payne's intention at all, and Mosby's precipitate departure proved difficult for Payne to interpret.

While Mosby was spending the evening at the Capitol Hill home of Barbour's railroad-magnate brother, John, Payne's second was with Barbour, objecting heatedly to Mosby's plan of fighting in Maryland. Payne, he said, would under no circumstances fight a duel in "Radical jurisdiction." He would meet Mosby at a spot near Buckland, between Warrenton and Gainesville, and take his chances with his own people afterward. He expected Mosby to be there by eleven the next morning. Tell Mosby, added Payne's second, that Captain Payne wishes to use Virginia squirrel rifles at forty paces.

Word of the challenge had by this time leaked out, and

Keith, after making a quick arrest of congressional candidate Barbour, telegraphed District police to pick up lawyer Mosby. He also sent a party out to get Payne.

That night, Mosby, unable to sleep, wandered for a time on the Capitol porticoes, then wended his way to the Congressional Hotel, where he could usually find an acquaintance or two. While talking to friends there, he was seized by District detectives and taken to jail—bail set at $5,000. Payne, too, was soon picked up, and held at Warrenton under $10,000 bond.

The patient Keith now roped Eppa Hunton into helping him draft a solution, and within days an agreement that saved face for both parties was signed. One of the document's more optimistic resolutions was that the parties should "speak to each other when they meet as though friendly relations had not been interrupted."[56]

A newspaper commented cynically:

> We are rather inclined to think well of Colonel Mosby's idea of settling his political differences by . . . the duello. That is the only kind of logic likely to be conclusive with him. . . . It is allowable to wish, but impossible to hope, that a fire-brand of his sort can be quenched in any ordinary way. Some men are like fleas; no half-way measures will suffice with them. . . . Now that the cruel war is over, [Mosby] is bestowing upon the unhappy Democrats of Virginia the same sort of attention . . . he gave to Grant and Meade. . . . His attacks, now as then, are made by preference upon the rear. . . . He knows perfectly well what he is about, and is the most serviceable partisan Grant has in Virginia. His object is to disorganize.[57]

Despite Mosby's efforts to get Barbour elected, the Democrat-Conservative tide in Virginia was welling up more strongly than ever, and unaffiliated candidates had almost no chance. Hunton won with ease. The Conservative tide was in fact washing across the entire South, lapping at the steps of the Capitol itself. In 1874, Radical control of the Congress was broken for the first time since the Civil War.

The going for Mosby was getting especially tough (he even had a falling out with the Barbours now), and he was forced to become more discreet in the use of his pipeline to power.

On May 2, 1875, he wrote to the President: "I wd call in person to see you but my appearance at the White House wd occasion a great deal of newspaper criticism which I know wd be as annoying to you as to myself."[58]

By November, the social pressures in Virginia had become overwhelming. He closed up his well-established but neglected Warrenton practice and opened a law office in Washington, where he knew he would probably starve. He never again had an office in Warrenton, and returned there only on weekends to be with his family.

The summer of 1876 was one that Mosby assuredly preferred to forget. Death came twice more—bringing the loss of everything he held dear. His wife Pauline died in May; she was followed in death a few weeks later by an infant son, Alfred, born the previous March.

A letter written in June to attorney Lunsford L. Lewis, soon to be president of Virginia's Supreme Court of Appeals, indicated Mosby's disinterest in what was happening around him. "The severe affliction I have suffered," he said, " . . . has utterly disqualified me from actively participating in . . . a canvass." But the historic presidential campaign of 1876 was raising steam and he could not keep his political inclinations totally in check—"I am nonetheless cordial," he added, "in the support of Hayes and in a quiet way will give him any influence I may have."[59]

In spite of Mosby's dual tragedy, his support for Hayes was somewhat more cordial than he was letting on to Lewis, for on the same day it was reported in the *New York Herald* that he had already met with Grant and Secretary of War Cameron on the subject of the coming election. "The President," stated the *Herald,* "manifested a great deal of interest in the carrying of Virginia for Hayes and Wheeler, and Col. Mosby told him it could be done. He will go into the work actively and energetically."[60]

The scandals that had been revealed in the very fabric of Grant's two administrations had made it plain that America needed a reform President, and reform candidates sprouted on both sides of the political fence. A hard core of "Stalwarts" was pushing for a third term for Grant (at heart, Mosby was in this camp), but Grant's time was past. At the tension-filled Republican Convention in June, Rutherford B. Hayes, reform governor of Ohio, was nominated on the seventh ballot, with New York's unknown William A. Wheeler as his running mate. The Democrats, meeting in St. Louis two weeks later, at first found themselves upstaged by the Sioux and Northern Cheyennes—who immortalized George Custer that week—but they managed at any rate to nominate their own reformer, New York governor Samuel J. Tilden. Tilden was remarkable not only for a face that seemed to denote the continual proximity of unpleasant odors but also for having sent "Boss" Tweed to the penitentiary.

Since both Hayes and Tilden were proven reformers, the campaign had to be carried out on other levels, and the Republicans hastened to haul the "bloody shirt" out of the closet. ("Every man that shot Union soldiers was a Democrat. The man that assassinated Abraham Lincoln was a Democrat. . . . Soldiers, every scar you have got on your heroic bodies was given you by a Democrat.")[61] Tilden was able to take slightly higher ground, having eight years of Republican misrule to look down upon. He had a treasury of unparalleled scandals at his disposal, and, of course, the unmatched severity of the recent depression: in 1873, 5,000 business failures, 89 railroads defaulting on their bonds, probably an equal number of business failures in the first half of 1876, and many, many more in between.[62] The ground had been well prepared by the Republicans for a Democratic victory, and when November came, this is precisely what the country got. Tilden won the presidency by a small majority of the popular vote.

Unfortunately for Tilden, however, his popular mandate was not enough to bring him to the White House. He needed a majority of electoral votes, and in this department he was failing by a single vote. Hayes, after the undisputed portion of the votes had been counted, found himself shy of the mark by twenty votes.

Not all the electoral votes were undisputed, however. There were, in fact, precisely twenty votes in dispute, from four states: Louisiana, South Carolina, Florida, and Oregon. Tilden needed only one of these votes to win; Hayes needed them all—and thanks to the strictly partisan vote of a fifteen-man electoral commission convened to decide the issue over the coming months, he was to get them. Tilden, with a clear moral right to the White House, would be denied the presidency by a single vote.

In spite of Mosby's avowed intent to campaign "quietly" for Hayes, in the end he did so openly though not so flamboyantly, perhaps, as he had stumped for Grant. The month after Hayes had been nominated, Mosby wrote to him, begging the candidate to show immediately some special interest in the South. "Mr. Greeley captivated the South by a few kind words," he reminded Hayes. "Why cannot you do the same and thus heal up the wounds of war? To that end my best efforts shall be directed."[63]

In August he mailed Hayes a copy of a lengthy letter he had written to a fellow Southerner in defense of the Republican ticket. The letter had been printed in the *New York Herald* alongside one by aging firebrand R. Barnwell Rhett, South Carolina journalist, in favor of Tilden. "The Democratic papers in the South," he told Hayes in an accompanying note, "are very indignant with me for unmasking their purposes."[64]

The *Herald* editor, however, was by no means indignant. On the contrary, although supporting Tilden, he lauded Mosby and his stand. "We are surprised," he said, " . . . to find in Colonel Mosby, who has always been known to us as a cavalryman and guerrilla chief, a writer of peculiar piquancy and power. His letter is an able political manifesto." Rhett and other Southerners were then chided for their failure to recognize that support of Hayes was a way of disarming Northern Republican animosity—Mosby's very strategy. Southern men, noted the *Herald,* have "made war upon every measure proposed by the North," and "in every contest the North won, as was inevitable." Southerners were wrong, the paper concluded, in labeling men like Mosby "scalawags" for selecting their own party with independence of mind.[65]

Mosby opened his written defense of the Republican ticket by noting that although he'd been a Confederate soldier, he had ceased to be one about eleven years previously, when he became a citizen of the United States. He continued:

The sectional unity of the Southern people has been the governing idea and bane of their politics. So far from its being the remedy for anything, it has been the cause of most of the evils they have suffered. So long as it continues, the war will be a controlling element of politics; for any cry in the South that unites the confederates reechoes through the North, and rekindles the war fires there. . . .

Do you not see, then, that as long as we keep up the fight on the old lines, with the same allies and same battle cries, the North will be suspicious of our good faith! . . .

I concur with you in a desire for a change in the policy of the national government towards the South, but that can only come from a change in the attitude of the Southern people towards the administration.[66]

Speaking of the likelihood that a majority of Southerners would vote for Tilden, he declared: "If they are bent on breaking their necks, I don't intend to assist them; neither can I see what good it would do them for me to break mine." Then, using a two-word expression that he is credited with coining, and that was to take hold for a century, he asked: "But suppose Hayes is elected with a *solid South* against him; what are you going to do then?"[67] He went on:

Four years ago I urged the Southern people, if they really desired peace and reconciliation, to bury their passions and resentments, and support the man who was not only the representative of an overwhelming majority of the North, but was the most powerful . . . of our foes. I have seen no cause to change my opinions or to regret my course. Many things have since occurred which no one deplores more than I do. . . . The responsibility is with those who adopted the fatal policy, "Anything to beat Grant." In the conflict they invited Grant to beat them. Having predicted all sorts of evils to result from the election of Grant, they have done all in their power to make their predictions come true.

You speak of the bitter hostility of the North toward the South. Well, four years of hard fighting is not calculated to make men love each other; neither is an everlasting rehearsal of the wrongs which each side imagines it has suffered going to bring us any nearer to a better understanding. Peace can only come with oblivion of the past.[68]

"From a chronic habit of complaining," he added, "[the Southern people] too often injure a good cause by mixing up real with imaginary wrongs." After stooping to a few irresistible *ad hominems,* he concluded: "I know very well the measure of denunciation which the expression of these sentiments will receive from the people in whose cause I shed my blood and sacrificed the prime of my life. Be it so."[69]

In late September, Mosby suggested to Hayes that he send the reform Republican Carl Schurz on a swing through the South. Public sentiment in Virginia, he told Hayes, was "in a very plastic state" and in a condition "very easily impressed" by a speaker like Schurz. "I think," he added, "you will be much nearer having a 'solid South' than Tilden."[70]

Hayes replied to Mosby from Columbus, agreeing that "sound speakers of national reputation [could] probably do good" in Virginia, and promising to place the Virginian's views "in the proper quarter."[71]

Mosby continued to hammer away at his theme that the South, by rejecting Grant, had become its own worst enemy. In a *Philadelphia Times* interview in early October he said, "[Grant] has only returned their fire. . . . Of all men he was the most magnanimous." And speaking of the carpetbag plague, he added:

> So far these fellows have been a necessity, for Grant couldn't be expected to appoint to office men who had but just emerged from a bloody feud with the government. . . . These leeches had to be resorted to. . . . They brought with them corruption and are now perpetuating it, and will grow worse until the Southern people prove their right to govern themselves by sustaining the Administration. . . . The attempt to solidify the Southern political forces is going to make a solid North against the South.[72]

Shortly after this interview appeared, Mosby's temper reared again, and he challenged another Warrenton man to a duel. The target of his ire this time was Lyttleton Helm, one of Captain Payne's seconds two years before. Fortunately for both parties, this "meeting" did not come closer to materializing than had the others, since the challenged party, evidently cut from rugged cloth, insisted on double-barreled shotguns at twenty paces.

The affair grew out of a remark Helm had made in the presence of one of Mosby's sons regarding "traitors to their country," and a "hurrah for Aleck Payne." The meaning was veiled too thinly for Mosby's taste, and he demanded satisfaction. When Helm rather cavalierly explained his original remarks, Mosby sent his second with a reply that the explanation was "perfectly satisfactory."[73] Astounded that Mosby did not wish to fight, Helm shrugged it off as just another Mosby fiasco.

Whether related to the heat generated by the disputed election returns or not, it was in November 1876 that Mosby decided he had to get his motherless children out of Warrenton. That month he closed up his home and moved them closer to Washington. "I did this," he explained to a friend, "because I was not there to protect them and as long as they were there they were daily subjected to mortification and insult on my account. . . . The people of Warrenton avoided me and my family as if we were stricken with the plague. You can see then the great wrong I was doing my children to keep them there."[74]

The tension surrounding the contested election dragged on through December; late that month, Mosby, relaxing in his Washington office, spoke about the election and other matters with a reporter from the *New York Herald.*

"Mosby is a good talker," remarked the newspaperman. "Not very fluent, perhaps, but what he says is generally worthy of attention. His intelligence is far above the average of what may be found in Congress, which is not, after all, much of a compliment."[75]

After a few words defending Hayes's title to the presidency, Mosby hit his accustomed stride on the topic of Southern obduracy:

I think the fight made on [Grant] by the Southern white men has been the great blunder of our Southern politics. I have had many conversations with him, and I know that he was able and willing to do more for the Southern people than any man in the United States if the Southern politicians would have permitted him. . . .

My idea was to build up a party in the South opposed to the sectional disunion democracy. The South for the last ten years has suffered under many evils and grievances, and the cause of it all has been . . . the attempt to make a Solid South. . . . It has driven the white men of the South into one political party in alliance with the Northern Democracy, and it has solidified the Negroes on the other hand and given that element a prominence in our politics which it never would have had otherwise. . . . The Solid South idea has actually compelled the Negroes in states . . . where they were in a majority to take possession of the government.[76] [This particular point seems to have been either rhetoric or imagination on Mosby's part, for Negroes were not in *control* of state governments at any time anywhere in the South.][77]

Not only that, [the Solid South idea] has compelled the administration to be on the side of the Negro, and thus given color to the idea that Gen. Grant was attempting to elevate the Negro over the white man, when he never had any such purpose. . . .

The governing idea of the Southern politicians . . . is revenge. They would not be willing to accept any benefits from the Republican party. . . . The greatest offense Gen. Grant can in their eyes commit is give a Southern gentleman an office, because it deprives them of all ground of complaint. . . . If a Southern man accepted office under him he was ostracized. . . . He became an outlaw in society.[78]

Mosby was asked about the attitude of the South toward him. The Southern attitude, he answered, was "bitter and vindictive," the weapon of choice against Republicanism in the South being "social ostracism."[79]

"You will not see it or feel it," he said, "while making a flying trip through the country, but it exists, and even few brave men can stand against it." He pulled out a freshly clipped editorial from a Culpeper paper, an item that touched on his recent removal of his "interesting lot of children" from Warrenton and his "foolish and unwise" course of action preceding it.[80]

The Democratic editor, said Mosby, made a remarkable distinction between the proper way to treat *Northern* Radicals who have settled in the South ("courteously and kindly"), and Southern Radicals—the kind, he quoted, "who have always professed to be with their own people and then . . . go with the radical party." These, said the editor, were quite properly "held in contempt and ignored." Mosby recounted how one of his former officers, in financial need, had recently asked him for a job in government. "I obtained a position for him in Richmond," he said. "He wrote back that he could not take it and live there."[81]

"That is the spirit of the South," concluded Mosby emphatically. "To say so will make them howl in Virginia, but let them howl."[82]

An experience earlier that month had demonstrated clearly the contempt in which he was now held in the South. He'd gotten a telegram from Wade Hampton, just elected governor of South Carolina. Hampton, a paragon of the class that most despised Mosby, would never have darkened the door of a Grant or Hayes White House (he'd turned down a chance to meet Grant with Mosby three years earlier), but he needed a favor from a Southerner who would do so. Racial violence had rocked South Carolina the previous summer—Hampton had in fact been propelled into office by the aftershock—but the reins of power were for the moment slack: Hampton had not yet been inaugurated. He telegraphed Mosby of his pious concern "that the Constitution be obeyed," which, translated, meant that he wanted Washington to recognize his newly elected Democratic statehouse but not to interfere in South Carolina's current crisis. The state, he said, would be under control as soon as he took the oath of office.[83] His message, in effect, was: "Tell Grant, 'No Federal troops.' We'll solve our own problems."

It was a plea from the part of the South that had done Mosby most damage, but he waded into the swamp again: he pocketed Hampton's telegram and headed for the White House. Arriving at seven on a crisp December evening, he was told that the President could not see him as he was having dinner. "I gave the man my card," wrote Mosby later, "and told him I would wait in the hall. He returned with a message from General Grant, asking me to come in and take dinner with the family. I replied that I had already dined. Then Ulysses S. Grant, Junior, came out and said, 'Father says that you must come in and get some dinner.'"[84]

Mosby, somewhat embarrassed, went in, and over dinner outlined Hampton's predicament. Grant listened. He had just come from a visit to the perennially ill "Little Ellick" Stephens, and thus may have been even more disposed than usual to assist an old rebel. He assured Mosby that Hampton needn't worry. He was growing tired of sending Federal troops into Southern states anyway, and promised to use military force only if anarchy threatened.

As on the previous occasion when Mosby had gone on a "secret" mission in behalf of a Southern old boy, so here the word of his mission got out, and his dispatcher suffered great loss of face. Virginia papers lampooned Hampton for having stooped to seek Mosby's help. The outcry was so great that Hampton felt constrained to publish an explanation. He hadn't realized, he said, how "odious" Mosby was to the Virginia people, and had he known, he would never have sought his help. "Hampton used and then abused me," concluded a much-saddened Mosby. "He did not appeal to any of the so-called true Virginians to help him."[85]

"My political experience," he said, summing up, "suggests the fable of 'belling the cat'—one man to incur all the danger and risk while others keep under cover and enjoy the benefit."[86]

On Friday, March 2, the Electoral Commission announced its decision: Rutherford B. Hayes was the nineteenth President of the United States. Only some last-minute economic concessions to an angry South averted what threatened to become a new civil war.

The country knew by this time where Hayes stood on two major issues: Federal troops on Southern soil, and civil service reform. Troops, he had said, would be removed immediately following his taking office; civil service reform would be instituted as rapidly as possible. Many Americans were pleasantly surprised at the forthrightness of such an apparently unassuming man. Perhaps most surprising of all was Hayes's declaration that he had no intention of serving more than one term in the White House.

The new President was inaugurated on Sunday, March 4. Although detractors insisted on paying him homage as "His

Fraudulency, the President," he took immediate control and quickly made good on the first of his campaign promises. By April the few Federal troops remaining in the South had been withdrawn, in effect allowing the final bricks to be laid in the wall of the solid South. Democratic (i.e. counter-reconstructionary) governments blossomed at once in the few states where Radicals had still held the reins, and the "undoing of Appomattox" that had been feared a decade earlier was virtually complete. The South was more solidly Democratic than ever, the Negro was back "in his place," the planter aristocracy had practically resumed control of Southern affairs, and the South was finally making a comeback on its own terms.[87]

To show that he was as serious about civil service reform as about ending reconstruction, Hayes courageously named reform leader Carl Schurz Secretary of the Interior. To please the South, however, he named Tennessee's David M. Key to the patronage-rich position of Postmaster General. He bent over backward not only to bring a mix of philosophies into his cabinet but to "kill the Southern brethren with kindness." In this he received enthusiastic support from Northern business interests, which viewed the South as a fertile field for Northern investment. By September, Hayes, Key, and Hayes's distinguished Secretary of State, William M. Evarts of New York, were off on a goodwill tour of the South, hobnobbing with Wade Hampton and other old-boy politicians who had gotten into office by suppressing the black vote. The President considered the journey such a smashing success that a year later he went south again.

Mosby, having already called on the newly retired Grant at the home of Hamilton Fish, where the ex-President was now staying, showed up at the White House the Saturday following Hayes's inauguration "merely to pay his respects," according to a newspaper account. The colonel and the former brevet major general reminisced about the war in the Shenandoah, where Hayes had served for a time. "He and Col. Mosby," said the *Baltimore Sun,* "exchanged some jocular remarks on the alternate games of hide and seek in which they and their respective commands had indulged." When the talk got around to politics, Mosby expressed hearty approval of the new President's planned "vigorous prosecution of peace."

Still the optimist, he predicted that the solid South would quickly dissolve under such a beneficent policy, and that the Southern people would without fail respond to his overtures.[88]

Mosby's own overtures were not going unnoticed. A letter to the *New York Tribune,* written prior to the Hayes inauguration but published afterward, warned that Mosby was doing irreparable harm to the *Republican* party in Virginia. He'd somehow succeeded in "getting control over" Grant, said the writer (a carpetbagger), and "for the last . . . two years, it [had] been impossible for a Federal soldier to get an appointment if Mosby knew of the fact."[89] It appeared that Mosby had finally succeeded in winning the distrust of both parties in Virginia. He had little turf left to stand on.

Mosby, the letter went on, was "not entitled to the respect of any decent man in this country." He was "captain of the hardest set of men . . . ever collected in one company on this continent"—the writer had evidently not heard of W. C. Quantrill—and was regarded "by even the rebels . . . as a thief and a robber." He was planning, said the correspondent, to exert even greater influence under Hayes. "Union soldiers," he concluded," hang their heads in shame and say, 'Has it come to this?'"[90]

Other letters came to Mosby's defense, one even giving him credit for Hayes's Southern pacification policy: "That [Mosby] advanced ten years ago the idea upon which [this policy] is founded is a matter of history."[91]

Letters about Mosby came to the President himself from both North and South, most urging him to have nothing to do with the Virginian. A Philadelphia man told Hayes, "Neither Republicans nor Democrats here or in the South like Mosby."[92] A friend of the President's from northern Virginia bemoaned the fact that Mosby was riding so high with the new administration—that he was, in fact, reported to be more influential with Hayes than anyone else in the state. "Mosby and his men," he said, " . . . we considered as a band of outlaws."[93]

"Don't place too much confidence in Col. Mosby," he warned the President. "Don't give him more confidence than a repentant sinner is entitled to."[94]

Hayes listened, but seemingly with only one ear. Mosby

was a valuable adviser on Southern affairs and worthy of attention as such. Hayes, moreover, could not fail to be impressed, as Grant had been, that Mosby's chief concern seemed indeed to be the South and not himself. He had never sought personal preferment, Hayes knew, and in fact had rejected offices whenever offered. The President decided he should probably be cautious in his relationship with the Virginian, but he would not cut him off.

In May, Mosby dropped into the White House twice in one weekend to talk on a favorite theme: appointments in the South. He wished to fill the soon-to-be-vacant postmastership at Richmond and the post of internal revenue collector at Petersburg with his own choices. Hayes's reform sentiments notwithstanding, he knew he was in debt to Mosby, and assented: the positions would be filled as he wished. Mosby was very pleased, since his candidate for the Petersburg job had succeeded in displacing the Maine carpetbagger incumbent— a man under the protection of the "Plumed Knight" himself, Maine's powerful Senator James G. Blaine. "Col. Mosby was in fine spirits over his success," reported the *Baltimore Sun*.[95]

One of the top items on Hayes's reform agenda was that of the consular service. The *Philadelphia North American* described the coming sweep in an April article, which noted how consulships in the past had been tools of personal enrichment only and had had nothing to do with advancing the nation's commerce. "It can be set down as a rule now," the paper concluded optimistically, "that for consulships politicians need not apply."[96]

The same paper a month later decried the abysmal ignorance of U.S. consuls, ignorance especially of foreign languages and the principles of commerce. About the same time, the *Milwaukee Sentinel* detailed some of the changes planned by Secretary Evarts, who was arguing that commercial experience and language ability should be requisites at most consulates. In other places—the Far East, specifically—where judicial duties were of greater importance than commercial duties, men with legal backgrounds would receive preference. The *Sacramento Daily Union* crowed that incompetents would at last be purged from "that longtime refuge for broken down political hacks, adventurers who have tried every other business and failed in it, and needy *litterateurs.*"[97]

The growing pressure for reform of the consular service seemed at the time to have little bearing on Mosby, who was currently engaged in watching another gubernatorial race shaping up in Virginia and devising new ways of carrying on his private reconstruction of the South.

On January 16, 1878, Mosby was given a wild turkey dressed for the roasting pan. He put it to better use, however, than having it cooked for himself: he shipped it off on the same day, with his compliments, to Ohio's powerful congressman, James A. Garfield. Garfield, primed by the bird, was evidently receptive to a request made of him by Mosby two days later, for within the week a similar idea seemed to be taking hold in the White House and elsewhere.

"I am informed," Mosby had written to Garfield, "that a vacancy is about to occur on the bench of the Court of Claims." After allowing that an ex-Confederate could probably not hope to be appointed to such a position, Mosby suggested an alternative: move a man from the Attorney General's office into this vacancy. His unspoken suggestion was that a Southerner might then be slipped into the less visible post vacated by this man. "I would be greatly obliged," he cagily told the former Union general, "if you would support this to the President."[98] A weary Mosby, of course, at last had himself in mind as the lucky ex-Confederate.

On January 22 a message from the Treasury Department appeared on the desk of Hayes's secretary, William K. Rogers, mentioning the President's recently stated "desire to do something for Col. Mosby," and then describing a similar shuffle of offices to what Mosby had advanced to Garfield. In the meantime, Garfield, with a number of well-known attorneys and Federal judges, "strongly urged" Hayes to slip Mosby into the Assistant Attorney General's slot, and before long he was in fact offered "an important Federal office." The job offered, however, was in the Internal Revenue Service. This was not quite what Mosby had had in mind, and he turned it down.[99]

There seemed to be nothing Hayes could offer that Mosby would take—except perhaps a foreign assignment. By late summer 1878, Hayes, with further prodding from Garfield, had spoken with Mosby about a consular post and had found him surprisingly receptive. On August 7, he wrote to a subordinate: "I have offered Col. Mosby Canton. . . . Please inform Col. M. as to the emoluments, advantages, etc., etc."[100] By early December the talk had shifted from Canton to the great trade center of Hong Kong, and by mid-month the forty-five-year-old widower, ex-Confederate guerrilla, and father of six had been confirmed by the Senate as the new United States consul in Hong Kong.

He would have to leave his children behind—the oldest, nineteen, the youngest, seven. But he had had trouble supporting them once he left Warrenton (he didn't seem to have more business than he could attend to was his enigmatic comment once about his practice in Washington), and leaving the country might be the only way to assure them of steady support. The children would be cared for by his brother, sisters, and by friends in Washington, Alexandria, and Warrenton. His mother would also help when possible.

It would in fact be nearly seven years before he saw them again, with the exception of Beverly, who was eventually to join him in the Orient.

Without a doubt, Virginia Democrats broke out the champagne when they heard the news. Hayes himself probably breathed a sigh of relief that a potentially troublesome man had been removed from the scene, and to a place where he could do little damage. Outside his family and small circle of friends—Keith, perhaps Hunton, some ex-rangers, and a few others—it is doubtful that many tears were shed. Certainly few Southern tears fell. Of the handful of congratulatory letters and telegrams he received as he was packing, the one Mosby cherished most was not from a Southerner but from Union general William Wells—the Vermonter who, as a young major, had crashed through a plaster ceiling onto his rangers' heads one day in a long-dead world, when all were young and knew how to laugh.

He left for San Francisco shortly before Christmas 1878, no one dreaming how soon they would be hearing from him again.

Mosby's brother and wartime adjutant, Willie, photographed two years after the war. The two brothers remained close for their entire lives. *Credit:* The Memoirs of Colonel John S. Mosby

Mosby during the mid-1870s, when Reconstruction was in full swing. He was a practicing attorney at the time, and a frequent guest at the White House. *Credit: Chicago Historical Society*

Mosby's home in Warrenton, purchased for $3,700 in 1867. Persecuted for his political stance, he was to close it up nine years later and leave Virginia. *Credit: Library of Congress*

TOP LEFT: Mosby as he appeared while serving as U.S. consul at Hong Kong. His tenure was stormy, causing tremors not only throughout the Orient but also in far-off Washington. *Credit: The Huntington Library*

TOP RIGHT: Mosby in 1889, during his sixteen-year attorneyship at the Southern Pacific. With few opportunities to shoot from the hip, he regarded these as the most exasperating years of his life. *Credit: Manuscript Department, William R. Perkins Library, Duke University*

LEFT: Mosby at the age of sixty. His final crusade was not to begin for eight more years. *Credit: Mosby's Rangers*

BELOW: The waterfront at Hong Kong, as Mosby saw it upon his arrival in January 1879 to begin his tour as U.S. consul there. *Credit: BBC Hulton Picture Library*

ABOVE: Charles W. Russell, Justice Department jack-of-all-trades, married Mosby's sisters Lucie and Lelia successively. Russell, Mosby's superior at Justice, had for some time to bear Mosby's censure for the old rebel's ouster in 1910. *Credit:* National Cyclopaedia of American Biography

MIDDLE: Bartlett Richards, Nebraska cattle king, relaxing at home two years before Mosby's arrival in the West. Mosby was in the van of a force that was to hound Richards literally to his grave. *Credit: Nebraska State Historical Society*

BELOW: Land seekers in Nebraska around the time of Mosby's tenure as special agent for the General Land Office. Free land attracted droves of Easterners, and cattlemen scrambled to protect their own interests any way they could. *Credit: Nebraska State Historical Society*

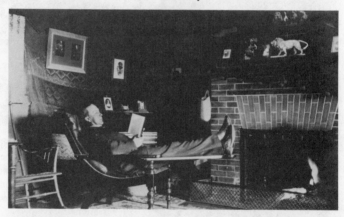

Will Comstock, Bartlett Richards's partner and brother-in-law, surveying the men's Nebraska Sandhills domain from a Studebaker buggy. Comstock was sent to jail as a result of investigations opened earlier by Mosby. *Credit: Nebraska State Historical Society*

ABOVE LEFT: Joseph Bryan, Southern publisher, industrialist, philanthropist, had as a young man served with Mosby's rangers. He and Mosby grew very close in their old age. *Credit: National Cyclopaedia of American Biography*

ABOVE RIGHT: The former guerrilla was a familiar figure on the streets of Washington. He is pictured here at the age of seventy-three, while an attorney for the Department of Justice. *Credit: Museum of the Confederacy*

LEFT: Taken in 1915, this photograph shows an eighty-one-year-old Mosby, one-eyed, flanked by his two eldest grandsons, Spottswood *(left)* and Mosby Campbell *(right)*. In his final years Mosby carried on a voluminous correspondence with these young men, who were among his closest confidants. *Credit: Manuscripts Department, University of Virginia Library*

9

THE CHINA COAST

My advent on the China coast . . . will be remembered with as
great horror by some of the American consuls as some of the
typhoons that have strewn its coasts with wrecks.
                                    —John S. Mosby to James D.
                                    Blackwell, September 6, 1879

HE SEA AIR was brisk but held a hint of warmth to
come as the *City of Peking* steamed toward the loom-
ing islands, and the knot of land-starved passengers
bellied up against the rail to drink in the rich view.
Off the starboard bow jutted the dark bulk of 1,800-foot-high
Victoria Peak, white clouds billowing up behind it and splendid blue-green bays sparkling at its feet. As the ship nosed
into the Orient's finest harbor, the city of Victoria was revealed above a forest of junk masts that bobbed and bowed at
anchor in the steamer's mountainous wake. Other junks could
be seen maneuvering clumsily about the harbor, or lumbering
among nearby islets on errands whose purpose could only be
guessed at. Squat gunboats of Her Majesty's Navy, and an
occasional man-of-war from France, the United States, or the
Empire of China—all with flags snapping smartly and funnels
belching thick, ashy smoke—were making way amid scores of
merchantmen from many lands. The busy harbor changed its
face by the moment, as the wind and a fickle sun played
across its surface. To the north, across the watery expanse,
could be seen the low spit of Kowloon, gateway to a still
largely unknown and forbidding China.

As the *City of Peking* approached its anchorage, Mosby and
the other passengers pushed forward to crowd aboard a steam
launch now coming alongside. When the launch finally eased
up against one of Victoria's great stone wharves, he heard the
first strains of the muted but bewildering cacophony that he
would hear for the next six years: giggling sampan girls vying
with one another for customers to Kowloon; the harsh gabble

of Chinese stevedores muscling chests of opium into position beneath cranes; richly garbed mandarins berating pigtailed coolies; a sprinkling of Indians and various species of European, each group chattering in its own way.

After a brief but restrained welcome by the American vice-consul, H. Selden Loring, who was accompanied by a few Englishmen curious to meet the Confederate guerrilla, Mosby was led from the wharves into the heart of a new world.

Across Queen's Road and a short distance inland, past several sturdy specimens of colonial government architecture and reassuringly Christian temples, he found shady avenues climbing abruptly onto the skirts of the mountain, becoming more like dense-foliaged stairways than streets. Wealth abounded here. There were lofty homes with covered green balconies—places festooned with creepers, ribbed with colonnades, studded with porticoes, all radiant in the pleasant winter sun. Standing away from the neatly groomed Caucasian settlement, however, was Asia. Here the newcomer's senses reeled in the jumble of large painted houses that was the Chinese quarter, redolent with unknown odors, gay with the daubed ideographs of vendors or their products, and crisscrossed by an assortment of crowded defiles.

The Virginian had seldom seen so many people rushing about in so little space. Chinese and Westerners alike were borne past him in gauze-curtained, green-canopied sedan chairs, held aloft by sweating and half-naked bearers. Cone-hatted coolies, like human horses, picked their way through the throng drawing jinrickshas. A few Westerners or Chinese merchants forced passage on horseback, or occasionally in light carriages with outriders, paying little heed to the disturbance they caused. Portuguese or Italian nuns and priests, somber splotches on a sea of rustling color, scurried along past gambling houses and brothels. The stench from great tubs of liquid manure in transit vied for the visitor's attention with the varied odors manufactured by itinerant cooks. A continuum of chatter flowed from stalls of birds'-nest sellers, sharks'-fin dealers, bean curd vendors, jadestone dealers, cinnamon sellers, or traders in sesame oil, ginseng, or joss paper. Punctuated by energetic exchanges in pidgin between Chinese hucksters and hiccuping Western sailors, the talk merged into a wall of undecipherable sound.

Everything was color, sound, odor—overstimulating to a rustic American fresh from a month at sea—and the new consul was pleased to be finally conducted to his quarters and allowed to sleep.

In 1879, the Crown Colony of Hong Kong—"Fragrant Harbor" in Chinese—consisted of two geographically separate entities: the twenty-nine-square-mile Hong Kong Island, first occupied by the British in 1841 and ceded to them in perpetuity the following year; and the tiny Kowloon peninsula, a scrap of seacoast in mainland China's Kwangtung Province, ceded to the British in 1860. Each cession had been made by the Chinese on the heels of a sound European drubbing in the two so-called Opium Wars, conflicts precipitated by the Western "barbarians" in the interests ultimately of defining their relationship with the Empire.

Aside from Victoria and a few fishing villages, the island in 1879 was still largely uninhabited, but—taken with Kowloon—the colony as a whole could number 150,000 souls. Nineteen out of every twenty were Chinese.

Mosby's new island home lay on China's underbelly near the mouth of the Pearl River. From here, he was told, it was seventy-five miles or so to the upriver commercial center of Canton, and forty miles across the river's broad mouth to the Portuguese colony of Macao. Peking, the seat of Chinese empire, lay more than 2,000 miles to the north. The colony, it was explained, had a monsoon-type climate, with high rainfall and tigerish summer heat—he would assuredly find summers a trial. Its lifeblood from the beginning, he knew, had been shipping, and its virtue continued to be the plethora of opportunities afforded here for making money.

Unlike other British colonies, Hong Kong had never been a settlement to which the British migrated to make homes, but rather to make money. If they brought with them their lawn tennis, amateur theatricals, formal balls, and horse racing, it was only to have something with which to while away the nonproductive hours before returning to England. The colony was the nerve center of a commercial rather than of a territorial empire and, as such, tended to attract a footloose population, both Westerners and Chinese. As a place to make money it was a magnet to businessmen, pirates, and thieves of every nationality and social station, from the virtuous merchant princes of Jardine Matheson or Russell and Co.—both of which grew fat on the opium trade—through a hodgepodge of seedy government types, to real seagoing pirates and the littered riffraff common to any seaport.

This bustling, brawling colony of transients, center of various forms of iniquity and disease, was ruled by proper British forms. But, as it happened, the forms were at this time breaking down. Mosby had arrived during the governorship of Sir John Pope-Hennessy, an aristocratic Irish Catholic who was engaged in throwing away nearly forty years of British social gains by daring to concern himself with the rights of the "heathen" Chinese under his administration. Mosby had in fact been warned upon arrival that the whites of Hong Kong were barely speaking to the renegade governor. When the new consul presented his credentials at Government House, however, he found, not surprisingly, that he and the independent-minded Sir John hit it off quite well. It was one of the few satisfying relationships he was to develop in the Orient.

Those at home who had rejoiced at Mosby's entry into what they considered a fitting though overdue oblivion must have been shocked in April 1879—only four months after his submergence—to see him surfacing again in the press. They smiled, however, when they read on.

"Col. Mosby," sneered one paper, typical of several, "brings the manners of the saddle into the salons of the diplomats, and has won more conspicuousness than distinction." A Hong Kong source was quoted to the effect that Mosby was breaking the rules of a place where "all the pomp and pageantry of a miniature court" was maintained, the specific complaint being that he had refused to dress in "the proper costume of polite society" for certain required social functions. The colonel seemed, it was observed, "better fitted for duty as a guerrilla than for official station." [1]

"His conduct in Hong Kong since his arrival there," the

piece continued, "has not only not been satisfactory to the American residents, but has been exceedingly objectionable to the English and . . . other nationalities." As coda, the editor offered a well-worn display of journalistic amazement that Mosby had been able to trade upon "the credulity of two Presidents" without ever having done a thing to merit their confidence.[2]

This journalistic obloquy, it developed, represented more than a casual slander. The charge that Mosby was acting in official circles "as he would in a Virginia bar-room" proved to be the opening salvo in a major effort to get him discredited in Hong Kong as quickly as possible, since he was threatening to upset a number of carefully laden applecarts on the China coast.[3]

On settling down to examine the previous consul's books shortly after taking office, Mosby had noted some peculiarities. Pulling out pencil and paper, his suspicions deepened. His predecessor, David H. Bailey, evidently with the connivance of Vice-Consul Loring, had over the past eight years been bilking the government of thousands of dollars. Given the shabby reputation of U.S. government agents in China, Mosby became all but convinced that Bailey and Loring too were part of the "ring," a known network of embezzlement and shady speculation apparently headed by U.S. Minister to China George F. Seward, nephew of Lincoln's distinguished Secretary of State.

What made matters sticky, however, was that Mosby's own boss was a Seward: Assistant Secretary of State Frederick W. Seward, son to the renowned Secretary and cousin to George. In addition, F.W. Seward was the cherished protégé of the reigning Secretary, William M. Evarts. Mosby decided he would leave the Seward implications unmentioned, but he determined to inform the Department at once of his suspicions about Bailey.

Less than three weeks after taking office, he wrote to Frederick Seward—a man whose feeling toward Mosby was doubtless colored by the beating he'd received from ex-ranger Lewis Payne during Payne's April 1865 attempt to assassinate his father. "I desire to call the attention of the Department," wrote Mosby, "to a question of interest both to myself and the government."[4]

There was a problem, he said, with the reporting of fees collected for consular services. The U.S. consul at Hong Kong, Mosby reminded Seward, was expected to certify, for every Chinese emigrant to the United States from Hong Kong, that his or her emigration was voluntary—in other words, that they were not part of the nefarious "coolie traffic," and, in the case of women, were not emigrating for immoral purposes. Fees had always been charged for such certificates, Mosby noted, but "by a strange coincidence," for emigrants shipping on U.S.–flag carriers over the past eight years the "expenses" for the shipboard examination had always equaled the fee (the government getting nothing) and for emigrants shipping on foreign-flag carriers the fees were quite openly pocketed.[5]

Even the fees for examination on board the U.S. vessels, hinted the new consul, must have been pocketed, since the examination was so absurdly simple that no expenses were possible. A whole shipload of Chinese could be examined in an hour. Bailey's "expenses," Mosby explained, appeared in the form of chits from one Peter Smith, an "illiterate keeper of a sailors' boarding house," who had carried out the examinations in Bailey's behalf. Suggesting that Bailey was pocketing most of what Smith had receipted, Mosby noted that Smith was the sort who would take $100 for a whole year of such work and consider himself well paid. Bailey had, said Mosby, been made at least $30,000 richer over the past eight years by this deceit; in other words, he had about doubled his salary. "I would like very much to be allowed to retain these fees," continued Mosby, "if it can properly be done; but I do not feel justified in appropriating them in the absence of instructions from the Department."[6]

There would no longer be any "expenses" charged to the government for shipboard examination of emigrants, he assured Seward, since he would be conducting all such examinations himself. Mosby would await the Department's decision as to whether either these "official" fees, or the "unofficial" fees for examination aboard foreign-flag vessels, should be turned in.

He had loosened the first log in the jam, but had picked a particularly slippery one in the matter of fees. As Hong Kong's *China Mail* put it: "If there be two things under heaven upon which men in China do agree they are that American consuls are most miserably paid . . . and that fearfully and wonderfully vague notions prevail as to the scale of fees chargeable upon their official acts."[7] The further question of what a consul *did* with the fees once collected was even more deeply shrouded in mystery. The accepted practice was not to ask questions either out on the front lines or back in Washington, where it was commonly accepted that the fee system helped the consular service to support itself.

Consulates, however, had the potential for being far more than self-supporting. They were places where one could get rich, and as such were avidly sought. So great was the tide of seekers for America's three hundred consular outposts following Hayes's inauguration that Secretary of State Evarts had made the tongue-in-cheek proposal of carving "Come ye disconsulate" over his office door.[8]

A new consul, usually selected for past political services if not for more casual reasons, frequently had several surprises in store for him at his new post. The first for many was that no consulate existed, and that they would have to rent quarters in which to establish one, for which they usually were required to pay part of the rent out of their own pocket. The second discovery was that commercial towns were dreadfully dull, and the work of the consul hardly more glamorous. The third was that it was impossible to promote American commercial interests by circulating among the merchant class, since one could not socialize on a $4,000-a-year salary.

With distant Washington averting its gaze, pocketing fees was the logical answer. Large sums of money besides fees were handled in some consulates—funds for the relief of distressed seamen, for example, or for the administration of estates of intestate Americans dying abroad. The "morality" of appropriating such monies was usually not even considered, and from here it was an easy step to resetting fee schedules, doctoring records, and a skein of further "irregularities." Special Treasury Department Inspector De B. Randolph Keim, in his whirlwind inspection of all United States consulates in the early seventies, had noted serious abuses everywhere; all were in full flower at Hong Kong when Mosby arrived a few years later.

Mosby, conscious that he'd been sent to the East by a self-proclaimed reformer, and himself constitutionally incapable of perceiving moral issues in shades of gray, had no qualms about pursuing the matter.

What made Mosby's pursuit of Bailey especially alarming to some was that Bailey had recently been nominated to the consul generalship at Shanghai, and was at this time in Washington awaiting confirmation by the Senate. Bailey had, however, an even more vital purpose for being in Washington: to help convince the public and a hostile Democratic Congress that U.S. Minister to China George Seward ought not to be impeached for high crimes, as a congressional committee had just recommended. It was hardly a propitious time for Bailey's own honesty to be called into question.

George Seward, formerly consul general himself, had always had troubles when honest men were sent to China, but he'd proven capable of handling them all until John C. Myers of Reading, Pennsylvania, was sent in 1876 to replace him at Shanghai—the thirty-six-year-old Seward being moved that year into the minister's chair at Peking.

Myers had noted at once that Seward and his vice-consul, Oliver B. Bradford, seemed to live far beyond their means. He soon found out why: they were at the head of a "land ring," a scheme of speculation in land and capital-intensive projects within China. Their actions were in violation of the provisions of the Burlingame Treaty of 1868, by which the United States had forsworn all intention to interfere in Chinese affairs. Moreover, they were also immersed in various shady practices involving the funds of the United States, as the consular books demonstrated clearly.

Myers turned Seward and Bradford in to the State Department, and was promptly suspended for his troubles. His successor, G. Wiley Wells, ex-congressman from Mississippi, met a similar fate when he, too, demonstrated excessive zeal in the pursuit of reform. Both Myers and Wells resorted to Congress for redress.

By the time Mosby was leaving for Hong Kong, Congress

was amassing reams of testimony for the impeachment of George Seward. Among the several charges: extortion of illegal fees and embezzlement of U.S. funds. In March now, with Bailey stretched on tenterhooks over his own appointment and Seward on the verge of impeachment, Mosby's damaging letter about Bailey arrived at the State Department. It was quietly slipped into Fred Seward's desk drawer.

While Mosby naively awaited a response to his dispatch, his curiosity about the other men in the East became aroused, and he began to cast about for more game. He did not have to look far. Merchant ship captains and naval men—the most honest class of men in the East—had begun to speak freely to him of their experiences with American consuls. The names that seemed to crop up most frequently were those of David B. Sickels, U.S. consul at Bangkok, and his vice-consul, a one-time Hong Kong vagrant named Torrey. Mosby made use of Gen. T. C. H. Smith, a Hayes intimate, to open fire on Sickels and Torrey.

Sickels, he explained to Smith in early March 1879, was "simply a weak incompetent man," completely under the control of Torrey. He was now no longer even in Bangkok, said Mosby, having moved permanently to Singapore, and leaving Torrey in charge behind him. Mosby told Smith of a letter recently arrived from Bangkok addressed simply to "U.S. consul at Hong Kong." On opening it, he said, he had seen that it was for Loring, but having just fired Loring, he felt justified in reading on. Torrey had congratulated Loring on the fortune he'd been able to accumulate at Hong Kong, pointing out that he himself had had far fewer opportunities for plunder. The only "fat thing" Torrey claimed to have gotten recently, reported Mosby, was a $480 bribe. "It was just such a . . . letter," he noted, "as one pickpocket would write to another."[9]

"The fact is," he declared, "nearly all the American consulates out here have a horrible reputation." They're a "scaly set" he added, and "a disgrace to the country." He felt "humiliated every day" at being obliged to deal with many of them.[10]

Three days later he tacked on a postscript:

In Bangkok, the favorite way of making money is to send out
the marshal and have a large lot of Chinamen arrested for
some imaginary offense and fine them from $100 to $500 and
then the consul pockets . . . the fine. . . . If the President does
not clean out this Augean stable it will be subject of congressional investigation. Better let his administration get the credit
of it than the Democratic party. I write this as his friend.[11]

Two days later he added a second postscript, describing
"another example . . . of the demoralization of the U.S. consular services in the East."[12] Here Mosby was referring to the
opium trade. In order to ship opium to the United States from
Macao—a perfectly legal practice, he reminded Smith—one
needed a consular certificate. Since no U.S. consul resided at
Macao, it was customary to ship opium through the port of
Victoria for certification by the American consul there. There
was, of course, a fee expected for this service, Bailey having
settled on the modest sum of $10,000 per year. Mosby had
already, he said, been offered this fee by the Macao shipper,
who assumed that the same system obtained. The shipper was
dumbstruck when the new consul informed him he could have
a certificate for $2.50.

Encourage the President, Mosby told Smith, to take an interest in this kind of "rascality." "It is much better," he reit-
erated, "for the President to root out the corruption here than
to leave it to a congressional committee. I intend to see that it
is done."[13]

By the end of April he was able to forget temporarily that
he'd still not received a straight answer from Washington. The
reason: U. S. Grant, nearing the end of a world tour begun
two years before, was coming to Hong Kong.

On April 30, Victoria Harbor was abuzz with traffic as the
1,000-ton U.S. corvette *Ashuelot* and a number of American
and English merchantmen dressed ship and stood to, awaiting
passage of the *Irrawaddy,* bearing the ex-President, his wife
Julia, his son Fred, and John Russell Young, an American
journalist Grant had added to his entourage in England.
Mosby clambered aboard the *Irrawaddy* almost before it had
anchored, the former Confederate, in a strange twist, now
representing the U.S. government to citizen Grant. A number

of U.S. consuls and high-ranking Chinese officials followed
Mosby aboard, all gathered at Hong Kong to welcome the
great general on his first China landfall.

After the introductions had been performed by a bubbling
Mosby and all the proper things said, the party climbed into
the launch for the short trip to the *Ashuelot,* standing to with
yards manned and firing an ear-splitting salute. As Grant's
party was being piped aboard the double-ended side-wheeler,
the Chinese corvette *Nissing,* not to be outdone, hove to and
fired its own salute to the former American President. It was
a banner day.

With the shipboard formalities completed, Mosby ushered
Grant and his party into the launch once again to steam into
Murray Pier, where at the head of a stairway festooned with
evergreens and colorful shields and draped with the flags of
the United States and Great Britain, Sir John Pope-Hennessy
waited beneath a bamboo arch. As the general stepped onto
the pier, an honor guard of the Twenty-seventh Enniskillens
braced and presented arms, while Pope-Hennessy, taking
charge now, shepherded his renowned guest along a lengthy
row of tall British officers, dumpy mandarins, and dignified
prelates of both English and Romish persuasion. Grant was
then assisted into a sedan chair, to be borne along a police-
lined road from the landing to the governor's home, where he
would stay for the next few days. All knew they were entertaining not only a past President but quite possibly the next
President of the United States.

For Mosby it was probably the high point, emotionally, of
his entire tour as U.S. consul. He breakfasted with Grant,
attended banquets at his side, and almost co-hosted the general's stay with Pope-Hennessy. They talked about the war—
Mosby even producing a renegade Virginian, never properly
paroled, for Grant's pardon and benediction—and they
talked about the consular service. Grant had just come from
Bangkok, and verified much of what Mosby had heard elsewhere. He advised Mosby to go directly to Hayes with his
complaint (Mosby had actually done so a few days before),
and promised to see the President about it himself when he
returned to Washington.

Grant's stay was short. On May 5, Mosby and Pope-

Hennessy joined his party in the launch for the trip to the *Ashuelot,* standing by to carry the visitors up the China coast. After a soldier's farewell, Mosby and the governor headed shoreward, but drew up when the *Ashuelot,* evidently at Grant's request, commenced firing twenty-one guns. When the firing died, the small figure on the deck lifted his hat to his hosts, and the launch turned once again to shore.

It was Mosby's last sight of his most special friend.

June saw a marshaling of the new consul's forces. By now he had a letter in hand from Pope-Hennessy, which he sent off at once for publication in the States, expressing the governor's "astonishment" at the stories circulating about the American consul's "costume at Government House."[14]

"You have often done me the honor," said Pope-Hennessy, "of being a guest at my table, and I need hardly say there is no one in this country whose social qualities and high character I more fully appreciate."[15] Judging by the low esteem into which the governor had fallen among his own countrymen, he doubtless meant every word.

Mosby's February dispatch to Fred Seward was not, it turned out, to see the light of day, and Bailey was confirmed as consul general that summer. But by this time word of Mosby's reform efforts had begun to leak out about the Orient. "The [new] consul," said the *China Mail* in July, "has evidently made up his mind to place things consular upon an entirely new platform. . . . Col. Mosby is . . . a man amongst men, and certainly he seems to be a consul among consuls. . . . Even if tact and discretion cannot be laid at [his] door . . . he may fairly be accused of strict honesty and ultra exactness."[16]

The praise was all the more meaningful for having come from the *Mail.* Shortly before, Mosby had won a court case against the editor of this paper, who had sued him for non-payment of a subscription. The new consul's position was, incredibly, that his predecessor had had no right to charge the government $24 a year for a newspaper for his personal use. He was therefore canceling the subscription, and refused to be held responsible for the arrears. After listening in amused silence, the British court found in the consul's favor, and worldly Britons swallowed in disbelief.

While Mosby's official correspondence was hopelessly one-noted, his letters to family and friends reflected more varied concerns, especially those of the absent father. In July he wrote to twelve-year-old Virginia Stuart about some "tiger's claws jewelry" he was sending for her birthday in September. Trying to keep his hand in as paternal referee, he told her that twenty-year-old May was to be allowed to wear the jewelry for the season at Fauquier Springs, but that she was to return it to Stuart at summer's end. He'd also be sending her a camel's-hair shawl, bought recently from a "Hindoo," and he hoped she'd received the dresses.[17]

"I feel a great deal of uneasiness about Johnnie," he confessed to his daughter. "I fear he thinks he is now a grown man since I am away, and that he is going to give himself up to idle habits. All the children but he wrote to me." He urged her to read and to study—"otherwise people will be cheating you all your life." Abbott's *Histories,* Marco Polo's travels, *Stories from Vergil* were among his recommendations. Like any disgruntled parent, he groused: Johnnie's lack of attention both to his handwriting and to his teeth bothered him, and neither Johnnie nor Bev knew how to fold a letter. He warned Stuart to take care of her money.[18]

"I dine out every Sunday evening," he told her in an abrupt change of subject. "Have two invitations today. I very often breakfast and dine aboard the American ships with the captains."[19]

"Mrs. Grant," he added, "told me to give her love to all of you all. I want May to go to see her when she goes to Washington."[20]

Describing his consular problems, he told Warrenton attorney James D. Blackwell in September, "I certainly have a great deal to try my patience and you know I haven't much of that." Despite the consulate's scenic location on the shore—a place where he could relax on his veranda and watch a parade of ships from many nations—he claimed to be less happy in the consular service than he'd been in the military or in law practice. "It seems," he said, that I am fated like Ulysses always to be in a storm, never to see sunshine and rest. I thought that if there was a spot on this earth where peace could be found, it would be on an island on the China coast and here I expected repose for a short time from strife. But my doom has followed me. . . .

Knowing as you do my restless temperament, you may judge how irksome life is to me shut up on an island with a horizon of about two miles in extent. . . . The population is as varied as the hues of the kaleidoscope. I believe I've seen every species of the human race here including Darwin's "connecting link." . . . I never enjoyed better health than I have here. I take a sea-bath every night and sleep as sound as a log.[21]

In spite of occasional tensions with the colonial authorities, he remarked, his relationship with the British, and especially with the "Catholic Irishman" governor, was very pleasant. But he could not abide British bureaucracy. "The red tape system," he declared, "is here carried to perfection. Hong Kong must have been the original of Dickens' circumlocution office."[22]

He told Blackwell of his desire to see more of China, to get off the island. So far he'd been only to Macao, whose wharves, "once populous," were "now almost deserted."[23]

"The only point of interest," he continued, in reference to the Portuguese colony,

is the garden and grotto of Camoëns, where he composed his great epic—the Lusiad [*sic*]—that celebrates the discoveries of Vasco da Gama. Being a poet yourself you can sympathize with my feelings when I stood on the spot consecrated by the genius of the poet and listened to the wild music of the waves that inspired his song. . . .

Well, now that I am no longer among you to create discord, I suppose Fauquier enjoys the peace and pastoral felicity described by Vergil in . . . his Eclogues. . . . I certainly do not wish to disturb your serenity or postpone the coming of the millenial [*sic*] year. If, however, it will not be a signal for war I want to get a furlough next year and come home. I am anxious to see my children who are all that makes life dear to me. I have many old friends who have never turned against me in adversity. . . . I wd cross the ocean to see them once more.[24]

By midsummer Mosby's original dispatch, to the mild consternation of the State Department, had found its way to the press. To the Department's further discomfiture, it was learned that Mosby had also been writing directly to President Hayes on such minutiae as the difference between "official" and "unofficial" fees. Seward had tried to quiet Mosby by assuring him that it was an accepted practice for a consul to pocket certain fees; but the new consul, uncomfortably for the Assistant Secretary, persisted in a righteous stance.

The Department's hand was gradually being forced, and Evarts finally ordered an investigation of affairs at Hong Kong. To stack the deck against Mosby, however, the investigator was to be Gen. Julius P. Stahel, friend of both Bailey and Seward, and Mosby's one-time cavalry nemesis in Loudoun County. General Stahel was presently U.S. consul at Hyogo, Japan. "Don't this look rather odd?" wrote Mosby to his daughter Stuart, when he heard of Stahel's assignment.[25]

Stahel arrived in August to inspect the books—having stopped off first at Shanghai to speak with Bailey—and Mosby gave him an earful. Bailey had not only been charging exorbitant fees and defrauding the government of them all, said Mosby, but he had also been up to his eyebrows in various other schemes, usually in league with Peter Smith, bilking shipmasters and seamen alike of large sums of money. The only provable part at present was that he'd stolen $40,000, Mosby declared, but there was much more.

After examining the books, Stahel saw that he had no choice. He reported to Washington that Consul Mosby's charges were true, to the letter.

"It is perfectly evident," wrote Mosby in August to G. Wiley Wells, former consul general, and one of George Seward's original accusers, "that the Seward influence put Bailey at Shanghai to cover up Seward's tracks, and that Bailey left Loring here to do the same service for him."[26] He reported that George Seward's secretary of legation, the Chinese-speaking ex-missionary Chester Holcombe, was beginning now to agitate in earnest, spreading the word among Far East consulates that Mosby was bad medicine. A movement was apparently mounting to have the consul at Hong Kong removed before Seward (who had come within a whisker's breadth of being impeached) could be sucked into another investigation.

"Now, as I have had nothing to do with Seward's matters," continued Mosby, "but was simply prosecuting Bailey, this shows how intimately their causes are blended." He predicted that Seward, who had returned to China after his successful Fifth Amendment–based defense, would shortly have his neck on the block again, this time in company with Bailey. "I am in for the war," announced Mosby, "and intend either to purge the public service of these scoundrels or go out myself."[27]

Being in for the war, he called up heavier artillery—now in the form of the prepotent Boston brahmins John M. Forbes and his merchant son, William. Mosby's connections with the Forbes family were complicated and interesting. William H. Forbes had succeeded his father in the Orient as head of the immensely successful mercantile house of Russell and Co., and was, as such, a business acquaintance of the American consul. He was, however, the same Major Forbes of the Second Massachusetts Cavalry who had driven a saber through Mosby's coat in a bitter cavalry engagement years before.

William asked his father to speak to Evarts in Mosby's behalf, and in mid-September Forbes senior did so. "My correspondent in China," he announced to Evarts, "writes me that somebody is trumping up charges against Mosby, which they do not believe have any foundation. . . . I have, on the whole, a good deal of faith in [Mosby], from what I have seen of the man and from what I hear from China."[28]

Newspapers were beginning to stir in Mosby's behalf, smelling fresh Seward blood in the offing. "The latest revelations in the matter of Bailey . . . ," declared the *National Republican* in late September, in reference to Mosby's now-publicized accusations, "only emphasize the unfortunate position in which the State Department is placed by its efforts to shield Seward, Bradford, and Bailey."[29] Evarts had refused to release Stahel's findings, it was said, and he and Fred Seward were at present giving conflicting stories about Mosby's original dispatch: Seward admitting its possession by the Department prior to Bailey's confirmation and Evarts refusing to do so.

"This is a very unhappy complication," continued the *Republican*, "for it is very strongly charged that the Department shields Bailey because Minister Seward must stand or fall by the former."[30]

The *Milwaukee Sentinel* summarized:

Mosby . . . makes specific charges against Bailey . . . of assimilating $40,000 of the money belonging to this government. But in the face of this Bailey is made consul-general at Shanghai. Minister Seward tries to screen Bailey, as he is in the same boat with him. Mr. Evarts doesn't appear to desire the investigation and punishment of these men, and it is time for Mr. Hayes to give the matter his personal attention. . . . They must be brought to trial, . . . not shielded.[31]

By this time those in the know could no longer discredit Mosby by defending the indefensible, and they began to concentrate more on his methods. He was actually reporting to the President, it was announced, and refusing to observe channels of authority. The *Hartford Evening Post* offered the opinion that the Department would have to refrain from enforcing these kinds of rules against him:

There has seemed to be family and other influence at work in the State Department to shield Minister Seward, . . . and if Mosby should be turned out because of his activity in the matter, it would incline people to think that he was sacrificed because of his zeal in pursuit of a corrupt official, rather than because he had disregarded the rules of the service. People would honor Mosby for the course he has taken, and coming home with a fistful of facts he would become an exceedingly troublesome customer for the Seward family. No, we do not think Mosby will be dismissed just at present.[32]

Anti-Mosby propaganda found its way to the press as well. In a publicized letter subheaded "Mosby Rampaging Around the Orient," Mosby was ridiculed for having "organized himself into a widespread smelling committee," to sniff through all the consular corners of the East. Worse than that, repeated the writer—apparently an administration insider— Mosby was violating "official etiquette" in reporting to everyone, including the President, who, it was alleged, didn't want to be bothered with such stuff. The President had been forced to impress upon the colonel, it was noted, that "he had a 'boss,'" and "was no longer engaged in the partisan ranger business." Mosby considered, continued the complainant, that he had "authority express and unqualified from the Chief Magistrate to exercise a vicarious supervision over American affairs throughout the length and breadth of pagan land." His purpose, it seemed, was to make a national reputation as a reformer out of this "cloud of fragrant scandal."[33]

But the press, having seen much of Washington and little of Mosby, was coming down largely on the consul's side. On September 26 the *Philadelphia Times,* edited by Stalwart Republican Alexander K. McClure, noted how the impeachment proceedings against Seward had been "beset at every step with obstacles interposed by trusted officers of the State Department."[34]

"It is probable," continued the *Times,* after remarking on Seward's triumphant and boastful return to China,

> that the case against him would have been dropped sure enough but for the accident of our getting one honest man into a Chinese consulate. Col. Mosby is that man and it seems he is to be made to suffer for his honesty. . . . Is it not time that Mr. Evarts were taking the matter of Seward and Bailey into his own hands? A man like Mosby cannot be punished for honesty without the world knows all about it.[35]

Fred Seward, possibly running a little scared, determined at this time to get on top of another Mosby-raised issue before it got out of hand. In early October he asked the consul at Hong Kong to make his charges against Sickels and Torrey, at Bangkok, more specific.

He had demonstrated an inability to read lawyer Mosby's fine print. "I have preferred no charges against the Bangkok consul," answered Mosby innocently. The charges, he said, were being brought by the master of the *Alice C. Dickerman,* who had already written to presidential secretary Rogers on the subject. "His letter," he sniffed, "is the foundation of your official action."[36]

"It is true," he told his superior,

I wrote a private letter to Mr. Rogers in which I expressed
pretty freely my opinion of the consul and vice consul at
Bangkok based on common report and general reputation out
here. . . . I believe that I said Sickles [sic] was an idiot and
. . . Torrey . . . was about as fit to be in the consular service
as . . . Capt. Kidd. I have no apologies to make for having
expressed this opinion.[37]

In an October letter to *Philadelphia Times* editor McClure,
he supplied the information that Bailey had stolen not $40,000
but probably $100,000 from the government, concluding that
there was "no hope of any remedy except in Congress."[38]

"All the power of the State Department is against me," he
told McClure, "and in all probability the next mail will bring
my recall."[39]

"I want you to open your guns on them," he exhorted,
"and call for an investigation by Congress. Nearly all the consuls out here are of the same class as Bailey. . . . There is an
abundance of game out here if they will only hunt for it."[40]

Two weeks later the game began to flush, although from an
unexpected quarter. Assistant Secretary Seward, pleading
overwork and poor health, turned in his resignation at the end
of October. "The friends of Mr. Seward . . . ," the *Cincinnati
Gazette* hastened to explain, "indignantly repel the insinua-
tion thrown out . . . that the charges pending against his
cousin, the Minister to China, influenced his resignation."[41]

Mosby claimed to know the real story. A few weeks after
the Assistant Secretary's resignation, he confided to Warrenton attorney E. M. Spilman that after having so many road-
blocks thrown in his way by the Department, he'd at last had
to "turn" on Fred Seward "and expose him along with the
others whom he was trying to protect."[42]

"If he had remained in office until Congress met," declared
Mosby, "I would have had him impeached. He saw what was
coming and got out of the way."[43]

In later years he related to U.S. Senator from Virginia John
W. Daniel that after he'd discovered Fred Seward trying "to
shield the rascals," he'd written privately to Hayes, exposing

the Assistant Secretary. "Hayes," he asserted, "discharged him from the State Department."[44] Following his resignation, Seward disappeared from public life.

About this time—December 1879—Mosby determined that the renewal of an important friendship was past due. He was, after all, being gradually forced into the role of an enemy of the administration, of one who outreformed the reformers, and doubtless felt that he could be burning some important bridges behind him. On Christmas Eve he wrote to Congressman James A. Garfield. "I just drop you a line," he said, "to ask you not to be affected by anything you may see in the newspapers prejudicial to me in reference to exposures I have been compelled to make of corruption in the consular service in the East. I regret the necessity of having to make these things public."[45]

After explaining away his recent rebuke from Hayes, he hastened to protest again his Republican loyalty, unaltered by his pursuit of Republican crookedness:

> The Republican party can only be injured by these things by attempting to cover them up. No man is less disposed than I am to aid the Democrats. I am now, as I was on the day I called to tell you "Goodbye"—for "Grant-Garfield" for the next presidential ticket. I hope to be home in time to help assure that result. . . . For the kindness you have always shown me I shall always be grateful.[46]

By January 1880 Fred Seward's place had been taken by John Hay, a man later to write a memorable chapter in U.S. diplomacy as Secretary of State, but never to become a friend of Mosby. Mosby urged Hay at this time to speak both to William H. Forbes, on his way now to Washington, and to Capt. George H. Perkins of the U.S.S. *Ashuelot,* who could fill him in on Bangkok, especially. "Capt. Perkins informed me of things he saw down there," he said, referring to the Bangkok consulate, "that would disgrace a Modoc Indian."[47]

There was no notable softening of Departmental attitude with the coming of John Hay. Mosby continued to be treated as a crackpot, yet the grass-roots appeal of his crusade meant that he could not be easily dislodged. Prying him out of the Orient was in fact the last thing the Department wanted: he would be far more dangerous prowling about congressional corridors than bottled up on Hong Kong Island. Probably for this reason Mosby's continual pressure for a furlough was ignored. He was harassed in more subtle ways as well: denied money for law books, despite similar allowances made to his predecessor; denied money for boat hire; forced to beg funds for chair hire and other assorted budgetary scraps.

The pinpricks came not only from Washington but also from his colleagues in the Far East. These attacks were instigated, Mosby was sure, by Chester Holcombe, the "renegade missionary" at Peking. It is likely that David Sickels, now living in Singapore, was also involved in the campaign, since the sniping came principally from the U.S. consul at Singapore, Adolph Studer.

Unfortunately for Studer, he was not as adept as Mosby in the use of pen as rapier, and he made a serious blunder besides: in the course of one of his anti-Mosby rantings to the Department, he spoke pejoratively of Mosby's military record, and even labeled him anti-Yankee. The State Department kindly forwarded a copy of Studer's remarks to Hong Kong, and Mosby smacked his lips as he picked up his pen. "Mr. Studer," he wrote to Washington in February,

informs the Department that he served in the Union army, and he imagines me to be his enemy on that account. In other words, that while long ago I was reconciled with such soldiers as Grant, Sherman, and Hancock, I am unable to forgive a warrior at Singapore. Now, the fact is, that I never knew he had been a soldier until I read his letter.

I am informed he is a Swiss, and I have no doubt that with the characteristic aptitude of his race, he went to the highest bidder and fought, if he did any fighting, . . . for provender and pay.[48]

To the charge that Mosby was ashamed of being classed with the U.S. consuls of the East he pleaded guilty, with the qualification that he never meant this to embrace all U.S. consuls in the East—only men such as Bailey, Loring, Sickels, Torrey, and Studer. "I have said," he emphasized, "that these men have so degraded the consular service that I felt humiliated at being placed on the same level with them."[49] He requested the Department to forward a copy of his remarks to Singapore.

While carefully avoiding any appearance of acting under pressure from the "crackpot" at Hong Kong, the Department was nonetheless preparing to clean out the Augean stable in the Far East. Secretary Evarts's later reputation as a civil service reformer was about to be established. Grant and John R. Young had briefed Evarts in January about Sickels and Torrey, and by February 1, newspapers were predicting imminent "beheadings" in the Orient.

In March, Garfield wrote to assure Mosby that despite what he'd been hearing, Hayes really found no fault with his conduct. Mosby answered at once, pressing Garfield to have Hayes act immediately at Bangkok, and then informing him of the latest in subtle tortures being applied. Secretary of the Treasury John Sherman had just removed one of Mosby's sisters (the only member of his family holding office) from the Light-House Board. "I see," he went on,

> that Sherman in an interview disclaims all responsibility for my appointment. I readily acquit him of it. No one ever suspected him capable of doing so creditable a thing. . . .
> I want you to say to the President for me never again to tell a consul that his place is worth more than the base salary. Many construe it into permission to make the place worth what it is said to be. Now I have been here over twelve months and my unofficial fees have not amounted to $100. I have sent a dispatch to the department recommending the abolition of all unofficial fees, as allowing consuls to retain any class of fees is a source of great demoralization in the service.[50]

Moving to the upcoming presidential campaign, he commented: "Of course, I and all my friends are for Genl. Grant, yet the contingency may occur of the withdrawal of his name." The compromise candidate in such an event, he predicted, would be Garfield. "I have written to all my friends in Va.," he said, "to go for you in this event."[51]

"I regret," he added, "that the President did not take the advice I gave him when I first came here as all the scandal would have been avoided and he would have got great credit for reforming the service. I suppose, however, that he was thwarted by the State Department, which has done everything to obstruct me." He hoped to be coming home soon. "I have seen enough of the East," he declared, "and the emoluments of this position are not sufficient to justify my separation from my children."[52]

By now the journalistic chorus was rising against Evarts for his handling of the Seward matter. "Mr. Evarts," noted the *Washington Post* in March, " . . . seems infatuated with the idea of being the special defender . . . of all the legally uncon-victed violators of law that disgrace his Department, es-pecially those bearing the name of Seward." Evarts, said the *Post,* was in favor of holding back the second Seward's resig-nation, which was already in hand, until impeachment should again become imminent, while Hayes was bent on getting on with it and installing a new man at Peking as soon as possible. "[Seward's] official misconduct and villainy," crowed the *Post,* "have disgraced the nation abroad as none others of its accredited representatives have ever done."[53]

The chief executive prevailed, and it was shortly announced that George F. Seward, after many years of meritorious ser-vice, etc., etc., had resigned his post at Peking. Two Sewards had been brought down. Only Bailey and a few other "ras-cals" remained on the roost.

Mosby sensed change in the wind, and perhaps was begin-ning to see that the power for continued change would ema-nate not from Grant but from Garfield. He began now to badger Garfield about consular matters, pressing for a con-sulate to be opened at Manila (it later was), and for the clos-ing of five consulates in China, including those of Canton and Tientsin. He was coming to be depicted in the U.S. newspa-pers as a man "holding the fort" for reform in an administra-tion that professed reform ideals without pursuing them. "Col. Mosby," remarked the *San Francisco Chronicle* in April, seems just now to be a particularly sharp thorn in the side of our mild and virtuous "civil service reform" administration. . . . [He] seems to be one of those restless, inquisitive spirits, who feel that they have a mission to look into things, and get at their true inwardness. Instead of being content to draw his pay, take things easily, and shut his eyes and ears, . . . he keeps a bright lookout, and is always wanting to understand the working of the machinery.[54]

After noting that Mosby's investigations had not "had the effect of endearing him to Secretary Evarts," the *Chronicle* commented that far from being "chagrined or disappointed" by the result of his "inquisitorial labors," he seemed rather to enjoy it all. "His present attitude toward the powers that be at Washington," said the paper, "is one of open defiance." In sum, it was a "very pretty fight" as it now stood, but "at the latest advices the colonel appeared to be master of the situation."[55]

In May, Mosby felt constrained once again to set his Republican credentials right with Garfield. The United States press, he assured his correspondent, was wrong in attributing to him the claim that the administration had ever threatened him with dismissal. Only the China "ring" had worked for this, although with the apparent blessing of the State Department.

By the fall of 1880 Garfield had in fact become the presidential nominee, and Mosby saw his chance to accomplish something big. It was U. S. Grant all over again, with the difference that this particular leader had greater potential as a reformer—at least in Mosby's opinion. He subjected the nominee to another harangue on consular reform. Frequent inspections of consulates should be carried out, he wrote to Garfield in October, by a newly created office of Inspectors of Consulates. Furthermore, he repeated, several consulates in China should be shut down. Then there was the matter of ignorance of law within the walls of the State Department, which might be remedied by the creation of a Solicitor's Office there. "The ignorance and stupidity," he said,

of those who send out instructions from that Dept. to consuls on questions of law is frightful. They didn't even know at the State Department that we went to war in [*sic*] England in 1812 to settle the question whether or not a seaman on the articles of an American ship was entitled to the protection of the Govt., no matter whether he was native or foreign—in other words was an American seaman. In a late dispatch I had to inform the Department that they had reversed the decision of that war.

"What I have written," he warned Garfield in conclusion, "is not for public use but only for your own private information."[56]

By now Bailey's resignation had been secured, as had Sickels's at Bangkok, the President having "at last swept the China coast," in Mosby's words.[57] Judge O. N. Denny, formerly consul at Tientsin, was put in Bailey's place at Shanghai, and the Kansan Gen. John A. Halderman, a Grant crony, installed at Bangkok. "The President's new appointments in China," chirped Mosby to Garfield, "are all first-rate men. You may tell him I have just received a letter from Gen. Haldeman [sic], . . . who says that he found all that I had reported about the rascality in [Bangkok] to be true."[58]

In November, Garfield was elected by the slimmest of margins, his plurality being something like 9,400 votes out of 9 million cast. Even his large electoral victory was hollow: two pivotal states, New York and Indiana, had been carried only by strict party discipline and a barrage of hard cash. But he had been elected, and following the election Mosby got to the point directly. "I now venture to make a few suggestions," he wrote, adding with uncharacteristic humility, "which you can take for what they are worth."[59]

His theme this time was to be politics. "I hope you will not insult your Southern friends," he began, shedding his diffidence rather quickly, "by putting a Democrat in your Cabinet." Nor, he said, should Garfield invite a Southerner of any stripe to join his cabinet. "Of course," he added,

I am in favor of the most liberal policy towards the South consistent with justice. I think, however, with a Cabinet of stalwart Republicans who are from the North and have the confidence of the party you can pursue a much more liberal Southern policy. . . . [Postmaster General David M.] Key, by accepting a place in the Cabinet did a good thing for himself, but he brought no strength to the Administration and had no powers to do anything for his section. . . .

You now have a grand opportunity to nationalize the South. I think this shock will shatter the solid South. You should direct your policy toward building . . . out of the fragments of the wreck . . . a new Republican party at the South. But while trying to win new friends don't commit Hayes' error of turning the cold shoulder on those who supported you.[60]

He would be home soon, he told Garfield, having no intention of remaining beyond Hayes's administration. "I never would have come here," he confided,

if I had not been grossly deceived about the value of the place. My predecessors made fortunes here but by dishonest methods. To me the office has been worth nothing beyond its salary and I shall return home after an absence of two years as poor as when I came. . . . The salary of this office does not justify a longer separation from my children, neither is it sufficient to allow me to bring them here.[61]

He wished to get back into law practice when he returned, but allowed that he would need help. "To enable me . . . once more to get a foothold at the bar," he told the President-elect, "and a start in the race of life I shall ask you to give me the position of Assistant Atty-General for which Judge Bond and many other friends urged my appointment."[62]

Two weeks later he was at it again: "Dear Genl: I venture to add a few more suggestions." The subject once more was consular reform, this time some suggested structural revisions to the service in China, including a variation on the newly revived idea of a secretarial corps. Mosby preferred to call the members of this corps "cadets"—a half-dozen salaried pupils in Peking to do secretarial work and study Chinese at the same time. "We need a staff of well-educated and reliable interpreters very much in China," he wrote. "These pupils . . . would not only become good Chinese scholars but qualified to act as Secretary for any Legation, which would be a step towards civil service reform."[63]

He suggested his one-time adversary but now respected colleague Julius Stahel as Assistant Secretary of State, referring to Stahel as "one of the few consuls out here that has reflected honor on the country."[64]

"The State Department needs overhauling," he added, "and renovating. It needs above all an able law officer—some of its decisions on law questions would 'make the angels weep.'" His final word: "Do not commit yourself to . . . Southern leaders until they have given hostages for their good faith. Otherwise they will use you and abuse you as they did Hayes. . . . I know them well."[65] His present intention, he told Garfield, was to be home by March.

Throughout these continuing efforts to insinuate himself into national politics at home and consular reform abroad, Mosby also strove to be father to his absent family. In June 1880, with the assistance at home of his now-widowed mother, he was arranging for nineteen-year-old Beverly's entrance into the University of Virginia. "My boy," he assured Prof. Francis H. Smith, previously one of his own teachers, "is a little headstrong and wayward but I think you will find him a boy of very correct principles and I commend him to your care."[66]

In October he was fretting that Bev had chosen to board off campus instead of on campus with Professor Holmes, as his father had wished. Bev was not taking the right courses either, Mosby told Smith. The boy didn't seem interested in natural philosophy. "I will, however," he added,

> be very well satisfied if he can get through on Literature and Chemistry. . . . I do not want him crowded and whatever he learns I want him to learn well. As I am so far away I hope you will give your special attention to him and not hesitate to advise him just as if he were your own son. He has a wayward disposition but at the same time is . . . very susceptible to kind influences.[67]

Seventeen-year-old Johnnie was also on his mind. Living with Mosby's brother Willie in Bedford County, he was a student at Bellevue High School, and his father had hopes of sending him, too, to the university. In a letter to Johnnie shortly after New Year's, 1881, Mosby explained that the reason he had not come home yet was that he had still not received a furlough and was reluctant to quit without having something better to go to.

"There has been a great sensation in H.K.," he told his son, shifting topics. Peter Smith, the sailors' boardinghouse keeper he had mentioned previously in connection with Bailey, had recently sued him for slander, and the case had just been tried in a British court. "I defended myself," he proclaimed, the affair proving to be "a greater sensation than a new opera."[68]

"The jury and spectators loudly applauded me," he reported, in a tone calculated to catch a teenager's attention.

The old judge in a tan wig and gown just like Justice Shallow in the Merry Wives of Windsor tried to look wise and solemn, rammed his bandana down his throat and almost burst with laughter. The novelty of my speech was that it was delivered in such a different style from the drawling humdrum style of the English. They are more excited over it than Pinafore and the Governor and several lawyers told me today that it is the best speech ever made in the Colony. . . . The jury found a verdict in my favor. I made the fur fly from Peter but he roared with laughter and a captain told me today that Peter said, "It was better than a theater."

"My health is excellent," he assured his son, "and the climate delicious. I go to a ball this week. . . . Kisses for my babes."[69]

Mosby was ebullient with Garfield's ship of state about to ease into the water. In February he confided to Halderman, "I don't think that there will be as much sentiment or talk about reform with Garfield's administration as with Hayes' but more practical work."[70] Stahel, he hoped, would soon be named Assistant Secretary, then Mosby would get his long-awaited furlough and could go home to an influential position under his friend Garfield's wing, quitting the East and the consular service.

In April, while waiting for Department appointments to shape up under the President's new Secretary of State, James G. Blaine, he shipped off some gifts to the White House: a teapot and two boxes of tea from a Portuguese merchant friend and a Japanese dressing gown from a group of American shipmasters in port. The wife of the *Amethyst*'s captain, he told the President, had just had a baby boy on board ship, christened James Garfield Slocum, and the parents wished him to procure Garfield's photo and autograph.

By July 25, his furlough had been approved; but by then everything had become ashes. Mosby's dreams had been blasted on the second of the month by a revolver shot in Washington that left the new President with a bullet in his back.

Garfield lingered throughout the sticky Washington summer as doctors attempted to find the bullet, and the nation waited. Mosby seems not to have realized the seriousness of Garfield's condition, since in mid-August—when Garfield was beginning to fail—he wrote to a friend to secure an audience with the President for a sea captain friend on his way from Hong Kong to the United States.

On the evening of September 20, however, Pope-Hennessy's secretary called at the consulate to deliver a Reuters telegram announcing Garfield's death. Mosby's personal grief found immediate support throughout the English colony. The British, on the day following the announcement, dropped flags throughout Hong Kong to half-mast and commenced the mournful discharge of minute guns from shore batteries and from the warship *Victor Emmanuel,* on station in Victoria Harbor. "Men who never saw the President," reported Mosby to Third Assistant Secretary Walker Blaine—the Secretary's son—"speak of [this sad event] in the tone that they would of a brother's death. . . . On every ship in the harbor the drooping ensign announced the loss which not only our country but mankind had sustained."[71]

By the twenty-second, orders had arrived from the U.S. admiral at Yokohama, and the single U.S. naval vessel in port, the 420-ton screw tug *Palos,* commenced firing guns every half hour from sunup to sundown.

James Garfield was buried at Cleveland on September 26. With his passing, Mosby was condemned to live on at Hong Kong, unless dismissed by President Arthur.

Chester A. Arthur was the second man to don the mantle of the U.S. presidency in the wake of an assassination, and many were uneasy about his investiture. Having won his political spurs in the nation's richest pork barrel, the New York Customshouse, he was viewed by a large segment of the population who happened to know anything about him as another run-of-the-mill ward heeler. One could never have gotten this idea, however, from his personal appearance or bearing. He was dignified and handsome—one of the most elegant men ever to occupy the White House. Moreover, despite his background as a Stalwart, he was far more interested in reform than he was given credit for. It was to be under Arthur's administration, not Hayes's or Garfield's, that the first concrete steps toward civil service reform would be taken.

Not only did Arthur not dismiss Mosby; with prodding from Grant, he seems to have considered promoting him. Grant, some time after Arthur had taken the oath of office, had handed the President a written recommendation that Mosby be named U.S. consul general at Shanghai. "But at the same time," Grant later explained to Mosby's brother-in-law, fledgling attorney Charles Wells Russell, "[I] stated to the President verbally that I thought Col. Mosby would be much better pleased with a position at home, and suggested two positions—one of them assistant attorney general and the other district attorney of Virginia."[72]

By early March, Arthur had taken the matter under advisement. But as predicted by Grant, Mosby grew balky at a new Far Eastern assignment. He asked Russell, who had married his sister Lucie shortly after his departure for the Orient, to explain his feelings to the President. "He doesn't want Shanghai," Russell told Arthur in May, "since the slight increase of salary would be more than offset by the increase of expenses."[73]

"If he is to stay in the East," he continued, "he prefers to stay in Hong Kong, but he is anxious to return to this country, unless he could be assigned to some first class post in Europe."[74]

There the matter ended, and Mosby resigned himself to remain on the island for the duration of Arthur's administration.

Mosby had arrived in the Orient at a critical point in Chinese-American relations. The "heathen Chinee" had been welcome enough in the American West when there was gold to be mined or a railroad to be built; but after the gold was dug and most of the railroads running, Californians found themselves competing with an increasing number of "Celestials" for a dwindling number of jobs. By the late seventies the temperature of American racism was climbing, and not just in California. The *Daily State Gazette,* of Trenton, New Jersey, after noting in December 1878 that the Chinese were "almost as innumerable as the sands of the sea," proclaimed: "They might populate every foot of our available territory as densely as New Jersey, and scarcely miss the emigration from their Empire." The Chinese was labelled "a sort of predacious scavenger"; he was "frugal to squalid meanness" and lived contentedly "on offal that would feed the American's pigs." He was alleged to be "addicted to brutish vices," and to possess no element of character that would make him a desirable addition to the American population. Put limits on such an "impure human flood," cried this lantern of truth, "that it may not defile the entire body of our social seas."[75]

The less strident *Chicago Tribune* pointed out the following month that the American people, "with the best of intentions [could not] close their eyes to the radical differences between the Chinese immigrants and every other race or class" seeking America's shores. They bring wages down, argued the *Tribune,* by working for so little, and "the women they bring with them almost entirely belong to the prostitute class."[76]

Other papers took a more enlightened stand, the *Cleveland Leader,* for one, soundly pointing out that the Chinese were not "a colonizing people" and were "quite willing Christians should remain Christians."[77]

"There is just as much danger," said the *Leader,* "that the Caucasians will overrun China and drive out the natives as there is that the Chinese will drive out the Caucasians on this continent."[78]

The *New York Sun,* in February 1879, sensibly drew attention to the growing China trade that would be harmed by anti-Chinese measures in the United States:

San Francisco's Chinese imports are seven times what they were in 1870. . . . The export trade of San Francisco is also

greater with China than with any other country in the world.
. . . All the exports of San Francisco combined to Great Britain in the year 1877 were eight million dollars less than its exports to China.[79]

James G. Blaine himself was, like most Republicans, a cheap-labor man and therefore until now in favor of this unending supply of Celestial bodies. Yet, again like most Republicans, he was being forced by the realities of politics into a protectionist stance. Around the time that Mosby was leaving for the Orient, Senator Blaine had been telling a dinner party in Washington: "A people who eat beef and bread and who drink beer cannot labor alongside of those who live on rice, and if the experiment is attempted on a large scale the American laborer will have to drop his knife and fork and take up the chopsticks." Treat those who are already here, he hastened to add, "kindly and fairly and honestly," but "the throwing of [U.S.] ports wide open to an unlimited immigration of Mongols" was, in his opinion, an entirely different matter.[80]

The right of Chinese to emigrate to the United States had been guaranteed, with certain minimum controls, by the Burlingame Treaty of 1868. But by 1879 anti-Chinese sentiment was so high in America that in January of that year the House passed a restriction act as if unaware that the Burlingame Treaty existed. Less than a month later the Senate passed a similar version. No ship was henceforth to be allowed to land more than fifteen Chinese in the United States. (Under the new bill, cracked the *New York Times,* the Chinese would have had difficulty in staffing their Washington mission.) As expected, Hayes vetoed the bill at once, and Congress was unable to override; but the Chinese government—not previously noted for its concern for Chinese nationals abroad—developed some ruffled feathers over America's cavalier attitude.

Chinese immigration continued unabated, with approximately equal numbers returning from America as departing for it. The number of Chinese in California therefore promised to remain manageable, and the threat to American culture, religion, and morals fairly stable.

By February 1880, however, the nation's temperature had risen further, especially in California, which now passed a law of dubious constitutionality prohibiting the hiring of Chinese. Threats of violence escalated at the same time, becoming so serious that the Chinese consul at San Francisco that spring sought and received Federal troop protection for terrorized Chinese in his city. "Chasing pigtails" was becoming an accepted Western sport, and the phrase "not a Chinaman's chance" came to take on a sinister meaning.

George Seward having recently been relieved of his duties as U.S. Minister at Peking, there was no American envoy with authority to slow the deterioration of Sino-American relations. Hayes by now realized that the problem had to be handled from the top. In mid-year, therefore, he sent a three-man commission to Peking to renegotiate the Burlingame Treaty, hoping to be able thereafter to do legally what was now being attempted illegally—namely, keep the "heathen Chinee" out of the land of the free and the home of the brave.

Since virtually all Chinese emigrating to the United States departed from Hong Kong, it was Mosby who was required to certify the majority as acceptable immigrants, and it was therefore not long before he was embroiled in the Chinese immigration question. With the aid of interpreters, he conducted all examinations of emigrants personally; not surprisingly, however, undesirables occasionally slipped through. The few women who emigrated were always subjected to the closest scrutiny in San Francisco, and by early 1882 Mosby had come under fire for allowing too many Chinese prostitutes onto America's shores.

In a vigorous defense of his screening efforts, he wrote to the collector of customs at San Francisco in May of 1882 that for every woman desiring to emigrate, he required character witnesses from the prestigious Tung Wah Hospital committee; and, he added, some of the women had even been vouched for by the Chinese consul at San Francisco himself. He could not hope to do more. Always a believer in the value of a stiff offense, he now turned the question around. "The women who get my certificates," he remarked,

are much better than a majority of the white women who
come from San Francisco to Hong Kong. The China coast is
overrun with California prostitutes who are much more demoralizing in China than Chinese cheap labor and lewd
women in California. . . . I am no more responsible for the
number of Chinese going to the United States than you are for
the number of San Francisco whores continually coming to
Hong Kong.[81]

Writing two weeks later to Assistant Secretary of State
John C. Bancroft Davis, he pointed out that he had to rely
exclusively upon Chinese testimony in judging women applicants, emphasizing that he had rejected many women on the
advice of Chinese merchants. "A woman's virtue," he said,
"is a mystery which it is very hard to determine; even in
American society it is very difficult . . . for any woman to
prove her own virtue. The only rule to govern society is that a
female's virtue is presumed until the contrary is proved." In
San Francisco, he added, it seemed that the opposite theory
prevailed, that "on account of race prejudice," Chinese
women were presumed whores unless they could prove otherwise. "From my knowledge of the Chinese," he declared,
"[this] is very unjust to them."[82]

He would now have his little revenge on the San Francisco
collector. If you read the law, he told Bancroft Davis, it says
nothing about the need for a consular certificate for women
emigrating to the United States aboard a *foreign* vessel, only
aboard U.S.-flag carriers. He had been certifying such
women, he said, only for the convenience of the shipmasters,
who were afraid to arrive in San Francisco without these papers. But he would do so no more. From now on, he announced, it would be up to authorities in California—at least
with respect to women arriving on foreign ships—to separate
the virtuous from the wicked if they could.

Mosby had recently forced the Department to swallow an
even more bitter pill. To the great relief of foreign shipmasters, he had wrung an admission out of Washington that,
despite the practice of the past twenty years, no consular fees
were legally chargeable for Chinese emigrants sailing to
America aboard foreign vessels, but only for those aboard
U.S.-flag carriers.

"It seems almost incredible," commented the *China Mail*,

> that large firms . . . who have representatives in America
> should have continued to pay a levy of this kind without ascer-
> taining whether or not it was legal. But so it now turns out to
> be . . . and the official to whom the credit of the discovery was
> due is the man whose interests are more likely to suffer than
> those of any other party concerned. . . . If any proof were
> needed that the present consul of the United States at this port
> deserved well of his countrymen and others, this last act of
> justice and fair dealing would satisfy the most exacting of crit-
> ics. Whatever else Col. Mosby has done, . . . he has reclaimed
> the U.S. consulate here from "ways that were dark" to a
> straightforward and honest position among the consulates of
> his country.[83]

These issues were soon to become dead, however. In early
May Congress, acting now within the framework of a renegotiated treaty, passed another exclusion act. President
Arthur, who had vetoed a draconian anti-Chinese bill the previous year, decided he had to let this one pass. With few exceptions, no Chinese were to be permitted to enter the United
States for a decade.

Mosby, less interested in the factors or philosophy behind a
law than in obedience to it, requested detailed instructions on
how it was to be carried out. Gone were all thoughts of defending the morals of Chinese women, and gone was the satisfaction of foreign shipmasters at their recent triumph, as
Mosby made ready to assist in the exclusion of Chinese from
the United States. Until the new law had been explained thoroughly, however, he continued to certify emigrants. The
Philadelphia Evening Telegraph that summer arched an editorial eyebrow at this business in an item entitled "Must Mosby
Go as Well as the Chinese?"

> Mosby, it appears, has not been complying with the anti-
> Chinese regulation of this great, free Africo-Caucasian govern-
> ment, but has been signing and sealing . . . emigration papers
> without the slightest regard for the prevailing anti-Chinese
> sentiment on the Pacific coast and in Congress. The Pacific
> coast is therefore incensed at Consul Mosby, has commenced

to attack him, and we may shortly expect to be entertained with imperative demands for his recall.[84]

The consul at Hong Kong eventually not only stopped his certification of emigrants, but soon entered into a three-year-long battle with Washington over "irregularities" he perceived in the new law's enforcement.

Although Mosby's exile was made considerably more palatable in January 1883 by the arrival of his twenty-two-year-old son Beverly, in the capacity of vice-consul, he kept up a dyspeptic fire on anyone who appeared to deserve it. Annoyed, for example, with the Spanish authorities at Manila for insisting upon an exclusive right to issue bills of health to American vessels clearing Manila for the United States, he argued to the Department that issuing bills of health for such ships should be the prerogative of the American consul there, not the Spaniards. "It is no business of the Spaniards," he snapped, "to take care of the health of the people of New York."[85]

He gave advice freely on the uses to which the navy should be put in the Far East. As early as 1880 he had been pressing the Department to exert its influence for the redistribution of the Asiatic Squadron, advocating that U.S. men-of-war be occasionally seen among the Philippines, and around Hainan, Java, and Borneo. Three years later he repeated the suggestion, urging that the navy move a portion of its fleet away from Japan, where there was little threat to American interests, to the South China coast, where there was such a threat. "Japan, I admit," he said, "offers more attractions as a pleasure resort for naval officers."[86]

In 1884 he renewed the request, urging that some warships be sent down among the Marshall-Carolines and Palau islands. The Germans, he pointed out, had a stranglehold on trade in that region. "I think," he continued, "the United States Navy should be utilized for practical purposes and made to extend our commerce." Hinting again that the navy looked upon Kobe and Nagasaki as a Far Eastern Newport or Fort Monroe, he added, "Japan is a sort of paradise for naval officers. They can spend all their money there in curios, and dance every night on shore with 'sweethearts and wives.' Our

Asiatic Squadron is now cruising in the inland sea of Japan. . . . There is scarcely more need for the presence of a naval force . . . in Japan than in Europe." A few men-of-war, he repeated, should be detached to cruise among "the savage races of the Pacific Islands," as pioneers of "civilization and commerce."[87]

He advocated American expansion into China, pushing (not unlike George Seward before him) for a ground-floor American presence in Chinese railroading and other internal projects. No one, he said, knew how to build railroads as Americans did. If China should continue on the path of internal improvements being embarked upon at this time, he predicted—exhibiting now a flawed understanding of both the Chinese and the American character—the tide of Chinese emigration would be reversed, and Americans would be flocking to China.

He took his superiors to task for what he perceived to be a false understanding of the renegotiated Burlingame Treaty, specifically as related to the opium trade.

Opium had been used from time immemorial in China as a medicine, but had gradually become a vice. By the 1830s senior Chinese officials and generals assumed that 90 percent of their staffs were opium smokers. Because of drug abuse, business slowed, the standard of living fell, and public services broke down. The British, not noticeably burdened by a desire to preserve Chinese well-being, were by midcentury supporting the Chinese habit amply with Indian poppy, filling 10 to 15 percent of British Indian coffers with the revenues.

By the Treaty of Tientsin, following the Second Opium War, China forswore all interference with the British opium trade, and American traders gained similar privileges. In 1880, however, the Chinese, in return for immigration concessions made in the renegotiated Burlingame Treaty, insisted upon a restriction on the American opium trade (really a rather painless one for American interests), forbidding the importation of opium into China on American vessels.

Mosby, not having found the State Department top-heavy with legal talent, soon struck out on his own in interpreting the new treaty's opium clauses.

In answer to a query from Russell and Co. about the legality of doing business as usual with opium, Mosby declared that nothing had changed, since the treaty provisions were not self-executing. To become operative, he maintained, they required the enactment of appropriate legislation in both the United States and China, assessing specific penalties for nonobservance. In the absence of such legislation, he told the firm, the opium trade could be carried on as before.

In July 1884, the *Hong Kong Telegraph,* noting that Mosby's opinion was in direct conflict with that of the U.S. Minister at Peking (since 1882, Grant's extremely able protégé, John Russell Young), confidently came down on the side of Mosby—"one of the most astute lawyers of the United States."[88]

On July 9, lawyer Mosby wrote to the Department about journalist Young's, in his opinion, erroneous views of the treaty. When Mr. Young spoke of "the law" against the opium trade, argued Mosby, he spoke of something that did not exist. "American citizens," he continued, "would lose a great deal while China would gain nothing by the enforcement of the opium clause of the treaty. Just the same amount of opium would be brought into China." He went on to blame foreigners in China for trying to drive Russell and Co. out of the Orient with prattle about treaty violations. "In a moral point of view," he added,

> the trade in opium is no worse than that of spirits or tobacco which is a source of large revenue to our government. If the United States government wants therefore to embark on a purely humanitarian policy it would be better to teach temperance to the Chinese not by precept but example, by making the manufacture and sale of whiskey and tobacco a crime.[89]

Returning at predictable intervals to the theme of fee abuses, Mosby by 1884 was arguing strenuously for the abolition of *all* fees at consulates, and for their collection at customshouses or other easily controllable points. He traced all the evils of the consular service to the union of two functions in one office: trade promotion and revenue collection. Attending to fees, he said, was not only a temptation but a time-waster. "Consuls have little or no time," he told the Department in November 1884, to look after the real commercial interests of the country; they are mostly engaged in performing clerical work and in the petty details of accounts and returns. . . . I would be much better employed in gathering commercial information to be sent home, or in discovering new channels for American enterprise. The consular regulations seem to me to have been ingeniously devised for the purpose of reducing the usefulness of a consul to a *minimum*. A great many think that the end has been accomplished.[90]

By this time Mosby had given up altogether on getting a sound answer to his questions about fees, and was remanding almost all fees to the Treasury. He would sue the government for them at a future date, and allow a court to decide what the State Department seemed incapable of deciding.

The attention of the Far East in the early eighties was riveted on the war brewing between France and China—a dispute centered largely upon the question of who would control Annam (Vietnam). Li Hung-chang, governor general of Chihli, superintendent of northern ports, and virtual leader of China in its relations with the West (the "Bismarck of the East," in one foreigner's opinion), had tried to head off war with superior French forces by treaty in 1882 and 1884, but to no avail.[91] Anti-foreign rioting had broken out in several ports in September 1883, and by December French and Chinese troops had actually engaged in combat. The following June a French military detachment was massacred in a place called Bac-lé.

The French now had the war they wanted, and proceeded, in Mosby's words, "practically [to reduce] the whole of Tonquin and the Kingdom of Cambodia to the condition of a French province."[92] By early August, the port of Keelung, Formosa, was under French bombardment, and two weeks later most of China's modern fleet was destroyed in a surprise attack at Foochow. The war gradually came to engulf the whole of South China, even reaching into Hong Kong. In January 1885, when the French man-of-war *La Galissonière* put in to Victoria for repairs, the port exploded in a harbor-workers' strike and British authorities were forced to refuse to repair the French ship. While anti-French riots flared in several other Chinese ports, she limped off to Japan. In the wake of this incident, Hong Kong's governor—since 1882, Sir George F. Bowen—declared Hong Kong a neutral port.

It was in the midst of these events that the wily Li Hung-chang (in Grant's opinion one of the most impressive leaders he had ever met) cabled the fifty-one-year-old Mosby to offer him command of his growing regional army. Li's was but one of several loosely coordinated armies in China, but since Li was assuredly the *primus inter pares* of Chinese viceroys, Mosby may have stood to gain by the association. The offer was, he said, the highest testimonial he received during his stay in China, and must have been tempting. Grover Cleveland, the first Democratic President in two decades, had just been elected, and Li perhaps knew that Mosby had already sent in his resignation. He offered the ex-guerrilla a chance now to do what he did best: command troops in the field. "I decided to decline . . ." said Mosby,

> for sentimental reasons. I had never admired the soldiers of fortune who go around poking their noses into other persons' quarrels, and the idea of being a mere adventurer went against me. Then there is a sort of traditional friendship between the Virginia people and the French. . . . I kept the offer a profound secret while the war was in progress.

Noising it about would, he felt, have been tantamount to "a public acknowledgment of China's weakness."[93]

After the peace process had been set in motion, in 1885, he mentioned the matter in passing to the French consul at Hong Kong and promptly forgot about it. The French, however, did not forget. Several months later he received an official dispatch from the French Minister of Foreign Affairs at Paris, offering warm Gallic gratitude for Mosby's reluctance to march against France.

As the brief war wound down, life went on as usual in Hong Kong. The only notable event for Mosby was the international birthday party he threw in February in honor of George Washington, attended by the governor as well as by a number of foreign consuls and by former Yankee cavalryman Forbes. With a band from the American flagship playing national airs, everyone toasted everyone else and their respective heads of state throughout a long and apparently memorable evening.

During the period prior to Cleveland's inauguration a Treasury Department circular had been printed, ostensibly to clarify the procedure to be followed by U.S. consuls in certifying Chinese adjudged exempt from the restriction act of 1882. Since almost all emigration was from Hong Kong, the circular was, in effect, addressed to the U.S. consul there.

When in January 1885 the Chinese consul at San Francisco, F. A. Bee, quoted this circular as his authority for requesting exemptions for a number of Chinese wishing to emigrate from Hong Kong, Mosby put his foot down. In the first place, he said, he took orders from State, not the Treasury Department; and secondly, even if he owed allegiance to Treasury, he felt that a U.S. consul at Hong Kong had no business acting on exemptions. This was the business of the Chinese government, or at least of a U.S. consul accredited to that government (he himself being accredited to the British government). "As the Circular . . . is clearly *ultra vires,*" he told Assistant Secretary Alvey A. Adee in April, "I pay no respect to it. . . . I shall certainly not volunteer to do this work."[94] Because of this directive, he declared elsewhere—one "unauthorized by law and a piece of pure Department legislation"—large numbers of Chinese were coming to the United States, virtually nullifying the restriction act. He would not obey it.[95]

Such insubordination might in other days have resulted in his being cashiered. But coming at this time it could do him no harm, for a more pliant man had already been named to succeed him: Dr. Robert E. Withers, one-time standard-bearer of Virginia Conservatives, later the state's lieutenant governor, and never a special friend of Mosby.

Upon learning of his replacement by Withers, Mosby dashed off a letter to Grant, telling him that he'd soon be home, out of a job, and could Grant please do something to help him get started.

By mid-July Withers had taken over the consulate, and the Mosbys, father and son, were impatiently awaiting the July 29 departure of the *City of New York*. On the twenty-eighth, however, Mosby received a devastating cable: Ulysses S. Grant had died a few days before. "I felt," he wrote, "that I had lost my best friend."[96] He had surely lost all his prospects.

Grant had been discovered, the previous autumn, to have throat cancer. Working on his *Memoirs* throughout a winter and spring made hellish by pain, the general bore his lot without complaint, slipping gradually downhill until unable to speak. In mid-June he was moved from his home to the cottage of a friend near Saratoga, New York, and Mosby's letter was forwarded to him here. It reached him literally on his deathbed.

On July 22, the day before his death, Grant scribbled a telegram which he ordered sent off to California's Leland Stanford, former governor and recently elected senator from that state and, more importantly for Mosby, president of the Southern Pacific Railroad. It was Stanford who, as president of the Central Pacific, had driven the ceremonial spike at Promontory Point, finally linking East and West by rail. The dying man asked Stanford, as a personal favor, to do something for Colonel Mosby.

When Mosby and his son, after a cheerless voyage, stepped onto the pier at San Francisco, a man approached and handed the elder Mosby a note from Senator Stanford, requesting him to call as soon as convenient. Mosby made his way to Stanford's office the next day, where he was given Grant's wire to read—probably the former President's final piece of correspondence.

It was quickly done. The ex-guerrilla and newly retired consul was assigned a desk in the legal division of the Southern Pacific Railroad, San Francisco, California.

10

ON THE SHOALS

The world moves, and I had to move with it.
—John S. Mosby, Letter to an
Unnamed Newspaper, April
10, 1897

ARLY IN THE MORNING of April 18, 1906, the trembling rind of earth supporting San Francisco began to buckle and crack. The violent tremor lasted less than a minute, but its effects were devastating. The city was soon ablaze, its wooden buildings awash in flaming coal oil from overturned stoves. Three days later, when the fire had spent itself, San Franciscans were faced with the task of rebuilding from scratch. Nearly five hundred city blocks had been destroyed, to say nothing of the toll in human life.

The Southern Pacific Transportation Co., until then proof against most forms of disaster, was not immune to the fire that raced through company files. Any hope of using these records to reconstruct the California career of John Mosby—who had left the Southern Pacific some years before—literally went up in smoke.

In light of the fact that he had expended considerable effort in trying to escape his staid existence at the Southern Pacific, dry employee records would probably not have been very revealing anyway. To be yoked in corporate harness with dozens of other attorneys and sent out to fight the daily battles of the railroad must have been galling to one more accustomed to a good cavalry charge or a lucky shot from the hip. As he put it, though, his poverty dictated, not his will.

Mosby lived in California for nearly sixteen years, still the alien, having no more home on the Pacific shore than he had in Virginia. Although he had obtained his position through Senator Stanford, he proved nonetheless able to weather the change of company presidents upon Stanford's death in the early nineties. The Southern Pacific's new president was the titanic Collis P. Huntington—the company's real drive-wheel from the beginning anyway—and Mosby, who had known Huntington for years (no doubt through Grant), had no fear of being put off the train as the grizzled old veteran put his hand to the throttle.

Huntington and Stanford were not the only giants to cross his path in these days. In the course of his work he came to know Mexico's ironfisted Porfirio Diaz, an acquaintance born of his frequent trips to Mexico on railroad business, and of his supervision of a monthly lottery in Juarez. He came also to know at least one colorful man of the future: George S. Patton, Jr., then a boy living on his parents' ranch near San Gabriel. One of Patton's biographers relates that Mosby and young Georgie used to go riding together frequently, and that many a Civil War action was refought by them under California skies.[1]

Mosby was fifty-one when he stepped off the boat from Hong Kong. Although his hair was by this time snowy-white, his body remained sinewy, and he seemed to have no intention of growing old. People meeting him for the first time still remarked on how little the apparently mild-mannered attorney seemed to fit his reputation.

But working as a corporate lawyer did nothing to dull his guerrilla instincts. The year following his arrival found him still enmeshed in the pursuit of Far Eastern "rascalities"—now through the agency of an Indiana senator named Benjamin Harrison—and he lost little time in opening on the United States government in the courts to reclaim the "unofficial" fees he had remitted to the Treasury while in Hong Kong.

In December 1887 his efforts in this area bore their first fruit: he was awarded nearly $14,000 by the U.S. Court of Claims. Rubbing the State Department's nose in the dirt was gratifying, but he had been seeking twice that amount, so in early 1889 he appealed to the U.S. Supreme Court. In its October term, 1889, the high court did as lawyer Mosby should have known it would do: it reduced the amount of his award. The money remained substantial, however—close to $12,000—and Justice Blatchford, in announcing the Court's decision, was lavish in his praise of the ex-consul for the exemplary manner in which he had handled the cloudy question of consular fees.

By August 1888, Mosby had zeroed in on Benjamin Harrison, now the Republican presidential nominee, urging him to send speakers like James Blaine and an Ohio congressman named McKinley on the Virginia–West Virginia stump route. In November he was advising President-elect Harrison, as he had advised earlier Presidents-elect, on how to fill cabinet posts. California's John F. Swift, who had been to China in 1880 as part of the treaty negotiating team, was high on his list, as was Judge Robert W. Hughes of Virginia, whom he had opposed vigorously fifteen years before as being too much of a fence-jumper to deserve being governor. Mosby himself, however, had jumped a few fences since then, and Hughes suddenly seemed good cabinet material—"the ablest man in the State," he told Harrison.[2]

The following month he wrote to his friend and general Eastern factotum, Benton Chinn, of an impish idea he intended to share with the President-elect. "I intend to advise Harrison," he told Chinn, "to make a test case and appoint some *negro* postmasters in Boston and other places. The north *in fact* never has accepted the constitutional amendments. A doctor ought to be willing to take his own medicine."[3]

There is no evidence that Harrison listened to Mosby on any of these matters, and Mosby soon grew sour on the Centennial President.

It was shortly after his arrival on the West coast that he realized he could make money for his children by writing. He began to write accounts of his guerrilla days for eastern newspapers, found them well received, and by 1887 had packaged a series of newspaper features into a book called *Mosby's War Reminiscences,* signing over all future royalties to his son Johnnie. Perhaps because he had few windmills to tilt at as a Southern Pacific employee, he now took up his pen with a vengeance in defense of past causes. He was merciless in his critiques of books by Longstreet and Fitz Lee regarding Civil War events which he remembered differently than they, and he now began a years-long effort to burnish the reputation of his friend and idol Jeb Stuart, tarnished since his failure to

appear at Gettysburg on time. Mosby's painstaking reconstruction of pre-Gettysburg events eventually became the
apologia *Stuart's Cavalry in the Gettysburg Campaign,* heavy
going for non-scholars, and dismissed today even by scholars—not as trivial, certainly, but as a case of heart running far
in advance of head.

It was his newly active pen that earned him an invitation to
lecture in New England at this time. While on tour there, the
Forbes family saw to it that he met all the "right" people: at a
banquet in his honor in Boston he found himself seated with,
among other luminaries, James Russell Lowell and the Oliver
Wendell Holmeses, father and son. It was the beginning of his
romance with New England.

By 1894, Mosby had been a California resident for nine
years, yet he still considered himself an exile, cut off from
friends and the scenes he loved. He therefore willingly accepted an invitation in January 1895 to his men's first reunion.
Greeting his former hellions in Alexandria, he was amused to
see how many of them had become clergymen. "Well, boys,"
he bellowed over their heads, "if you fight the devil like you
fought the Yankees there will be something to record judgment day." [4] But he was not one for reviving the past, and
never attended another reunion. "It is like taking ipecac,"
was his tart observation; he claimed to have "no taste or tol-
eration for [the] gush" of such occasions. [5]

A year later he was taking an active interest in the historic
presidential race then raising steam. "I am for *gold* and civilization," he announced to his friend, U.S. Senator John
Daniel of Virginia, "vs silver and barbarism," thus putting
himself squarely in the camp of Major McKinley. [6] By August
he had come out for McKinley in a statement considered so
eloquent that it was published as a Republican campaign document. Arguing against William Jennings Bryan's proposed
free coinage of silver, he observed that in Mexico, which
had free coinage, he'd never seen a piece of gold in circula-
tion—"By a natural law," he said, " . . . the cheaper always
drives out the dearer currency." As for Democrat Bryan's
Populist party following, they were animated, he said, by a
"lawless spirit," and he intimated that the country was in for

serious disturbances if this element of Bryan's people ever got the bit between their teeth.[7]

Just before the election he wrote to Chinn on the money question, protesting some of "Daniel's nonsense" about having a currency that would "stay at home."[8]

"I told [Fount Beattie]," he continued, tongue well in cheek, "that the old Confed. was the best for that purpose I have ever known, but I wanted a currency good for its face value."[9]

McKinley was voted in by a comfortable margin, and Mosby began to look to the President-elect for a ticket out of California, perhaps a consulate, perhaps something else. But the first year of McKinley's presidency was to be disastrous for Mosby. Not only was he continually to be thwarted in his effort to pry something out of McKinley; he was to suffer more serious setbacks as well.

In January 1897 his mother died, and taking advantage of his time in the East to help settle her affairs, he started spading some ground around the twenty-fifth President. In February he was asking Daniel to speak to his own senator—California's George C. Perkins—for him, in hopes of getting some leverage on McKinley. But he hedged his approach too closely, fearful of seeming to be just another office-seeker. He still considered, probably with justification, that he had a special claim upon the Republican party in light of what he had suffered for it. But McKinley, he knew, could have forgotten all this. The new President had, moreover, served in the Shenandoah Valley, and Mosby was not sure whether he might be harboring some hidden resentment against the former Valley guerrilla. If any apologies for past "misdeeds" were expected, Mosby knew he could not provide them.

By early March, however, he had called upon McKinley and found him "very cordial," as he reported to a Virginia friend. "Said that I used to make him miserable in the Shenandoah Valley," he added.[10] There was apparently no talk of appointments.

After the inauguration that month, he called on some former Vermont cavalrymen he'd last seen across a warm gun barrel. One happened to be the Green Mountain state's gov-

ernor, Josiah Grout, who as a young lieutenant had been seriously wounded in the wild morning melee at Miskel's farm,
April Fool's Day 1863, and another was the influential Senator Redfield Proctor, formerly Secretary of War, and on duty
at Fairfax Court House the night Mosby slipped in and kid-
napped General Stoughton. Both men assured him they
would push his case with McKinley.

Since he was to argue a railroad case in the Supreme Court
the following month, he stayed on in the East. It was a decision that proved to be ill-starred. On April 23, out for a carriage ride near Charlottesville with William Robertson's
daughter, he was kicked senseless by a skittish horse while
making some harness adjustments. The accident left him with
a fractured skull and a left eye become pulp. It did not take
doctors at the university hospital long to determine that the
eye had to be removed, and the surgery was quickly done.

He began his convalescence now, separated from a source
of livelihood that he didn't really want yet with no prospect of
a better one, in a land which he loved but in which he had no
place. He was sixty-three years old, and would now have to
make his way with only one eye. It was a sad prospect.

By June, probably self-conscious with his new glass eye or a
dark patch, he was pressing his case again at the White
House, and evidently by this time had received some definite
promise from the President. He was pushing at the moment,
somewhat pathetically, for a return to Hong Kong, the post
having recently become vacant; but before he knew it, the
consulate was given to someone else. Senator Perkins attempted to explain. "The President," he assured Mosby in
July, " . . . is very desirous of doing something for you, but
[said] that it was not quite clear to him what he could do. He
is besieged by thousands of applicants from every state of the
Union."[11] His "special relationship" to the Republican party
was evidently not clearly perceived by McKinley.

Perkins made a point of encouraging him, however, to
choose a vacant consulship to his taste, intimating that
McKinley would do the rest. But it never happened, and
Mosby grew daily more embittered, feeling that a promise
had been broken. He tended to blame not the President, how-

ever, but Secretary of War Russell A. Alger, who had made no secret of his loathing for the ex-guerrilla.

In mid-August he headed back to California, after an absence of nearly a year.

Three months later he turned up again in Washington, having come to argue a Supreme Court case—perhaps the April case postponed. He made it clear to friends that he had no plans to see McKinley on this trip, that it was purely business; but he did in fact stop at the White House before returning. It is possible that the President was feeling some pressure in Mosby's regard, since even newspapers were talking about the faithful Virginia Republican's lack of success with the new administration. Mosby had, moreover, been assured by friends in the Senate that the President remained "very friendly" toward him. But just before his scheduled meeting with McKinley, the President received word of his mother's stroke, and talk of an appointment became impossible. By New Year's Day 1898 he was back in San Francisco.

Whatever tiny corner of McKinley's mind was reserved for promises made-but-not-kept to John Mosby, by February even that space had been preempted by events of wider importance. On the night of February 15, the battleship *Maine*, flexing some American muscle by its presence in Havana Harbor, erupted in an ear-splitting explosion that hurled 260 American navymen to their deaths in water and fire. There was no evidence of sabotage, and appalled Spaniards even assisted in fishing survivors out of the water. But America, sated with thirty years of boring commercial pursuits and already maddened by tales of brutal repression in Cuban *reconcentrado* camps, was spoiling for something that would make the blood run a little faster.

Before long, recruiting officers were faced with ten applicants for every slot they had to fill. The words "Remember the *Maine*" bristled like marlinspikes from the pages of the Hearst and Pulitzer jingo-sheets, as the country rolled up its sleeves to "have at the damn Spaniards." To an America on the road to becoming the world's conscience, the explosion of the *Maine* seemed as good an excuse as any to clean things up in Cuba. The irrepressible Assistant Secretary of the Navy, young Theodore Roosevelt, had been waiting a long time for such a chance, and he was ready for more than a Cuban adventure. Largely through his efforts there was already a solid naval force on station in Asia—under an unflinching admiral—with orders that if war should be declared, the Spanish fleet at Manila Bay was never to leave the Asia coast.

Mosby, cynical about the war, remained nevertheless a knee-jerk patriot and offered his services to the government. While Congress was debating a possible war declaration, he telegraphed his friend Nelson A. Miles—ex-Union soldier, veteran Indian fighter, and now major general commanding the army—asking for a military appointment. Miles, himself receptive to the idea, nevertheless cautioned the sixty-four-year-old ex-Confederate that he would need some senatorial influence if he wanted to carry this one off. Mosby, stung, fired back, "I have no influence except my military record." [12] Pressed by the *New York World* to elaborate on his exchange with Miles, he said: "I was surprised to hear that congressional influence was required to secure the privilege of fighting the battles of the country. . . . I cannot imagine what any congressman could say that would add anything to the endorsements I have received from General Grant and General Robert E. Lee." [13]

Miles, struggling now with the bewildering details of finding food, clothing, weapons, and transport enough to send an untrained army to a tropical war, had no comment. "I fought against Miles," Mosby told the *San Francisco Call,* "against McKinley in the Shenandoah, and against Alger, and what the devil good can [California senators] White or Perkins do? Major McKinley knew me before he ever heard of White or Perkins." [14]

In a letter to the *Richmond Times* a few days later he explained that he was "indifferent about rank" and would be satisfied to go in as a lieutenant. Convinced that Alger was behind the official snub, he nonetheless resigned himself to it and began—*à la* Theodore Roosevelt—to raise his own company. The *Call* in late June noted that the old Confederate was drilling a light cavalry troop in Oakland, "instilling the same vim that he showed when at the head of his raiders." By

July 4 San Francisco papers were announcing a military concert and ball to be given under the auspices of "Mosby's Hussars," an event that California Governor James H. Budd and San Francisco's Mayor Phelan were expected to attend.[15]

By early August, however, the mini-war was nearly over, and Mosby's Hussars disbanded without having drawn a drop of Spanish blood. Mosby, against this war as much as he had been against the War of Secession, felt embarrassed but relieved. "After all," he told Daniel, "although I was rejected, I think I got the best of it."[16]

He complained again to Daniel about McKinley's not having kept faith with him, continuing, however, to direct his ire more against Alger than the President: "[Alger's] hostility," he told Daniel, "grows out of the fact that my men came upon his regiment burning houses in the Shenandoah Valley and shot all they caught—*which I would do again*. A few days after that Custer published Alger as a deserter. Alger is a nice fellow to be professing horror over Spanish atrocities."[17]

Unable to resist a parting shot at his friend Daniel's expansionism, he added: "As soon as the principles of the Declaration of Independence are applied for the benefit of the Malays and West Indian sambos I suppose the United States will go on another crusade in behalf [of] Hindoos and Irish, and try again to recover the Holy Sepulcher from the infidel."[18]

In December, a few days after the peace treaty with Spain had been signed, he wrote again to Daniel. "Everybody knew," he said, in reference to the brief war, "that humanity was a mask and pretext. Expansion, conquest, rapine, plunder—the object. (What became of the poor reconcentrados? I have never heard them mentioned since we went to war to relieve them and blockaded Cuba to keep them from starving.)."[19]

By January 1899 the United States—new owner of the Philippines—was discovering for the first time that it took more than payment of a little cash to buy a country. Partisan leader Emilio Aguinaldo, one-time ally against Spain, was making it plain that his people wanted Americans in their islands no more than they had wanted Spaniards. The real war for the Philippines was about to begin. "I am utterly opposed," Mosby wrote to ex-ranger captain Robert S. Walker that month, "to pay twenty millions for the privilege of governing a people who don't want us." In reference to another former ranger, Joseph Bryan (now owner of the *Richmond Times* and a director of the Southern Railway Co., among other corporations), he continued: "Joe Bryan insists on giving taffy to Aguinaldo. Aguinaldo says, 'I don't want your taffy but independence. All we ask is to be let alone.'"[20]

"I lived seven years in a British colony in two days' sail of Manila," he commented (one hopes humorously):

> I know how worthless colonies are. I was afraid to go to the Philippines. There is an earthquake or typhoon nearly every day. People live on native products—mangoes, coconuts, and bananas—dress like Adam did before he ate the forbidden fruit. So you see they would not consume much goods for clothes. Holding them will cost us a great deal and no benefit. Keep us always in danger of war. We will soon be, if we owned them, like the fellow holding the bear by the ears and calling for somebody to come and help him turn the bear loose.[21]

Later that month, during the heated congressional debate on ratification of the treaty, he complained to Daniel that the American presidency was being converted "into an Oriental monarchy" by seizing territories without constitutional right. "If we govern Asiatics," he added, "outside of the Constitution we will soon get into the habit of governing ourselves in that way too. What I dread is the reaction on our own institutions."[22]

In early February, with the treaty recently ratified by a one-vote margin and a wave of violence gathering momentum in the Philippines, he wrote to Daniel: "Our civilization is a very thin coat of varnish."[23]

News of jungle warfare and of both American and Filipino atrocities was leaking out of the islands by August, and he wrote to Walker:

> Joe [Bryan] has become a snorting expansionist. I have just read his editorial in which he says it is a duty we owe not only to ourselves but to the Philippinos to murder them because they refuse to acknowledge the validity of their sale to us at

two dollars a head. . . . I look upon the whole business as a piratical expedition. Captain Kidd was honest enough to fly the Black Flag; these people are hypocrites. Their motive is slaughter and plunder in the name of humanity.[24]

The following June, as the presidential race shaped up between McKinley and the perennially available William Jennings Bryan, Mosby wrote to Walker of his "strong reasons for personal resentment" against McKinley, and continued his criticism of the administration's course in Asia:

I am as bitterly opposed now as I ever was to our having colonial possessions. . . . Joe Bryan says that if we come away from the Philippines the Philippinos will go to cutting each other's throats. So he thinks we ought to kill them to prevent them from killing each other. I don't think Providence has imposed such a duty upon us, but I suppose Joe knows—he is a Christian. I am not.[25]

On November 6 he voted for McKinley.

By this time, with his children grown and needing him not at all, he was taking an active interest in the education of his grandchildren. May's two boys, John Mosby and Alexander Spottswood Campbell, were in high school; their grandfather was hoping to see them transfer to a private school in Virginia, Woodberry Forest, run by his friend Walker. He also seems to have felt some responsibility for educating sixteen-year-old Jack Russell, son of his deceased sister, Lucie, and stepson to his other sister, Lelia, who had married Jack's father following Lucie's death in 1884. Russell, now an assistant attorney in the Department of Justice, was advancing rapidly in government, but at the price, it seems, of frequent absence from home. Just before the *Maine* blew up, he'd been sent to Cuba to investigate the plight of the *reconcentrados,* and he later served as legal adviser to the Puerto Rican Evacuation Commission. He was soon to have even more important assignments.

Mosby was never close to Russell—"Russell . . . lives in the clouds," he once told Chinn—but he was very fond of Jack, and felt justified in stepping in.[26] He wanted Jack to go to

Woodberry Forest for a year with Mosby Campbell, as a bridge to the University of Virginia, where his father wanted to send him immediately. The elder Russell had disagreed with Mosby's view that his son was too young for the university, and had objected specifically to Woodberry Forest for, among other things, its lack of a Catholic atmosphere. "To that I replied," wrote Mosby to Walker, triumphantly,

> that neither is the university Catholic, and that I thought Jack would be as free to say his beads at Woodberry Forest as at the university. I also suggested that if they thought that Jack's faith would not stand the rude shock of contact with the outside world, they had better let him follow Abelard's example and go into a convent. Send Jack your catalogue.[27]

He was, he told Walker, grooming young Mosby Campbell for West Point.

Two deaths in August altered his scheming. The first was that of Huntington, his protector at the Southern Pacific, a death which left him with the prospect of imminent dismissal. The second was that of Robert Campbell, the Campbell boys' father, who died leaving virtually nothing to his family. May was postmistress in Warrenton—appointed by McKinley—but she could not now let her boys leave home. Young Mosby would work in the post office as clerk, she said, at least for the time being, and Spotty could not think of going away to school for the foreseeable future.

"If I retain my situation," Mosby told Walker in late August, explaining this turn of events, "and there is no change to my prejudice, I want to give both of May's boys a good start in life so as to enable them to take care of their mother."[28]

By February 1901, however, his worst fears had been realized: he had been turned out of the Southern Pacific. The sixty-seven-year-old attorney was beginning the new century out of a job, uprooted again, and heading east to an uncertain future, his only financial asset a life insurance policy.

11

GUTTERING CANDLE

It seems to be my fate like Ulysses always to be drifting in a storm.

—John S. Mosby to Joseph
Bryan, October 20, 1905

THERE WAS SNOW in the air as the express out of Chicago, brakes gently protesting, drew to a halt at Omaha. The elderly passenger who alighted from the rearmost car, a smallish man with a glass eye, muffler and collar already pulled up against the November cold, instantly became the center of a small hive of newspapermen who had been waiting for him, supperless, stamping away their impatience for an hour and a half in the falling snow. "I have come back here," the man announced in notably Southern tones, forcing the scribbling pack to match his brisk stride, "with instructions from the government—from President Roosevelt down to the Land Office—to clean out all the fences on government land and all the fraudulent homestead entries. Particularly those of subsidized soldiers' widows. If District Attorney Summers remains indifferent in the matter, I shall report so to the attorney general—as I have done once before. As for Special Agent Lesser's recent statement concerning the charges against *him,* this is simply an evasion of the real charge, which is stealing from the government by use of false and fraudulent vouchers."[1]

Further questions followed from the scurrying cluster of reporters as, grip sack in hand, the man strode purposefully into the street and finally, with a peremptory wave, made it plain that he was finished with them.

"Mosby Brings His Broom," shouted the *Omaha Evening Bee* in a front-page item next day—"Bears from Washington

Instructions to Sweep Away Illegal Fences." The *New York Times* proclaimed: "Report of Agent Mosby May Necessitate Explanations from Two Senators—One Official Already Removed." The *Washington Post* had contented itself with a simple play on words: "Col. Mosby's Charge."[2]

On the day following his return to Omaha, Mosby met with District Attorney W. S. Summers, his purpose being, he had told reporters, to see what Summers had presented or was planning to present to the grand jury then in session. After his own appearance before the federal jury, he would immediately push on to his post at Alliance, four hundred miles away—but stopping off at North Platte long enough to have a look at suspended agent Lesser's books.

It was the sort of high drama he loved.

Although he had been depicted in the press of both Colorado and Nebraska as riding around the prairie with a set of wire nippers alongside his buggy whip, the nippers were purely figurative. All knew by this time that Mosby's personal mandate from the President cut more cleanly than the sharpest nippers. He'd already cleared hundreds of miles of fences off government land in Colorado by personal persuasion alone, and while it was true that Nebraska cattlemen were not quite running scared, they were apprehensive. He was confident of repeating his Colorado performance here. In the cattle states he was by now as widely despised as the "four-eyed maverick" in the White House.

Barbed wire was a potent instrument for change in the American West. Perfected in 1874, it was at first beyond the reach of many at $20 per 100 pounds. But through the eighties and nineties production wheels became so well greased (in 1883, one Illinois factory was turning out more than 600 miles of the stuff every 10 hours) that by 1897 the price had tumbled to $1.80 per 100, and even less when bought by the carload. For the phalanx of eager farmers pressing across the Western grass seas to claim a free piece of land, barbed wire provided an easy way of staking out a 160-acre empire. The wire also discouraged trespass by the thousands of cattle that, in some areas, pastured on the surrounding range as far as the eye could see.

Drovers from the great cattle incubator to the south, Texas, soon found their way blocked by impassable steel tangles, and were forced to skirt further and further westward into the higher and drier shortgrass country. This inconvenience was not tolerated for long, however, and soon wire nippers found their place in a cowboy's belt, as easily reached as his six-gun. But the flood of settlers did not diminish—in fact it increased—and cattlemen watched as prime rangeland was broken up for wheat, corn, a few potatoes, and erosion.

It became obvious that even an army of cowboys with wire nippers and six-guns could not stem the invasion of these grass sanctuaries, so cattlemen did the only thing they could: they began to buy barbed wire themselves by the trainload, sent crews out to string it, and dared anyone to cut *their* wire. Apart from having been there first, they felt justified in their action by the very nature of the land. As one Nebraska paper put it: "It looks so much better to see great herds of cattle fattening on the rich grass than to see some poor devil with more muscle than brains, trying to farm and eke out a precarious existence where God never intended farming should be engaged in."[3]

The Cleveland administration had attempted to stop the fencing of government land by the Van Wyck Fence Law of 1885, but the law proved an empty letter. Devoid of Washington sinew, it was simply disregarded, and local officials, without the support of the Federal government, were not eager to shoulder enforcement responsibility. Fencing went on; some ranchers, individually or in groups, locked up a million or more acres or, more cleverly, closed off hundreds of miles of rivers and creeks, rendering surrounding uplands useless for homesteading. In some parts of the West, areas larger than Massachusetts and Delaware combined were enclosed. Public roads were barricaded, and "sodbusters" sometimes found their entire spreads locked up overnight behind a cattleman's fence, making them prisoners on their own land. Only the most reckless newcomer would expect to return home after nipping his way out. The warning was clear: "Get out, nester."

A latter-day sophistication of the cowmen was the hiring of Easterners to file adjacent homestead claims along well-watered, low-lying hay meadows, with an arrangement for subsequent deeding of these homesteads to cattle interests. A quasi-legal rind was thus created around the drier uplands— now useless to the settler—which could be grazed without fear of settler pressure. It was only quasi-legal, however, since as part of filing the claim, a homesteader had to swear intent to live on the land, and cattle barons were therefore paying Easterners by the trainload to perjure themselves. A favorite target of the cattlemen's smooth-talking agents was the enormous number of soldiers' and sailors' widows in America, women who could count their husbands' years of military service toward the necessary residency period—shortening the time to free and clear title. Combing military pension rolls became a ranch agent's full-time job.

The system had always been maintained by a felicitous combination of governmental neglect and threat of cowmen's violence. Colt, Winchester, and rope proved adequate to the task of day-to-day enforcement, and legislators, judges, sheriffs, and marshals could usually be purchased for the long haul. Land Office agents were seldom a problem. Object lessons in cattlemen's justice were usually graphic enough to deter transgression: a dried-out corpse doubled over a fence wire, a fresh one swinging by the neck from a tree limb. In 1878, not only were two Nebraska farmers hanged but their bodies were later burned, and the horror of the "man-burnings" caused many a nester to scurry back where he'd come from. Prairie farms were dotted with the graves of those who had run afoul of the cattle kings. Just ten years before Mosby's arrival in cow country, the war for the range had reached white heat in the tense confrontation between a small army of settlers and the cowmen's "Regulators" in northern Wyoming.

Then Theodore Roosevelt came to the White House. Viewed widely in the East as a simple maniac, men of the West understood him, they thought, and regarded him as a godsend. He had run cattle himself in the Dakotas, and he knew which end of a steer went through the gate first. With old "Big Teeth" in charge, ranchers believed, there would be a new Age of the Cow, and McKinley's assassination was therefore not deeply mourned west of Omaha.

By the end of 1901 the cowmen were not so sure. Four-Eyes Roosevelt (he'd once remarked that, in the Badlands, men seemed to equate the wearing of glasses with defective moral character) seemed bent on busting *all* kinds of trusts, including Western cattle spreads. He was not making sounds like a cattlemen's friend. Frightened cowmen buttonholed their congressmen with practiced authority and said they'd be willing to *pay* for the use of these lands if Washington would just leave them and their fences alone. They wanted a law passed, they said, which allowed them to lease government range.

In December 1901, a Congress that knew little of what went on on the other side of St. Louis obligingly legalized the cattlemen's land steal by passing a Land Lease bill. If the President signed it, cowmen would be allowed to keep their fences up and to operate, business as usual, on payment of a small fee. Cattlemen's clubs in Cheyenne and Omaha were awash with liquor in anticipation of a golden future. But the "bunch-quitter" in the White House (he'd once been "one of the bunch") wasn't fooled. He promised to veto the Lease bill, and reaffirmed his intention to tear down all illegal fences in the West if he had to send the whole U.S. Cavalry to do it.

The cavalry threat was, of course, pure Roosevelt. He had already begun to accomplish his goal in Colorado with just one man: Land Office Special Agent, Col. John S. Mosby.

When Mosby arrived home from California at the beginning of McKinley's second term, jobless, he renewed his efforts with the President, and was told to his pleasant surprise that a place would shortly be found for him in the Justice Department. He waited patiently, visiting friends throughout the spring and summer of 1901, and writing. He turned out a curious piece for an April issue of *Leslie's Weekly* entitled "The Dawn of the Real South," in which he made some rather bold predictions about the South's rise from the ashes of slavery and war to a preeminent position in the country. His reasoning was sound, and apart from his prophecy that Richmond would become the banking and commercial capital of the nation, his vision proved remarkably sharp. Among newspaper editors who cared to notice, the piece produced knowing smiles. It was only Mosby, at it again.

In July his efforts with McKinley paid off, but again his poverty, not his will, was forced to consent. He was given a position in the Department of the Interior, not Justice, and instead of being assigned an attorney's work, was made a special agent in the Department's General Land Office.

As November arrived, with McKinley now dead and Roosevelt in office, he found himself in a buggy under the lowering skies of northeast Colorado, condemned to several months of cowboys, coyotes, and a harsh Colorado winter. His job was to see that the old 1885 Fence Law started to get some attention.

However much he disliked being there, the job to Mosby was simple enough: Announce your intention and your authority; find the fences; round up some witnesses to swear out affidavits; send out notices to remove the fences; then see that the notices are obeyed. Apart from not realizing that he'd find no one willing to sign an affidavit against a cattle baron, or that he would not be backed by the Land Office if he did, he seems not to have understood that it was dangerous to touch fences in Colorado. In later years he claimed to have felt that his status as a U.S. officer protected him. But in light of the ongoing violence around him, he may have been naive and was certainly lucky. His main problem, as it happened, proved not to be threats from the Colorado cattlemen but the unwillingness of witnesses to come forward, and, to a greater extent, the lack of Interior's will to enforce.

By late February 1902, however, he had badgered his superiors into a sort of submission. Attorney General Philander C. Knox had been moved to issue "special instructions" to the U.S. attorney at Denver, Earl M. Cranston, who soon became remarkably zealous in his duties; Land Office Commissioner Binger Hermann was, for his part, persuaded by Mosby to produce a fencing circular for the education of all Land Office agents. To skeptical and snickering cowmen, Mosby made it plain that civil suits were not the only route to compliance, that the U.S. Cavalry was also an option.

Things gradually began to happen. First the giant Pawnee Cattle Co. started to remove its fences, and soon all the fences in northeast Colorado were being pulled down. By spring 1902, the crusty sixty-eight-year-old had succeeded in surviving the Colorado winter, much of which had been spent out of doors, and understandably had begun to look toward something more comfortable: in this case the vacant consulship in Havana. Despite his Washington proxies' intercession with Roosevelt, it proved to be a pipe dream. "I am not the least disappointed," he told Daniel after the post had been given to someone else. "I really did not expect to get it but the world never estimates a man higher than he estimates himself. . . . I have now succeeded in doing what I wanted—getting myself favorably before the President."[4]

After a July holiday in Washington, he left for his next assignment: western Nebraska. On arrival there in August he noted that Nebraska, where "the reapers [had] been few," promised "good pasture for a Special Agent."[5] Nebraska journals noted only "considerable uneasiness" among stockmen at the coming of a man who had done "as much as the drought toward destroying the Colorado range cattle industry."[6]

Before setting to work in the prairie's blast-furnace heat, the newly arrived Mosby took a searching look at the neighboring jurisdiction's land agent, W. R. Lesser. Lesser, he noted, had been in office throughout the entire period of the land frauds. Suspicious by nature, Mosby was on his guard, and with customary directness wrote expressing to Lesser his hope that they could get along with one another.

Lesser, transparently nervous, answered: "So far as getting along harmoniously, I do not quite understand why we should not—your work will not conflict with mine, you can handle your cases to suit your own ideas of right and justice, and I will go along as I have, doing the best I can, and as rapidly as possible."[7] It was the kind of answer guaranteed to prick Mosby's curiosity still further. Eventually it came to light that Lesser, responsible for the land districts around North Platte, spent most of his time at home in Iowa, not hesitating to present vouchers as though on the job in Nebraska.

By October Mosby was recommending Lesser's suspension, and by December 1902 Lesser would find himself indicted for fraud.

In the Nebraska Sandhills, an oasis of belly-deep grass and sweetwater lakes in the dry, shortgrass plains, Bartlett Richards was king. President of the bank at Chadron and one of the biggest cattlemen in the West, he had more political and business clout than any man between the Black Hills and Denver. The Richards family interests were vast. Richards's older brother, DeForest, governor of Wyoming at the turn of the century and formerly a carpetbag officeholder in Alabama, controlled about a half-million acres; in 1899 Bartlett himself had nearly three hundred miles of fencing on government land, locking up another half-million acres, and by the end of 1902 his Nebraska Land and Feeding Co. had reportedly fenced a piece measuring sixty by seventy miles—more than 2.5 million acres, or an area four times the size of Rhode Island. Another brother, Jarvis, owned land in Colorado and helped manage his brothers' holdings.

In Nebraska, Bartlett Richards was a natural target for the gathering inquisition.

Richards was not just another cattleman. To begin with, he was baby-faced—looking almost womanish—and had stayed away from the killing indulged in by his associates. He was known even for kindness to down-and-out nesters, objecting more to their quantity than to their personal attributes. He was, however, as tough and arrogant as the rest, surrounding his land with "dummy" homestead entries, brazenly putting down fence where he wanted, and daring anyone to get in his way. In a conservative society, he had the effrontery to marry his niece. No one who knew Richards was fooled by the baby face.

Richards had seen trouble on the horizon when the "bunch-quitter" had started talking fences. In February 1902 he had addressed the Nebraska State Cattlegrowers Association, pleading that a "grave danger" faced Western stockmen. In the Alliance and Sidney land districts alone, he reminded his hearers, over 6 million acres of government land was under fence, and about 350,000 head behind the fences. The total value of cattle and land, he estimated, was $18 million. But, he added, all this could be lost if the fences came down. Herds would run together, rustling would again become rampant, and chaos would come to a presently well-ordered world. Something clearly had to be done to convince the President to leave the fences alone.[8] All Roosevelt had to do was sign the Lease bill, passed just before the adjournment of Congress, and certain to be passed by the new Congress.

Richards and a few others decided that it was worth a trip east to see that the President did nothing so foolish as to veto a new Lease bill. And if a veto was in fact in the offing, they felt, the trip might at least help them to buy time before the inevitable and make the removal of fences an orderly affair. They knew that Roosevelt, himself a cowman, could not possibly be against their use of the range, or even fail to see the good sense of fencing it. It was the *legality* of the fencing that had him stuck, and they hoped to unstick him on this point.

The trip was a disaster. A testy Roosevelt told the cattlemen in his plainest vernacular what he thought of the Lease bill, and made it clear that more time was out of the question—they'd had since 1885 to pull down their fences. The meeting soon degenerated into a shouting match between the short-fused Richards and the equally volatile President, and the two had to be restrained physically.

The seething cowmen returned to Nebraska with Roosevelt's final words ringing in their ears: "Gentlemen, the fences must come down."

In April 1902 the President vetoed the Lease bill, and in August Mosby arrived in the Sandhills, borne there on a flood of rumors that once he got Nebraska as clean as Colorado, he would be moving into the cattlemen's Holy of Holies—Wyoming. One Texan, with apparently less at stake than the Richards family, viewed the possibility with amusement. "I sure want to see DeForest Richards' face," he drawled, "when that turncoat Mosby starts working on that carpetbagger."[9]

Mosby had been in Nebraska less than a month when he decided that the solution there was the same as it had been in Colorado: Persuade the district attorney to begin doing his job. He reminded his superiors of how zealous the U.S. attorney at Denver had become upon receipt of instructions from the Attorney General, and suggested that District Attorney Summers at Omaha would respond to the same stimulus. He described to Commissioner Hermann the forest of fraudulent homestead entries he'd found there in the names of soldiers' widows, and noted, "The fine Italian hand of one Bartlett Richards can be traced in all this business for by a remarkable coincidence all their entries happen to be in the same ranges and townships with Richards' fences. I shall notify him in a few days to pull down his fence." [10]

He did so on October 2, and by October 3 was headed east on a trip "arranged" by Nebraska Senator Joseph H. Millard, who saw that Mosby had to be removed from the state as quickly as possible and had taken steps to have him called to Washington. The trip, Mosby later observed, could not have come at a better time. "I accomplished more," he told reporters on his return, "in the six weeks I was in Washington than I could have done in six years out here in Nebraska. While here my hands were tied. I could not reach the proper persons. . . . I made several written reports, but they were . . . pigeon-holed." [11]

Emboldened by several conferences with the President, who told Mosby he would send a cavalry regiment to the Sandhills if necessary, he lit fires under everyone from Secretary of the Interior Ethan Allen Hitchcock and Attorney General Knox on down. "Those fences must come down or there will be trouble," Roosevelt had told him. [12] The Attorney General was at length persuaded to draft "special instructions" to the district attorney in question, and on the heels of this action, a confident Mosby drafted his own instructions.

He warned Summers from Washington that he would soon be hearing from the Attorney General, and advised him to get the "so-called widows" in front of a grand jury as soon as possible. "While the widows are technically guilty," he continued, "the real criminals to be punished are the men who hired them to commit perjury and fraud." Singling out a particular widow, he told Summers that although she had not named the person who had hired her and others to make fraudulent entries, it was obvious who the party was. "As Bartlett Richards' fence is located on their claims," he said, "no doubt he expects to be the chief beneficiary in the transaction and is liable to a criminal prosecution. . . . He should be summoned before the grand jury." [13]

On Mosby's well-publicized return to Omaha in late November, he found the grand jury in session and a large number of subpoenaed cattlemen, agents, and widows in town. A grand show was shaping up, and, true to form, Mosby was not shy about its orchestration. He told the press he would present "startling testimony" that would, without a doubt, "create a sensation," so that "a huge batch of indictments" would be returned. In answer to a question about an alleged sixty-two fraudulent filings made in one day for land within Bartlett Richards's fences, Mosby pointed out that the maximum penalty for just *one* such filing was $1,000 and a year in prison. "If Richards is convicted," he told the *Lincoln Daily Star,* "it will put him out of circulation for quite a while." He was asked if he thought the fences would really come down. "I do," he answered, "if there is cavalry enough in the United States."[14]

"The strange thing about this whole thing," observed the *Star,* "is that a special agent should make his business known in the newspapers in such a sensational way. . . . Such an official usually regards such a mission as confidential between the department and himself."[15]

Other papers were joining the chorus of questioners, one forecasting Mosby's early recall, another predicting that he'd soon have to admit to being the "biggest jerusalem mule" in the country.[16] A confident Mr. Lesser had been doing his part in late November, telling the press that Mosby was really just too old for the sort of work he was doing, that he lived in the past.

"I think that [Lesser] should be the last man to make such a complaint," snapped Mosby, "for since I have been in Nebraska I have started to tear down the illegal fences, have unearthed the wholesale illegal entries of land and have had him bounced. The cattlemen also seem to think that I live in the present. . . . I am 68 years old and . . . am fully able to perform [my] duty. . . . I know what that duty is."[17]

Shortly before his grand jury appearance, he was asked a crucial question: Did he think the simple notices he had served on cattlemen would stand up in court? "There is nothing difficult about such a notice," answered Mosby, "and they do not have to be . . . intricate. With such a notice as I have already served upon Bartlett Richards I have removed all illegal fences in Colorado."[18]

Something went wrong in the courtroom, however, and
Mosby's promised "batch of indictments" shriveled to just
one: Lesser's. The grand jury voted "no true bill" on all his
land cases, at least partly on the grounds of technical insuffi-
ciencies in the notices he had served. There was a wild eruption of joy in cattleland, as wealthy men who had been
driven, sullen, before a grand jury one day bared ugly fangs
against Roosevelt's man the next.

The "star performer" in what the *Alliance Times* unflinch-
ingly labeled a "tragedy" emerged from the courtroom
"baffled, beaten and raging in helpless anger." Allowing for a
dose of hyperbole in an editor with a heavy ax to grind, there
had clearly been a change in momentum, at least. A tremendous salvo was loosed against the "infamous fire-eater" for his
"personal, overweening, consuming ambition," and his desire
to look good before the President. "Once a guerrilla, always a
guerrilla," proclaimed the editor, gloating over Mosby's
"crushing, humiliating defeat" after his series of "sensational
interviews and statements," and his masquerade as "the great
upholder of the majesty of the law." Mosby's "war on the
cattlemen and the helpless soldier's widow" was over, and he
had been left to stamp in "impotent, senile rage." [19]

"We have fought him," concluded the editor with little de-
tectable humility, "and exposed him at every turn. . . . We
have fought him because he was seeking to destroy the very
basis of our prosperity, the vital resource of our country. . . .
We have fought him effectively and to a finish." [20]

The less strident *Lincoln Daily Star* reported that Mosby
was soon to be whisked away "to keep him from being eaten,
blood, boots, nippers and all, by the ferocious tribesmen who
inhabit the sandhill regions in western Nebraska." [21]

"He needs a rest," the paper concluded, "and so does
Nebraska." [22]

The Interior Department, regarding the result as a slip, not
a fall, announced that the case for fence removal would "continue to be pressed vigorously." To this the *Star* replied:

> If the "pressing" is done at the gun-straining range heretofore
> adopted by Colonel Mosby, the fences will be able to stand the
> strain, and remain steer-proof. So far the interior department

has done nothing more than to call Colonel Mosby a real cute fellow once in a while, and then call him to Washington to talk it over again. This plan tickles the colonel's vanity, and is easy on the fences.[23]

Nebraska's Senators Millard and Charles H. Dietrich were furious over the fiasco, which had their constituents screaming for the old rebel's blood. They saw to it that Mosby was recalled immediately and permanently—"banished" as he later put it, through theirs and the cattle kings' influence.[24]

But after Mosby's departure the curtain rose again, this time quietly. More careful men were sent to the West, and before the new year was out, Bartlett Richards and his English brother-in-law, William G. Comstock, had been indicted. Convicted late in 1905 of having nearly a quarter million government acres under their company fences, they asked for clemency on the grounds that the fences were even then being dismantled. A sympathetic court fined them $300 apiece, and sentenced them to six hours in custody of a Federal marshal—a period spent amid champagne, fine food, and friends at the local Cattlemen's Club, in rip-snorting celebration of having gotten off so lightly.

When the President heard of the sentence and subsequent partying, he "blew up like a North Dakota thunderhead," in the words of a noted Western historian.[25] He threw out the district attorney, fired the U.S. marshal, and nearly spit nails over his inability to touch a Federal judge. A second "Roosevelt Roundup" began, the President in effect telling his new team to do it once more, with feeling. A "whole herd" of ranchers and their agents were reindicted—now for the more serious crime of making fraudulent homestead filings—and Richards and Comstock again found themselves in the dock. No matter that the fences had already been taken down. The charge this time was "suborning and aiding fraud and perjury in the entry of public land."[26]

Roosevelt, plainly, was after Richards's head, and he got it. In 1906, community leaders Richards and Comstock were found guilty on the new charges, fined $1,500 apiece, and sentenced to one year in prison. The U.S. Circuit Court of Appeals upheld the conviction, and in December 1910, one-time cattle king Bartlett Richards entered the county jail at Hastings.

The whole affair was in fact a tragedy of sorts, for a few weeks before completing his sentence, the forty-nine-year-old Richards died.

Shortly after Mosby's removal, a letter of his to John Daniel surfaced in the Eastern press. It had been written during the grand jury proceedings in early December, and indicated a private softening on Mosby's part toward the cowmen—as though he had finally understood.

Unfortunately the change had come too late to prevent the catastrophe.

"I think some indulgence should be shown . . . " he had written Daniel, "but as an official I have no discretion but to obey instructions and execute the laws.

> [The fences] . . . certainly . . . should be removed; but as they were erected by an implied license and stood so long by the acquiescence of the Government, good faith requires they should be removed with as little damage to individuals as possible. Time should be given cattlemen to adjust themselves . . . just as Mr. Lincoln favored the gradual emancipation of the slaves. I am opposed to harsh measures.[27]

He recommended a congressional suspension of the Fence Law for six months or a year. Nobody, he said, would put up a new fence if it would have to come down in a few months, and cowmen would have time to pull down existing fences in an orderly fashion. The words could have been uttered by Bartlett Richards, but this new viewpoint received no attention in a hostile range press. At any rate it had no power to affect either his own or Richards's fate.

In December 1903, following Richards's first indictment, Mosby received a letter from Binger Hermann, Land Office commissioner during Mosby's explosive tenure in the West and now an Oregon congressman. "Those indictments at Omaha," said Hermann, "are based primarily, if not entirely, upon the good work which you accomplished there after so much sacrifice, and bitter attack from those who were friends of the violators of the law. . . . It is a long road that has no turn."[28]

Mosby's banishment was to Alabama. Despite having some family there, however, he found his new assignment the bitterest of all. He was charged now with pursuing trespassers on government-owned timber tracts, a job that seems to have left him with some leisure time, judging by the effort he was able to put into getting out of Alabama. He began dogging the President again for a transfer. His heart, he said, was set on the Justice Department's newly created section for investigation of interstate commerce and trusts, a business dear also to the heart of Attorney General Knox.

"The position I have in the Land Department," he told his friend Bryan in June 1903, "is a very distasteful one to me." He ticked off for Bryan the big guns he was bringing to bear on the White House for his transfer. Among them: Judge Lunsford L. Lewis, former president of the Virginia Supreme Court of Appeals, and a friend of Roosevelt's; both Virginia senators; and Senator Redfield Proctor of Vermont, former U.S. Secretary of War. Both Roosevelt and Attorney General Knox were coming under Mosby's fire, and he asked Bryan himself to open on the President when Roosevelt gave the commencement address at the University of Virginia in two weeks. "I am really in exile now," he told Bryan.[29]

Bryan, who proved to be the warmest friend Mosby ever had, was stirred. "It distresses me," he replied to his former commander, "to think that you feel that you are in exile, and I shall try to send a relief column to you." Bryan—sectionalist, expansionist, influential, wealthy, and a devout churchman—was everything that Mosby was not. But he said he would speak to the President and do whatever else he could. "I believe," he told Mosby, "that you are about the only man alive that I would be willing to ask anything from the president for."[30]

He wrote at once to Joseph Wilmer, fellow Virginian and close friend of Roosevelt's:

It is a pathetic thing to me that a man who was deservedly distinguished as he was and a man of such ability could be in the financial depression that he is in and having the feelings . . . of an exile. He is as thoroughly a rock-ribbed and honest man as I have ever known, and I believe that he has had the most abundant opportunity to make himself a fortune if he had chosen to do so at the expense of his character, but this he would starve before he would do. . . . I would . . . feel that I was conferring a favor upon Mr. Roosevelt in bringing his attention to so meritorious a person. . . . I don't intend to leave any stone unturned to get Col. Mosby [a] place in the Department of Justice.[31]

Bryan muscled other artillery into position, including Wall Street Banker George R. Sheldon, one of the President's New York confidants, and J. H. Beal, a Pittsburgh law partner of the Attorney General's. Both men wrote to Knox in Mosby's behalf—Sheldon reminding the Attorney General of Mosby's "claim . . . for consideration" by the Republican party.[32] William A. Jones, a Virginia congressman, also volunteered his efforts. By early July, Bryan was able to report that they were "certainly . . . enfilading [Knox] well."[33]

But October found Mosby still tramping about the Alabama pine forests, not an inch closer to his goal. He wanted to escape anywhere, even back to the West. "I have fallen in fortune so far from my former estate," he wrote mournfully to Bryan, "that I have a sense of humiliation here among Southern people. I did not feel it so keenly out among the cowboys of the West for I was not daily reminded of what I was."[34] By February of the following year his mood was even darker, and he was awash in pathos. "I am too old now," he told Bryan, "for the Southern people to atone for the wrong they did me. But you know that Columbus after discovering America was sent home in chains."[35]

Then, in March 1904, his spirits began to lift somewhat. After years of his own and Daniel's efforts, Congress had finally recognized the validity of a second Mosby claim against the government: reimbursement for 7,000 pounds of Mosby-owned tobacco, seized by the Union army in the postwar occupation of Richmond. Colonel Mosby would, the Congress voted, be allowed to press this claim in Federal court. (One year later he would be reimbursed nearly $4,000.)

In addition to this welcome news, Mosby was treated to the sight of the heaviest artillery in the North being trained upon the government in his behalf. Charles Francis Adams, Massachusetts renaissance man and long-time admirer of Mosby, in

February brought the Virginian's plight to the attention of the Bay State's powerful Henry Cabot Lodge (at the same time that Senator Lodge was being prodded by Supreme Court Justice Oliver Wendell Holmes, Jr., another Mosby advocate). "If he was promised a place in the Department of Justice by Pres. McKinley," Lodge told Adams, "he ought to have it, and I shall be glad to lay the matter before the President at once."[36] Now the renowned Southern novelist and dispenser of Roosevelt patronage in Virginia, Thomas Nelson Page, entered the ranks of the besiegers, and it became too much for Roosevelt. He determined to call in the old rebel and tell him what was wrong.

"Yesterday I called upon the President," wrote Mosby to Bryan on a visit to Washington in early May.

> He sent me a message to wait until the crowd had gone. I did so. He took me into a private room, sat down, and then began talking earnestly about his desire to put me in the Department of Justice. Said the trouble had been that Knox was not satisfied about my legal qualifications. He urged me to see Knox— talk with him—"then come to me and I will give you a letter to him." I could not understand what he meant by this. He seemed very earnest about it. But I shall not call on Mr. Knox to discuss my qualifications to enter the law department. I have too much self respect for that.

"The opposition to my appointment," he concluded, "comes from the Department, not from the President." He would, he vowed, return quietly to the Alabama forests.[37]

It is likely that corporation lawyer Knox, who had had dealings with Mosby during the fence crisis, was not eager to have such an unpredictable bull in his bright new antitrust china shop.

Mosby retained an unplayed ace, but one left unplayed by choice: his own brother-in-law and Justice Department fair-haired boy, Charles W. Russell. Russell was at that moment en route home from Paris, where he had just concluded successful negotiations with the French for the transfer of the New Panama Canal Company's assets to the United States in return for $40 million in U.S. gold. Mosby was even now staying at Russell's home in Washington, but had resolved not to bring his relative into play. Never comfortable with "Mr. Russell," as he always called him, Mosby preferred to keep his brother-in-law at a distance. He told Bryan at this time:

> Thomas Nelson Page thinks that my going into the Department of Justice rests entirely with Russell. . . . I shall not mention the subject to him. . . . I shall ask my sister also not to mention the subject or in any way seek to influence him. . . . I have had so many reverses of fortune that I will not be in the least depressed by failure. I shall still hope for something better in life.[38]

It is unlikely that Lelia could have been restrained from dropping a word to her husband. Two days after Russell's arrival Mosby was again closeted with the President, and three days later it was announced that Col. John S. Mosby was being transferred from Interior to Justice—not, however, to the budding antitrust division, but to the Bureau of Insular and Territorial Affairs, headed by Russell. And, it was whispered, not at a respectable $3,000 to $3,500 annual salary, but at $2,400. It had all the earmarks of a family job: scraping up a salary for a relative from departmental leavings. Knox was doubtless appalled but, on the point of leaving office anyway, he perhaps chose not to notice. Whatever Mosby's feelings were about the outcome, he accepted the appointment, immediately wiring his warmest gratitude to Bryan and others who had helped him. He then moved his few belongings to Washington.

After twenty-six years he had come home.

Throughout the aging warrior's personal struggles, he persisted in trying to manage the education of the fatherless Campbell boys, and in helping the rest of the family as well as he could. His daughter Stuart, married now, had children who needed money from Grandpa, and he helped his grown-up children as well. "Last week I sent Ada sixty dollars and Stuart ten dollars," he told Mosby Campbell in May 1903. "I couldn't send more because I had to pay life insurance."[39] His unrelenting attention to life insurance lay in some contrast to the attentions of his youth.

By September 1903 both Jack Russell and Mosby Campbell were at the university, and Mosby, true to form, was insinuating himself even into their search for housing. (As his sons had done before, the boys largely ignored him.) By this time young Mosby had proven his capacities at Woodberry Forest, and his grandfather had resolved to steer him toward mining and electrical engineering. But, stuck in the Alabama forests, he was growing despondent over his ability to be of real assistance to his grandchildren and confided so to Bryan, who stepped forward to assert very tastefully that he himself would see to the boys' education. "I beg to say," he told his former commander in October,

> . . . that I shall consider it a great privilege if you will allow me to unite with you in the education of your grandsons. . . . I have made it a rule ever since my boys left the university . . . to send a certain number of young men to college . . . and I don't know anybody's descendants who are better entitled to that opportunity than your own. . . . I want to be your partner in that business.[40]

Greatly relieved, Mosby accepted the generous offer, and a few days later Bryan sent his first tuition installment to the university. The Campbell boys' education was assured. To cheer up Grandpa Mosby still further, Bryan soon shipped him a birthday gift: a case of good Madeira he'd brought from London the previous summer.

One year later, with his life now somewhat on track, the ax fell again. His forty-five-year-old firstborn child—the Campbell boys' mother—died. He could not be consoled. "I want to be quiet," he wrote to Bryan, "and not meet strangers for you know that I am broken-hearted over the death of my child—the world now seems desolate to me. 'All things looked so bright about her that they nothing seem without her.'"[41] Bryan's efforts to distract him—even by a promise to send to London for some very special Madeira—were of no use. At December's end, bent and bowed, he confided to his friend, "It has been a sad sad Christmas for me."[42]

But hands were extended, some from unexpected quarters, and he was touched. The people of Warrenton, whose fathers had exiled him, petitioned the President that Mosby Campbell be allowed to fill his mother's government post until family debts could be paid. Bryan reassured him that money for his grandsons' education would be no problem. Expressions of sympathy arrived from the White House.

Mosby's first assignments for the Justice Department were in Alabama, a state that he knew well. As usual he maintained an extracurricular liaison with the President, apart from his official working framework, and in early 1905 he was sent—ostensibly at Roosevelt's request—to investigate a matter in Alabama which had the collectorship of the Port of Mobile at stake. Other Alabama assignments followed. In June the seventy-one-year-old investigator was sent by Russell to Indian Territory (present-day Oklahoma) to look into charges being brought against U.S. Marshal Benjamin H. Colbert—a former Rough Rider—and others, allegedly involved in land frauds against the Chickasaws. While there he turned up information which, it was widely reported, led to the indictment not only of Colbert, whom Roosevelt refused to rescue, but of several other territorial personages, among them a firm of lawyers from McAlester.

These attorneys, representing the Chickasaw and Choctaw nations in a potentially lucrative suit against the government, had, Mosby alleged, actually been misappropriating tribal funds. When the firm's three partners—George Mansfield, John F. McMurray, and Melvin Cornish—were indicted, he triumphantly wired the results to Russell. Russell's lack of enthusiasm for the proceedings stunned him. Pointing out that the evidence against the three was skimpy, and that there was the further question of bias among members of the grand jury, Russell cautioned his exuberant brother-in-law, warning that the men must get a square deal.

"Dear Mr. Russell," Mosby fired back,

I received your telegram asking for "a square deal" for Mansfield, McMurray, and Cornish. I think *every* man is entitled to a square deal; there has been no discrimination between Mansfield, McMurray, and Cornish and other criminals; they have the same kind of reputation among lawyers that Captain

Kidd had among sailors. . . . I feel very sure that if there is a
square deal they will land in the penitentiary.[43]

In the midst of the mild uproar over this case he returned to
Washington, but by the end of July was back, this time to
investigate land frauds against Indian minors. The territorial
press was ready for the colorful old fighter's second coming.
"Carrying an old-fashioned hickory cane," said one paper,
" . . . and walking as briskly and easily as if he were man of
30, Colonel John S. Mosby, whose renown . . . is known to
every schoolboy, has come to Oklahoma to unearth graft in
the Indian service."[44]

But while he was rummaging around for "grafters" in the
West, doors in Washington were being closed softly against
him, and something seemed wrong within his very family.
Russell, wiring him in mid-August that a "Special Attorney's
appointment" for him seemed "uncertain," tacked on the
searing postscript: "Stuart absent until end of month. She desires your absence."[45]

Upon Mosby's return from Indian Territory in late summer,
he found the world changed against him. Russell, apparently
annoyed by his pursuit of Mansfield, McMurray, and Cornish
(the case was dropped two years later for lack of evidence),
increased his distance from his brother-in-law—who still
seemed, after all, to be just a guerrilla in broadcloth—and
took a petty revenge. He began to ignore him, converting his
aged relative to an office fixture by giving him nothing to do.

It was an exquisite way to torture a septuagenarian. Mosby
was kept on at the Justice Department for five more years, his
"heart's desire" turning steadily to ashes.

12

THE DEFENSE
RESTS

I am now in "the sere and yellow leaf," and am seeking the
shade.

> —John S. Mosby to Alexander
> Spottswood Campbell, January
> 27, 1915

I N JUNE 1910 he was fired. With Roosevelt gone, a new
man in the Attorney General's chair, and Russell just
sent to Tehran as U.S. Minister to Persia, Mosby's toe-
hold in government simply eroded away.

He was, he was told, "superannuated"—too old for the
job.[1] His friend Keith, in his sixteenth year now as president
of Virginia's Supreme Court of Appeals, protested at once,
assuring Attorney General George W. Wickersham of Mosby's competence and particular merit; he'd met no man "with
a more acute and veracious mind than Col. Mosby," said
Keith. If Mosby hadn't thrown success away for conscience'
sake, he declared, he would have stood "in the front rank of
the bar of his day." Keith reminded the younger man of what
the old Virginian had sacrificed for the Republican party.[2]
Others spoke up, both to the Attorney General and to President Taft, but to no avail. He was seventy-six, and his working life was finished.

He blamed Russell more than Taft or Wickersham, but in
the end bared his neck with surprising good grace—"as grace-
fully as I did to the wounds I got in the war," he told a friend
that summer.[3] He had saved nothing, thinking his position
secure for life, and left office with a life insurance policy and
$40 in his pocket.

As heartbreaking as his final years were, both for him and for those who had to put up with him, they brought with them a certain fulfillment, a certain justice, a closing of circles ruptured long before.

He cared deeply for the nation, and was enormously pleased to see signs of a budding good feeling between North and South. The wound made sixty years before by his expulsion from the university was formally touched and healed. Southern friends long estranged came back to him. He made new friends, Yankees especially, who gave him the full measure of honor he had craved but missed from his own people. His attention, long distracted by the bitterness of reconstruction, by the exigencies of government service, and by the simple need to survive, was drawn inexorably backward to *the* event in his and the nation's life: the great fratricidal war of his youth. He persisted in trying to explain it to himself and to anyone who would listen.

In 1906 he again took to the rostrum in New England. The event was Grant's birthday, observed every year by Boston's Middlesex Republican Club. To the delight of his Yankee audience, he produced a fine eulogy of the nation's eighteenth President. To a clucking Joe Bryan he later explained that he was well aware of the controversy surrounding Grant's record as President, but that this was not the point. The point, he intimated, was that Yankees were now inviting Southerners among them, and were listening with respect to what they had to say. "The best on both sides," he said, "are praising both Grant and Lee."[4]

Outside Virginia he came to love New England more than any spot on earth—not for its climate, certainly, but for what he perceived as the openness of its people. "I have never before," he wrote to his son Beverly,

met such liberal minded people as the descendants of the Puritans. The word Puritan has been a byword of reproach in the South to designate a hypocritical, narrow minded bigot. Now it is remarkable that the two great Puritan soldiers of our war—I use the word Puritan not in the odious but in its original sense—were Southern men: Robert E. Lee, and Stonewall Jackson.[5]

The sons of the Massachusetts Puritans treated him like visiting royalty. They sent a Yankee colonel to Washington to escort him to Boston, then, upon his arrival, beefed up the escort with a number of his ex-prisoners—who seemed delighted. (One exuberant old fellow had to be persuaded by the embarrassed Virginian not to recount the details of his capture in a planned after-dinner speech.) He shared the lectern with Massachusetts Governor Curtis Guild. He was driven by automobile to Harvard, to Plymouth Rock, to Daniel Webster's home and gravesite, to the seashore to see fresh-caught cod. He was given a reception by some flinty old Yanks at Kingsley Post, Grand Army of the Republic. The high point of his trip, he said, was a seaside conversation with an old fisherman who remembered having fished with Daniel Webster. He met Emerson's daughter and the daughter of his friend Forbes, now dead. He visited Faneuil Hall. "They were so kind," he wrote of the Boston men, "I was sorry I ever captured them. Afterward I was sorry they didn't capture me."[6]

Six months after being fired, in December 1910, he went to Connecticut to deliver a series of lectures—invited by the brother of another former captive, one who had finished the war in the stockade at Andersonville. On this trip he was met at the New Haven depot by the dean of the Yale Law School, introduced at Waterbury by President Taft's brother Horace, and crowded wherever he went by people happy just to shake his hand or to touch him. In Hartford he was driven to the Colt's Arms factory, which he toured, entertaining his hosts with lively explanations of how he'd managed to get in the way of so many Colt's revolvers himself. "I never was half as well treated in Virginia," he told long-time friend Louise Cocke, "as I was in Connecticut."[7]

To Louise's sister Betty, still an unreconstructed Confederate, he wrote that his cordial reception was "evidence that the passions of the war had died out," and he hoped it would have "a good effect in the South."[8]

"I was ten days in Connecticut," he told Betty, "and did not hear a note of discord. . . . I confess that my animosity toward the North has long passed away. . . . My experience is that we are all the same kind of people."[9]

His men were slightly appalled that Mosby so willingly attended to such affairs in New England, New York, and even Toronto, while refusing to attend reunions of his own battalion. In 1906 he had attempted to explain why to ex-ranger Ben Palmer:

> The gatherings in the South [are] in [no] sense reunions—they are nothing but political meetings where demagogues go to spout and keep alive for their own benefit the passions of the war. If my men would have a real camp or bivouac in the woods where I could meet them and talk over the old days it would give me great pleasure to be with them. But I do not want to listen to Bloody Shirt speeches. . . .
> I have no intentions to ever go to another reunion, and it is useless to ask me.[10]

To ex-ranger Colie Jordan, who pretended not to have heard, he declared in 1909 that not only could he not stand the speeches and prayers at such assemblies, but that his men's reunions were plainly "political conventions in the guise of social gatherings."[11]

"I prefer healing the wounds of the war," he said. "I do not enjoy making them bleed afresh."[12]

Already convinced that the South was living in the past, he was more than horrified to learn that a group of ex-Confederates wanted to put up a monument to Capt. Henry Wirz, superintendent at Andersonville, who was executed at the close of the war. It was a perfect example of what he found most despicable in the South. Maybe prisoners were treated as badly in the North as in the South, he declared to his brother Willie, but nobody proposed building monuments to the "brutes" responsible. "I want the memory of all the brutes," he declared, "North and South, to sink into oblivion. By erecting a monument to Wirz the Southern people endorse his acts."[13]

He had less and less reluctance to speak about Southern failings. Slavery had been tolerated in the ante-bellum South, he said, because of sheer ignorance among Southern whites— a failing which he blamed on a lack of free and widespread education, fostered by the slaveholding class. "An enlightened public opinion," he declared, ". . . would not have submitted to the rule of a slaveholding oligarchy. . . . If there had been free schools in the South there would have been no war—the Southern people would have abolished slavery. . . . Slavery and general education could not live together." [14]

Parts of the Southern white population, he told his grandson Spottswood, had been not only ignorant but downright uncivilized. When he was a student, he said, the population in the mountains around the University of Virginia "was in about the same condition of barbarism that the Highlands of Scotland were in the time of Rob Roy." [15]

"There was no more volition," he continued, "in such people going to war than in the pigs they carried to market." [16]

As for Radical reconstruction, he told his grandson, it was not as bad as Southerners would have the world believe. "I went through it all," he said, "and was as restive under it as anybody. . . . When the yoke was removed and I was permitted to share under the government every privilege of a Union soldier my passion cooled and my reason resumed its sway. . . . My old sentiments about the Union returned." [17] ("As you were a product of Reconstruction," he had once told Keith, "I do not think it as bad as Joe Bryan's paper says it was." To a bitter Alabama man he had once remarked, "If there had been no Reconstruction Birmingham would still be a cotton patch.") [18]

He admitted that he, like Lee and all Confederates, had been guilty of treason in bearing arms against the United States government. It rankled him, however, to hear ex-Confederates deny the charge, as if it were somehow dishonorable. "Treason . . . ," he said, "is a legal and technical but not necessarily a moral offense. . . . When I hear Confederates deny that they were guilty of treason I tell them that the difference between us is that I am proud of it and they are ashamed." [19]

"It is a great error," he continued, speaking of the futility of attempting to justify the treason,

> to hold a soldier responsible for the merits of a cause in which he happens to fight; the side he takes is controlled by a power he cannot resist. The individual is no more at such a time than a straw in a cyclone.
>
> At Hong Kong an Englishman once remarked to me how

much he regretted the failure of the Confederate cause. Much to his surprise I replied that although I was a Confederate soldier and my family were slaveholders, yet I thought that it was much better for our whole country that slavery was abolished and the Union restored. "Then," he said, "you admit that you fought on the wrong side." I answered, "I do not—I may have fought on the side that was wrong, but I fought on the right side." . . .

It is very common for speakers at Confederate reunions to say that they have no apology to make for what they did in the war. . . . The French say that a man who excuses accuses himself. Why is it that Southern men are all the time pleading not guilty when nobody is indicting them? [20]

He continued in this vein to former ranger Sam Chapman. It was wholly unnecessary, he told Chapman, for Southern soldiers to go on trying to justify themselves before the North, for "Don Quixote never had a more imaginary foe." [21]

"Let Southern soldiers," he said, "get rid of the idea that their honor rests on the right of secession, or the righteousness of the pro-slavery cause. I prefer to let its ghastly memories pass away." He had once been infected by the madness, he admitted, and had run off "in pursuit of a phantom," but, he added, "time [had] cured many delusions." [22]

"I have always said," he later remarked in a more whimsical vein, "that the quickest way for southern people to get even with the Yankees is to marry them." [23]

Despite the agreeable closing of long-ruptured circles in his final years, old age was not kind to him. He shuffled about the streets of Washington, a familiar sight to all, a shrinking old man with a cane and black alpaca coat, close-cropped white hair, and one dead eye. His disposition grew more sour, and he became more of a trial to live with. If a conversation ceased to interest him, he walked away without excuse. If he could eat no more, or disliked what was served, he left the table without apologies. He was abrupt to the point of rudeness, and his lifelong habit of answering a question only after extended reverie became even more pronounced.

Part of his distance was caused by advancing deafness, a legacy, perhaps, of the years of thunderous battle sounds.

Physical problems compounded themselves: due probably to his deafness and crippled vision, he was knocked solidly to the pavement in 1907 by a hit-and-run cyclist. His body was breaking down in more serious ways as well. A urinary tract problem led to major surgery in 1908 and again in 1912. He also suffered from a persistent and annoying skin infection, which required a layering of powders and plasters into at least one sticky Washington summer.

His family took care of him, but, given his temperament, the effort was not without risk. His daughter Stuart, with whom he was not close, was nevertheless the one to take him in. Money dribbled in from various sources. His grandsons, once established in their professions, contributed; he earned money himself on speaking engagements, and in writing; he received a small advance from a publisher on his forthcoming memoirs (finished eventually by Russell and published posthumously).

Russell, whom Mosby at length acknowledged to be "very generous," attempted to help him, as did young Jack Russell.[24] But Mosby preferred accepting money from strangers who, he felt, gave out of respect, rather than from family, who gave out of charity. Virginia's governor, Henry Stuart, sent him $50 for his eighty-first birthday. Yankees occasionally dropped a check in the mail. But he found it impossible to hold on to a dollar. He hovered over daughters Ada and Pauline with money; sent an occasional twenty to his former servant, Aaron, in Brooklyn; always had something for a needy ex-ranger; borrowed against his life insurance to make loans to his grandsons; and paid for fifty-year-old Johnnie's hospitalizations when his son fell ill.

His sister Blakely was a great comfort and confidant. Daughters Pauline and Ada, both living in Baltimore, were there when he needed them. His sister Lelia, married to Russell, moved in other circles, but except for her years in Persia, was always nearby. Beverly had remained in the West. Johnnie, having lived many years in the West himself, had returned to take a job with the *Washington Post*—a job that he proved unable to keep. Victim of a gradually worsening throat ailment, he soon took up residence with George Slater, one of his father's old rangers, in the fresh air of Fauquier.

Mosby Campbell, an engineer now with General Electric, had moved to Schenectady, and both Spottswood and Jack Russell were practicing law in Manhattan.

When not prowling about the streets of Washington, alone or with Stuart's two children, the old soldier was hunched over a red damask-covered table in the center of his large but cluttered bedroom, writing. In 1908 he published *Stuart's Cavalry in the Gettysburg Campaign,* and began to devote full time to his memoirs, a work that was slowed considerably by his several bouts with illness. Nostalgia, as much as illness, had him in its grip, and he spent days wandering over the battlefields of the past: Manassas, and various fields in the Shenandoah Valley. He revisited Millwood, where he had dickered with the Yankees over terms of surrender, and spent a long while musing at the old chapel and cemetery there.

Modernity, at least certain aspects of it, he despised. "Buzz wagons" (automobiles) were anathema to him, and he expressed equal impatience with postcards and the turkey trot. Occasionally he put great energy into fighting modern trends. The best example of this was his long-time agitation against college football, a crusade that peaked for him in 1909 when a University of Virginia student named Christian was killed in a game against Georgetown.

Eppa Hunton, who, Mosby thought, was in a position to do something about football at the university, bore the weight of his tirade. Mosby accused the university of actually having murdered Christian by allowing such a "barbarous amusement" to go on. Football, said the ex-guerrilla chief, seemed no longer to be a student recreation but had become a profession. The sport developed, he said, "brutal instincts," and should be "no part of the curriculum of the university." He claimed to be astonished that professors had actually been part of the "vulgar crowd" cheering over "the mangled body of Christian."[25]

"One of the most disgusting features of the exhibition," he told Hunton,

was a priest—a disciple of Loyola—acting as director of the contest. It can't be much comfort to Christian's family that this Father said a Mass for the repose of his victim's soul. . . .

The main object of education should be to gain the empire of mind over matter. . . . The faculty of the university seem to have discarded the Baconian philosophy and to be trying to revert to a primitive state—putting muscle and prize fighters on top. But, say the defenders of such sport, it develops the *manhood of youth.* I deny it unless by *manhood* they mean mere physical strength. My sense of manhood is a sense of honor and courage; such qualities may exist in a weak body. . . . I can see no progress—rather retrogression—in a boy's going to a university to develop his muscle.[26]

If, without athletic programs to attract students, he added, universities would have to close their doors, then let them be closed. It was his opinion, he said, that severe physical exertion bore little relation to health or long life anyway, and certainly had nothing to do with courage. Athletes, he observed, had in his experience usually belonged to a class "invincible in peace and invisible in war."[27]

"During our war," he explained, "I often wondered what had become of the bullies and bruisers I had known."[28]

"I hope," he concluded, "the legislature will make these brutal games a felony."[29]

An uncomfortable Hunton harumphed his way through a reply, and Mosby continued the argument with Tom Bryan, Joe's youngest son, asking that if cock-fighting was illegal in Virginia, why wasn't college football illegal. "Why," he asked, "should better care be taken of a game chicken than a schoolboy?"[30] It was vintage Mosby, cutting against the grain—something like years before, when he'd been asked who he considered the ablest of the Union generals and had answered unblinkingly and in perfect sincerity, "McClellan, by all odds."[31]

The forest of family and friends that sheltered him continued to wither. Forbes was dead. Bryan went in 1908, Daniel in 1910. The ranks of his former rangers were thinning. In 1913 his brother Willie died, and in the summer of 1915 Johnnie succumbed to throat cancer. His two favorite children—his "idols," he called them—were now gone, and he was plunged in grief.[32] He refused to see even Cameron Forbes, late governor general of the Philippines, who had been planning a trip

with him to Aldie to go over the ground where his father had
been taken prisoner. Russell—not long back from Tehran—
would have to go with Forbes, said Mosby, for he wished to
see no one outside his family. "I do feel so lonely in the
world," he wrote mournfully to Mosby Campbell, "and hope
you can come soon to see me."[33]

He followed politics as closely as ever, turning against his
friend Roosevelt in 1912, when the wily New Yorker made a
new bid for the presidency. Roosevelt, locked that June in a
bitter and losing struggle with the Republican leadership for
the party's nomination, must be a "madman," said Mosby, to
"denounce as thieves and robbers the leading men of a party
he expected to elect him."[34] In November he climbed out of a
hospital bed to make the hundred-mile round trip to Warrenton—in one day—to cast his vote for Taft.

It was, of course, the Democrat, Woodrow Wilson, who
benefited from Roosevelt's obstinacy in running as a third-
party candidate.

Wilson, who had devoted little attention to foreign affairs
in his campaign, was faced with two imposing foreign issues
almost at once: instability in Europe and revolution in Mexico. During the President's period of "watchful waiting" on
the Mexican situation, as he weighed the consequences of
American intervention, Mosby—somewhat familiar with
Mexican affairs—volunteered his assistance in some way
(probably at the head of a regiment), and in August 1913,
Wilson patted the old firebrand on the head. "It was most
characteristic of you to make the offer you do," he told him,
"but . . . I do not see any reason to believe there will be any
occasion to avail ourselves of it. I hope, as I pray, that there
will be no intervention."[35]

Eight months later there was intervention, when Wilson
landed marines at Veracruz. A scant four months after this,
war broke out in the Balkans, flashed across the face of Europe, and Mosby volunteered again—this time with a tongue-
in-cheek proposal to King George V. His friend Nancy Lang-
horne of Lynchburg—now Lady Waldorf Astor, and soon to
be the first woman to sit in the British Parliament—carried his

offer to the king, who sent the old Virginian an equally tongue-in-cheek and gracious reply.

The Great War seemed to Mosby to be devastation for devastation's sake, and on a scale that would make it "break of its own weight" within six months. He abhorred especially the killing of civilians, maintaining that not even Sitting Bull would have thrown bombs out of zeppelins. "In our war," he declared, "we never attacked the non-combatant."[36]

He held strong views about the proper U.S. course with Mexico, views greatly at odds with his past reservations about American involvement in the Philippines. In the spring of 1916, with "Black Jack" Pershing massing his forces for a dash across the Mexican border in pursuit of Pancho Villa in the so-called Mexican Punitive Expedition, Mosby held forth for reporters on the "Mexican question." The President, he said, should never have dealt with either Carranza or Villa, then struggling for power in Mexico, and he should never have pulled the troops back from Veracruz after landing them there two years before. "The only way to handle Mexico," he announced unabashedly, "is to take it over. My views always have inclined to a quick occupation of the whole Republic."[37]

He had always felt, he said, that England, France, and the United States should simply have carved up Mexico among them, extinguishing the Republic—"not because of desire for conquest," he hastened to add, "but to eliminate all of [the] petty squabbling and to . . . forever put a stop to activities of such men as Huerta, Carranza, and Villa."[38] In 1916 this was not an astonishing viewpoint.

"I knew [Mexican President Porfirio] Diaz well," he concluded. "He was the only man of the day who was qualified to rule down there."[39]

The year before his death a final circle closed. The rift with the University of Virginia, which he'd attempted to overlook for more than fifty years, was sealed.

In January 1915 he was invited by university president Edwin A. Alderman to a gathering which, it was explained, would be a testimonial to ex-President Taft. He refused to go. "I haven't the slightest objection to meeting Taft," he wrote to Spottswood, "and no prejudice against him, but I thought it would look rather obsequious for me to go that far to be at an ovation for him."[40] Taft, of course, had been responsible for his removal from office five years before.

Then he found out that the "ovation" was planned for him as well as for Taft, and he was doubly glad of his decision. "They intended to give me a testimonial," he wrote to Mosby Campbell after the event, "that would be an atonement for their having expelled me from the university for shooting a bully. That determined me not to go."[41]

But the medal had been struck and had to be presented, so in mid-February an equally determined delegation from the university brought it to his home. "The Gift of Alma Mater, to Her Son," it read in part.[42] For all his bluff and bluster about Virginia ("All that Virginia ever did for me," he once said, "was to lock me up . . . in the Albemarle jail"), he was deeply moved, and felt now that the greatest injustice of his life had finally been righted.[43]

Alderman followed up with a letter assuring him that his name was held in great affection and honor at the university and that he would always be welcome there.

Softened by the medal, he succumbed easily to an invitation to speak on campus—the first time ever. As word of the May 1 address spread, old rangers dusted off their Civil War jackets and other memorabilia to be dragged to Charlottesville for Mosby's day in the sun. Ex-ranger Major Dolly Richards, de facto leader at most of the battalion's annual reunions, and grown distant from his former commander over the years, made plans to come over from Louisville. Ben Palmer was coming, as were William Chapman, surgeon Will Dunn (who produced a rusty old knife he'd once used to cut a bullet out of Mosby), and several others.

President Alderman pulled out all the stops, turning it into the most thrilling event of the old man's life—his "proudest recollection," he said—and leaving him deeply moved. "I now feel that I am a rich man," he told a friend afterward. His reception, he said, proved that he "possessed something more valuable than gold."[44]

"I came home from the university," he wrote, "with a much better opinion of the world than I ever had before. . . . The truth is this is a far better world than it has credit for being, and the older I grow I feel more charity for mankind."[45]

But it did not take long for the sadness to set in again, the petulance, the gloom—especially with his son approaching death—the craving for affection. He unburdened his heart two and three times weekly to his grandsons in New York, making petty demands upon them which young Mosby accepted with better grace than Spottswood, who seems to have liked his interfering grandfather best at arm's length. A few months before the old man's death, Spottswood all but ceased writing. "I am mortified that Spottswood takes no notice of me," Mosby wrote to young Campbell in March 1916. "He knows the deep interest I take in you and him." And a week later: "I do not like the way that Spottswood is treating me." A week after that: "I wrote to Spottswood . . . but I haven't a word from him. I do not understand his indifference to me." Then, wistfully, "There is another delivery about 11. . . . Maybe I will hear from him then."[46]

February 1916 broke drearily upon Washington, and a deteriorating Mosby spoke to a priest, formerly stationed in Warrenton, about getting him into St. Vincent's Hospital and Sanitarium in the mild sea air of Norfolk for two or three weeks. The sisters, he was shortly informed, would be delighted to have him, and on March 12 the old rebel boarded a boat for the trip south.

As usual in his travels, he enjoyed a steady stream of visitors in his retreat, including this time reporters, ex-rangers, and the daughter-in-law of Jeb Stuart. He was driven out to see Stuart's aged widow, Flora, as well.

Upon his return to Washington in April, he still did not feel well, and entered Georgetown University Hospital, only to move out after a short stay. "Papa is now at Garfield Hospital," wrote Stuart to one of her father's friends in early May, "and doing well. I apprehend no immediate danger and there is reason to think he will . . . entirely recover."[47]

But the old soldier did not rally this time. His three daughters and two sisters took turns at his bedside throughout the waxing summer heat. Russell came and went, and came again. The Campbells and Stuart's children—Beverly and

Pauline—came, as did his brother Willie's children, Hal and Bob. Jack Russell and his stepsister Lucie were there. They watched the old fighter sinking, but remaining conscious and clear-headed until the morning of May 30.

As the end drew near, one of his daughters stepped forward to pour the waters of baptism over her dying father's head, uttering through her tears the age-old formula of the Church of Rome, at whose fringes he had stood for most of his life: "I baptize thee, John, in the name of the Father, and of the Son, and of the Holy Ghost."

At 9:00 A.M. on Memorial Day, 1916, he died. Two days later his body, escorted by a uniformed guard, was taken by train to Warrenton to lie in state briefly in the county courthouse before being consigned to the earth. The governor sent a wreath, and three thousand persons attended the funeral.

He was buried in Warrenton, surrounded by the graves of his wife Pauline and his infant children, and not far from the new mound that covered his beloved Johnnie.

Fittingly, he rests on the brow of a hill.

NOTES

Full publishing details of all books and articles, MS collections, and government documents are given in the Bibliography.

1. SHIFTING SANDS

1. Mosby to Virginia Mosby, June 11, 1856, 9836, John S. Mosby Papers, University of Virginia, Charlottesville, Virginia. There is confusion on the issue of where Mosby first practiced law. Mosby claimed he opened a practice in Bristol in October 1855 (John S. Mosby, *The Memoirs of Colonel John S. Mosby,* edited by Charles Wells Russell, p. 11). This is supported by a notice in the *Bristol News* of September 4, 1855, in which his future services in and around Bristol are advertised (John Singleton Mosby Papers, Virginia Historical Society, Richmond, Va.). He is contradicted by his sister Florence, who says, summer 1866, "Col. Mosby commenced practicing law in Howardville [*sic*], a little town in Albemarle County" (Diary and Daybook of Florence Mosby, 1866, 9836, John S. Mosby Papers, University of Virginia), and by the above-mentioned letter to his mother of June 11, 1856, indicating that he was in fact practicing in Howardsville at this time. Perhaps he made an abortive attempt at a practice in Bristol in 1855, although it is not clear why.

2. Mosby to Victoria Mosby, December 17, 1856, John S. Mosby Papers, Library of Congress, Washington, D.C.

3. Virgil Carrington Jones, *Ranger Mosby,* p. 28. The fact of Johnson's presence was communicated to Jones by Mosby's eldest son, Beverly, as having been received from his mother.

4. Richard Hofstadter, William Miller, and Daniel Aaron, *The United States,* pp. 318, 320.

5. Mosby, *Memoirs,* pp. 16–17. The remainder of the conversation is adapted from p. 17.

6. Ibid, p. 18.

7. William Willis Blackford, *War Years with Jeb Stuart,* p. 14.

8. Susan Leigh Blackford, comp., *Letters from Lee's Army,* edited by Charles Minor Blackford III, p. 2.

9. *Fairfax Herald,* n.d. (4F49, Fairfax County Public Library, Fairfax, Virginia).

10. John S. Mosby, *Mosby's War Reminiscences and Stuart's Cavalry Campaigns,* pp. 6–7.

11. Mosby, *Memoirs,* p. 19.

12. Ibid., p. 21.

13. Ibid., p. 23; Mosby, *War Reminiscences,* p. 8.

14. Mosby, *War Reminiscences,* p. 8.

15. Ibid., p. 9.

16. Ibid.

17. Mosby to Virginia Mosby, June 18, 1861, John S. Mosby Papers, Library of Congress.

18. Mosby to Pauline Mosby, June (n.d.) 1861, 7872, John S. Mosby Papers, University of Virginia.

19. Ibid.

20. Mosby, *Memoirs,* p. 30.

2.   IN THE FORGE

1. Virginia Mosby to Virginia Cabell Mosby, n.d. (Virgil Carrington Jones, *Ranger Mosby,* pp. 17–18).

2. John S. Mosby, *The Memoirs of Colonel John S. Mosby,* edited by Charles Wells Russell, pp. 2–3.

3. Ibid., p. 2.

4. Charles C. Wertenbaker to William Sam Burnley, January 18, 1911, Box 2, Burnley Family Papers, University of Virginia, Charlottesville, Virginia.

5. Mosby to Burnley, n.d., Box 7, Burnley Family Papers.

6. Mosby, *Memoirs,* p. 5; Monthly Report Card, John S. Mosby, August 1, 1849, 9836, John S. Mosby Papers, University of Virginia.

7. Mosby, *Memoirs,* pp. 5–6.

8. Mosby to Reuben Page, June 11, 1902, Douglas Southall Freeman Papers, University of Virginia.

9. Certificate from the University of Virginia, June 28, 1851, 9836, John S. Mosby Papers, University of Virginia.

10. *Baltimore Sun,* January 15, 1911.

11. Commonplace Book of Robert G. Kean, March 30, 1853, 3070-a, University of Virginia.

12. *Baltimore Sun,* January 15, 1911.

13. Mosby to Louise Cocke, January 16, 1911, Mosby-Cocke Letters, University of Virginia.

14. Shelton F. Leake to Joseph Johnson, June 21, 1853, Mosby Pardon Material, Letters Receiged, Governor's Office, Executive Department, Virginia State Library, Richmond, Virginia.

15. A. Monteiro, *War Reminiscences by the Surgeon of Mosby's Command,* p. 12.

16. Mosby Pardon Material.

3. MANASSAS

1. Mosby to Pauline Mosby, July 12, 1861, 7872, John S. Mosby Papers, University of Virginia, Charlottesville, Virginia.

2. Mosby to Reuben Page, June 11, 1902, Douglas Southall Freeman Papers, University of Virginia.

3. Ibid.

4. Mosby to Pauline Mosby, July 24, 1861, 9836, John S. Mosby Papers, University of Virginia.

5. John S. Mosby, *The Memoirs of Colonel John S. Mosby,* edited by Charles Wells Russell, p. 49.

6. Mosby to Pauline Mosby, July 24, 1861, 9836, John S. Mosby Papers.

7. Ibid.

8. Mosby, *Memoirs,* p. 85.

9. Ibid., p. 86.

10. Mosby to Pauline Mosby, August 18, 1861 (Mosby, *Memoirs,* p. 87).

11. Susan Leigh Blackford, comp., *Letters from Lee's Army,* edited by Charles Minor Blackford III, pp. 56–57.

12. Virginia Mosby to N. F. Cabell, August 9, 1861, Box 47, Cabell Family Papers, University of Virginia.

13. Mosby to Pauline Mosby, August 10, 1861, 7872, John S. Mosby Papers.

14. Mosby to Pauline Mosby, November 3, 1861, 9836, John S. Mosby Papers.

15. Mosby to Elizabeth Mosby, September 17, 1861 (Mosby, *Memoirs,* p. 89).

16. Ibid.

17. Mosby, *Memoirs,* p. 93.

18. Ibid., p. 96.

19. Ibid., p. 98.

20. John S. Mosby, *Mosby's War Reminiscences and Stuart's Cavalry Campaigns,* pp. 17–19.

4. SUNRISE

1. John S. Mosby, *Mosby's War Reminiscences and Stuart's Cavalry Campaigns,* p. 21.

2. Ibid., pp. 21–22.

3. Mosby to Pauline Mosby, February 14, 1862, 7872, John S. Mosby Papers, University of Virginia, Charlottesville, Virginia.

4. John S. Mosby, *The Memoirs of Colonel John S. Mosby,* edited by Charles Wells Russell, p. 102.

5. Douglas Southall Freeman, *Lee's Lieutenants: A Study in Command,* 1:279–80.

6. William Willis Blackford, *War Years with Jeb Stuart,* pp. 59–60.

7. Mosby, *War Reminiscences,* p. 216.

8. Ibid., p. 22.

9. Mosby to Pauline Mosby, June 4, 1862, 9836, John S. Mosby Papers, University of Virginia.

10. Mosby, *War Reminiscences,* p. 221.

11. Statement of the Count of Paris (Mosby, *Memoirs,* p. 119).

12. Mosby to Pauline Mosby, June 16, 1862 (Mosby, *Memoirs,* p. 120).

13. James E. B. Stuart to George W. Randolph, June 20, 1862 (Mosby, *Memoirs,* p. 121).

14.   Robert E. Lee, General Orders No. 74, June 23, 1862, *The War of the Rebellion: A Compilation of the Official Records of the Union and Confederate Armies* (cited hereafter as *Official Records*), series 1, vol. 11, p. 1042.

15.   W. W. Blackford, *War Years,* p. 73.

16.   Mosby, *Memoirs,* p. 125.

17.   Stuart to Thomas J. Jackson, July 19, 1862, *Official Records,* series 1, vol. 51, part 2, p. 594.

18.   History of the Harris Cavalry (Mosby, *Memoirs,* p. 128).

19.   Mosby, *War Reminiscences,* pp. 243–44.

20.   Carl Sandburg, *Abraham Lincoln: The War Years,* 1:544.

21.   Mosby, *War Reminiscences,* p. 29.

22.   Ibid.

23.   Ibid.

5.   FOX IN THE HENHOUSE

1.   John S. Mosby, *The Memoirs of Colonel John S. Mosby,* edited by Charles Wells Russell, pp. 150–51.

2.   John S. Mosby, *Mosby's War Reminiscences and Stuart's Cavalry Campaigns,* p. 32.

3.   Mosby to Messrs. Powell, Chancellor, et al., February 4, 1863 (John Scott, *Partisan Life with Col. John S. Mosby,* p. 27).

4.   Mosby, *Memoirs,* p. 168.

5.   Ibid., pp. 159–60.

6. Mosby to James E. B. Stuart, March 11, 1863, *Official Records,* series 1, vol. 25, part 1, pp. 1121–22.

7. L. C. Baker, *History of the United States Secret Service,* p. 170.

8. Ibid.

9. Mosby to Thomas Keith, January 20, 1900, John S. Mosby Papers, Fairfax County Public Library, Fairfax, Virginia.

10. Mosby to Joseph Bryan, January 30, 1904, Folder 47–106, Joseph Bryan Papers, Virginia Historical Society, Richmond, Virginia.

11. Stuart, General Orders No. 7, March 12, 1863, *Official Records,* series 1, vol. 25, part 2, p. 856.

12. Robert E. Lee to Stuart, March 12, 1863, ibid., p. 664; Stuart to Mosby, March 27, 1863 (Mosby, *War Reminiscences,* p. 92).

13. Mosby to Stuart, March 16, 1863, *Official Records,* series 1, vol. 25, part 2, p. 667.

14. Lee to Jefferson Davis, March 21, 1863, ibid., p. 679.

15. W. H. Taylor, Special Orders No. 82, March 23, 1863, ibid., vol. 51, part 2, p. 688; Taylor to Mosby, March 23, 1863, ibid., vol. 25, part 2, p. 857.

16. Stuart to Mosby, March 25, 1863, ibid., pp. 857–58.

17. Charles F. Taggart to R. Butler Price, March 24, 1863, ibid., part 1, p. 65.

18. Mosby, *War Reminiscences,* p. 72.

19. Mosby to Stuart, April 7, 1863, *Official Records,* series 1, vol. 25, part 1, p. 72.

20. Mosby, *War Reminiscences,* p. 89.

21. Ibid., pp. 89–90.

22. Ibid., p. 92.

23. Ibid., p. 105.

24. Ibid., pp. 105–106.

25. Ibid., pp. 106–10 passim; Julius P. Stahel to Samuel P. Heintzelman, April 2, 1863, *Official Records,* series 1, vol. 25, part 1, p. 78.

26. Stahel to Heintzelman, April 2, 1863, *Official Records,* series 1, vol. 25, part 1, p. 78.

27. James A. Seddon to H. L. Clay, April 22, 1863, ibid., p. 73.

28. Scott, *Partisan Life,* p. 59.

29. Mosby, *War Reminiscences,* pp. 100–101.

30. Mosby to Stuart, prob. March 1863 (Scott, *Partisan Life,* p. 76).

31. Lee to Stuart, prob. April 1863 (ibid., p. 76).

32. Mosby, *War Reminiscences,* pp. 131–32.

33. Ibid., pp. 132–33.

34. Ibid., p. 134.

35. Ibid., pp. 138–39.

36. Ibid., p. 145.

37. Ibid., p. 146.

38. Ibid., pp. 148–49.

39. Ibid., p. 150.

40. Ibid.

41. Ibid., pp. 157–58.

42. Ibid., p. 162.

43. Carl Sandburg, *Abraham Lincoln: The War Years,* 2:99.

44. Mosby, *War Reminiscences,* p. 163.

45. William Willis Blackford, *War Years with Jeb Stuart,* p. 218.

46. Mosby, *War Reminiscences,* p. 165.

47. Ibid., pp. 166–67.

48. Ibid., pp. 176–77.

49. James J. Williamson, *Mosby's Rangers,* p. 75.

50. Douglas Southall Freeman, *Lee's Lieutenants: A Study in Command,* 3:208.

51. Lee to Stuart, June 23, 1863, in Clifford Dowdey and Louis H. Manarin, eds., *The Wartime Papers of R. E. Lee,* pp. 526–27.

52. Mosby, *Memoirs,* p. 216.

53. Alfred Pleasonton to A. A. Humphreys, August 2, 1863, *Official Records,* series 1, vol. 27, part 3, p. 830.

54. Charles R. Lowell, Jr., to J. H. Taylor, August 12, 1863, ibid., vol. 29, part 1, p. 69.

55. George A. Custer to Pleasonton, August 13, 1863, ibid., part 2, pp. 38–39.

56. Lee, Endorsement, August 18, 1863, ibid., vol. 27, part 2, p. 992.

57. Lee to Stuart, August 18, 1863, ibid., vol. 29, part 2, p. 652.

58. Seddon to W. B. Mallory, August 18, 1863, ibid., p. 653.

59. Diary of Virginia Mosby, August–September 1863, 9836, John S. Mosby Papers, University of Virginia, Charlottesville, Virginia.

60. Mosby to Pauline Mosby, October 1, 1863, 7872, John S. Mosby Papers, University of Virginia.

61. Mosby to Stuart, September 30, 1863, *Official Records,* series 1, vol. 29, part 1, p. 81.

62. Stuart, Endorsement, October 5, 1863, ibid.

63. Horace B. Sargent to A. Wright, September 2, 1863, ibid., p. 90.

64. Henry W. Halleck to H. S. Turner, October 28, 1863, ibid., part 2, p. 397.

65. John H. Alexander, *Mosby's Men,* p. 19.

66. Ibid.

67. Ibid., p. 21.

68. Ibid., p. 26.

69. Account of William H. Chapman (Williamson, *Mosby's Rangers,* pp. 486–87).

6. FIRESTORM

1. Thomas L. Rosser to Robert E. Lee, January 11, 1864, *Official Records,* series 1, vol. 33, p. 1081.

2. Ibid., pp. 1081–82.

3. Ibid., p. 1082.

4. Ibid.

5. James E. B. Stuart, Endorsement, January 18, 1864, ibid., p. 1082.

6. Lee, Endorsement, January 22, 1864, ibid.; Lee to James A. Seddon, January 21, 1864, ibid., p. 1113; Bill to Repeal Con-

federate Partisan Ranger Act, February 15, 1864, Frank Moore, ed., *The Rebellion Record: A Diary of American Events,* 8:422.

7. Bill to Repeal Confederate Partisan Ranger Act, February 15, 1864, *Rebellion Record,* 8:422.

8. Mosby to Stuart, March 26, 1864, *Official Records,* series 1, vol. 33, p. 1241.

9. U. S. Grant, *Personal Memoirs,* p. 407.

10. William Willis Blackford, *War Years with Jeb Stuart,* pp. 253–54.

11. Douglas Southall Freeman, *R. E. Lee,* abridged by Richard Harwell, p. 388.

12. Carl Sandburg, *Abraham Lincoln: The War Years,* 3:51.

13. Blackford, *War Years,* p. 258.

14. Grant to Philip H. Sheridan, August 16, 1864, 1:30 P.M., *Official Records,* series 1, vol. 43, part 1, p. 811.

15. Ibid.

16. Grant to Sheridan, August 16, 1864, 3:30 P.M., ibid.

17. J. H. Taylor to John M. Waite, August 18, 1864, ibid., p. 831.

18. Sheridan to Christopher C. Augur, August 19, 1864, ibid., pp. 843–44.

19. Sheridan to Augur, August 20, 1864, ibid., p. 860.

20. Augur to Sheridan, August 24, 1864, ibid., p. 898.

21. Taylor to Waite, August 28, 1864, ibid., p. 942.

22. Grant to Sheridan, August 26, 1864, ibid., p. 917.

23. John Scott, *Partisan Life with Col. John S. Mosby,* p. 320.

24. "A Horror of the War," *Southern Historical Society Papers,* 25:240.

25. Sheridan to Grant, September 29, 1864 (John S. Mosby, *The Memoirs of Colonel John S. Mosby,* edited by Charles Wells Russell, p. 304).

26. Grant to Sheridan, October 3, 1864 (Mosby, *Memoirs,* p. 305).

27. Henry W. Halleck to Grant, October 4, 1864, *Official Records,* series 1, vol. 43, part 2, p. 273.

28. Ibid.

29. Sheridan to Grant, October 7, 1864, ibid., p. 308.

30. Augur to Waite, October 6, 1864, ibid., p. 298.

31. Mosby to Pauline Mosby, prob. October 12, 1864 (Mosby, *Memoirs,* p. 309).

32. Halleck to D. C. McCallum, October 12, 1864, *Official Records,* series 1, vol. 43, part 2, p. 348.

33. Mosby, *Memoirs,* p. 314.

34. Ibid., p. 315.

35. Ibid.

36. Ibid., p. 316.

37. Scott, *Partisan Life,* pp. 336–37.

38. Mosby, *Memoirs,* p. 318.

39. Ibid., p. 328.

40. Mosby to Aristides Monteiro, February 19, 1895, John S. Mosby Papers, Museum of the Confederacy, Richmond, Virginia.

41. Mosby to Lee, October 29, 1864, *Official Records,* series 1, vol. 43, part 2, p. 910.

42. Account of Charles E. Marvin (James J. Williamson, *Mosby's Rangers,* p. 455).

43. Enclosure, Oliver Edwards to C. Kingsbury, November 7, 1864, *Official Records,* series 1, vol. 43, part 2, p. 566.

44. Mosby to Landon Mason, March 29, 1912, John Singleton Mosby Papers, Duke University, Durham, North Carolina.

45. Ibid.; Mosby, "Retaliation," *Southern Historical Society Papers,* 27:318.

46. Mosby to Sheridan, November 11, 1864, *Official Records,* series 1, vol. 43, part 2, p. 920.

47. Halleck to Sheridan, November 26, 1864, ibid., p. 671.

48. Sheridan to Halleck, November 26, 1864, ibid., pp. 671–72.

49. James W. Forsyth to Wesley Merritt, November 27, 1864, ibid., p. 679.

50. Sheridan to John D. Stevenson, November 28, 1864, ibid., p. 687.

51. Forsyth to Stevenson, November 30, 1864, ibid., p. 711.

52. Sheridan to Halleck, December 3, 1864, ibid., p. 730.

53. A. Monteiro, *War Reminiscences by the Surgeon of Mosby's Command,* p. 10.

54. Ibid., p. 16.

55. Ibid., p. 17.

56. Mosby, *Memoirs,* p. 337.

57. Ibid., pp. 337–40 passim.

58. Douglas Frazar to William Gamble, December 31, 1864, *Official Records,* series 1, vol. 43, part 2, p. 843.

59. Mosby, *Memoirs,* pp. 341–42.

60. Ibid., p. 342.

61. Ibid., p. 344.

62. Gamble to Taylor, December 27, 1864, *Official Records,* series 1, vol. 43, part 2, p. 831.

63. Gamble, Endorsement, January 1, 1865, ibid., p. 844.

64. Mosby, *Memoirs,* p. 346.

65. Sheridan to William H. Emory, December 31, 1864, *Official Records,* series 1, vol. 43, part 2, p. 844.

7. SURVIVOR

1. William Willis Blackford, *War Years with Jeb Stuart,* p. 283.

2. Ibid.

3. Ibid., pp. 283–84.

4. John S. Mosby to Pauline Mosby, February 3, 1865, 7872, John S. Mosby Papers, University of Virginia, Charlottesville, Virginia.

5. Ibid.

6. Quoted in John S. Mosby, *The Memoirs of Colonel John S. Mosby,* edited by Charles Wells Russell, p. 375.

7. Ibid., p. 374.

8. *Washington Evening Star,* February 13, 1865.

9. Quoted in Mosby, *Memoirs,* p. 353.

10. Blackford, *War Years,* p. 288.

11. Ibid., p. 292.

12. James J. Williamson, *Mosby's Rangers,* p. 376.

13. C. H. Morgan to Mosby, April 11, 1865, *Official Records,* series 1, vol. 46, part 3, p. 714.

14. Mosby to Winfield S. Hancock, April 15, 1865, ibid., p. 766.

15. Ibid.

16. The scene is adapted from A. Monteiro, *War Reminiscences by the Surgeon of Mosby's Command,* pp. 181–82.

17. Ibid., p. 182.

18. Ibid., p. 184.

19. Ibid., p. 196.

20. George H. Chapman to Morgan, April 18, 1865, *Official Records,* series 1, vol. 46, part 3, p. 830.

21. U. S. Grant to Hancock, April 19, 1865, ibid., p. 839.

22. Mosby to John S. Russell, December 16, 1899 (Mosby, *Memoirs,* pp. 370–71).

23. Monteiro, *War Reminiscences,* p. 204.

24. Ibid., pp. 204–206.

25. Ibid., p. 206.

26. Hancock to John A. Rawlins, April 20, 1865, *Official Records,* series 1, vol. 46, part 3, p. 868.

27. Mosby's Farewell Address, April 21, 1865, J. Henley Smith Papers, Library of Congress, Washington, D.C.

28. Mosby to Sam Chapman, January 12, 1907, Thomas Nelson Page Papers, Duke University, Durham, North Carolina.

29. Ibid.

8. PARIAH

1. *Washington Evening Star,* May 8, 1872.

2. The account of this meeting and its immediate aftermath is

based on the *Richmond Enquirer,* n.d. *(Alexandria Gazette,* May 16, 1872); John S. Mosby, *The Memoirs of Colonel John S. Mosby,* edited by Charles Wells Russell, pp. 392–94; U. S. Grant, *Personal Memoirs,* p. 372; *Brooklyn Eagle,* April 11, 1897; and Enclosure no. 1, Mosby to Francis H. Smith, March 23, 1904, Box 34, Tucker-Harrison-Smith Collection, University of Virginia, Charlottesville, Virginia.

3. *Richmond Enquirer,* n.d. *(Alexandria Gazette,* May 16, 1872).

4. Mosby to Aristides Monteiro, September 19, 1865, John S. Mosby Papers, Museum of the Confederacy, Richmond, Virginia.

5. Ibid.

6. *Washington Evening Star,* December 18, 1865.

7. Mosby to Monteiro, December 1, 1866, John S. Mosby Papers, Museum of the Confederacy.

8. Mosby to Monteiro, June 5, 1890, John S. Mosby Papers, Museum of the Confederacy; Mosby to W. Ben Palmer, May 9, 1906, Folder 1338–48, Section 19, Albert G. Nalle Papers, Virginia Historical Society, Richmond, Virginia.

9. *Washington Evening Star,* October 24, 1867.

10. *New York Post,* November 19, 1867.

11. Mosby to Pauline Mosby, November 20, 1867, 7872. John S. Mosby Papers, University of Virginia.

12. Henry Adams, *The Education of Henry Adams,* p. 255.

13. Ibid., p. 264.

14. Ibid., p. 276.

15. Ibid., p. 264.

16. Quoted in Hamlin Garland, *Ulysses S. Grant: His Life and Character,* pp. 402–403.

17. Mosby, *Memoirs,* p. 394.

18. *Missouri Vindicator,* n.d. *(Virginia Sentinel,* February 20, 1868).

19. Quoted in Garland, *Ulysses S. Grant,* p. 419.

20. Adams, *Education,* p. 266.

21. Mosby, *Memoirs,* p. 383.

22. Ibid., pp. 383–84.

23. Ibid., p. 384; *Philadelphia Press,* prob. 1867 (Mosby, *Memoirs,* pp. xxv–vi).

24. Mosby to Sam Chapman, January 12, 1907, Thomas Nelson Page Papers, Duke University, Durham, North Carolina.

25. Mosby, *Memoirs,* p. 380.

26. Ibid., p. 381.

27. Ibid.

28. Mosby to James Keith, January 27, 1906, John S. Mosby Papers, Fairfax County Public Library, Fairfax, Virginia.

29. Mosby, "Stuart in the Gettysburg Campaign," *Southern Historical Society Papers,* 38:196.

30. Grant, *Personal Memoirs,* p. 96.

31. These and other details of Mosby's family life are found in Virgil Carrington Jones, *Ranger Mosby,* p. 292.

32. Mosby to Pauline Mosby, December 19, 1870, 9836, John S. Mosby Papers, University of Virginia.

33. Enclosure no. 1, Mosby to Smith, March 32, 1904.

34. Mosby to James Lyons, June 1, 1872, Box 37, Brock Collection Huntington Library, San Marino, California.

35. Mosby to Lyons, June 6, 1872, Box 37, Brock Collection.

36. *Dictionary of American Biography,* s.v. "Stephens, Alexander Hamilton."

37. Mosby to Alexander H. Stephens, July 7, 1872, Alexander H. Stephens Papers, Library of Congress, Washington, D.C.

38. Mosby to Stephens, October 8, 1872, Alexander H. Stephens Papers.

39. *Washington Evening Star,* August 8, 1872.

40. *Washington Evening Star,* August 9, 1872.

41. "Mosby's Speech for Grant," Grant Campaign Pamphlets, California State Library, Sacramento, California.

42. Ibid.

43. Mosby to Joseph Bryan, October 5, 1908, Box 20, Burnley Family Papers, University of Virginia.

44. *Alexandria Gazette,* September 30, 1872.

45. Mosby, *Memoirs,* p. 389; Keith to George W. Wickersham, June 13, 1910, William H. Taft Papers, Library of Congress.

46. *Washington Evening Star,* November 8, 1872.

47. Mosby to Bryan, October 5, 1908.

48. Mosby to Lyons, July 31, 1873, Box 37, Brock Collection.

49. Mosby to Grant, August 31, 1873 (*Richmond Times-Dispatch,* January 31, 1904).

50. Enclosure no. 2, Mosby to Smith, March 23, 1904.

51. Ibid.

52. *Washington Evening Star,* April 4, 1874.

53. Ibid.

54. Mosby to Edward C. Turner, March 20, 1874, Edward C. Turner Papers, Duke University.

55. *Washington Evening Star*, June 15, 1874.

56. Mosby-Payne Agreement of August 24, 1874, William H. Payne Papers, Virginia State Library, Richmond, Virginia.

57. Unnamed newspaper, n.d., William H. Payne Papers.

58. Mosby to Grant, May 2, 1875, Benjamin H. Bristow Papers, Library of Congress.

59. Mosby to Lunsford L. Lewis, June 22, 1876, Box 143, Brock Collection.

60. *New York Herald*, June 22, 1876.

61. Quoted in John Hope Franklin, *Reconstruction: After the Civil War*, p. 212.

62. Ibid., p. 187.

63. Mosby to Rutherford B. Hayes, July 24, 1876, Rutherford B. Hayes Papers, Rutherford B. Hayes Library, Fremont, Ohio.

64. Mosby to Hayes, August 18, 1876, Rutherford B. Hayes Papers.

65. *New York Herald*, August 12, 1876.

66. Ibid.

67. Ibid. Emphasis added.

68. Ibid.

69. Ibid.

70. Mosby to Hayes, September 26, 1876, Rutherford B. Hayes Papers.

71. Hayes to Mosby, September 30, 1876, Rutherford B. Hayes Papers.

72. *Philadelphia Times*, n.d. (*Alexandria Gazette*, October 9, 1876).

73. *Warrenton Index,* n.d., William H. Payne Papers.

74. Mosby to Turner, November 21, 1876, Edward C. Turner Papers.

75. *New York Herald,* n.d. (*Alexandria Gazette,* December 26, 1876).

76. Ibid.

77. Franklin, *Reconstruction,* p. 133.

78. *New York Herald,* n.d. (*Alexandria Gazette,* December 26, 1876).

79. Ibid.

80. Ibid.

81. Ibid.

82. Ibid.

83. Enclosure no. 1, Mosby to Smith, March 23, 1904.

84. Mosby, *Memoirs,* p. 395.

85. Enclosure no. 1, Mosby to Smith, March 23, 1904.

86. Ibid.

87. See Franklin, *Reconstruction,* pp. 218–27.

88. *Baltimore Sun,* n.d. (*Alexandria Gazette,* March 12, 1877).

89. *New York Tribune,* March 16, 1877.

90. Ibid.

91. *Alexandria Gazette,* March 20, 1877.

92. A. Metcalf to Hayes, March 20, 1877, Rutherford B. Hayes Papers.

93. John P. Dutton to Hayes, May 4, 1877, Rutherford B. Hayes Papers.

94. Ibid.

95. *Baltimore Sun,* n.d. (*Alexandria Gazette,* May 21, 1877).

96. *Philadelphia North American,* April 10, 1877.

97. *Sacramento Daily Union,* May 17, 1877.

98. Mosby to James A. Garfield, January 18, 1878, James A. Garfield Papers, Library of Congress.

99. R. O. Smith to William K. Rogers, January 22, 1878, Rutherford B. Hayes Papers; Mosby to Alvey A. Adee, August 26, 1884, General Records of the Department of State, Record Group 59, M108, roll 15, National Archives and Records Service, Washington, D.C.; and unnamed newspaper, prob. July 1878, White House Scrapbooks, 46:110, Rutherford B. Hayes Library.

100. Hayes to unnamed, August 7, 1878, "Mosby, John S." Folder, Applications and Recommendations for Public Office, Hayes, Garfield, and Arthur Administrations, 1877–85, RG 59, Legislative and Diplomatic Branch, National Archives.

9. THE CHINA COAST

1. *The Press,* n.p., April 8, 1879, White House Scrapbooks, 56:96, Rutherford B. Hayes Library, Fremont, Ohio.

2. Ibid.

3. *Cincinnati Commercial,* October 2, 1879.

4. Mosby to Frederick W. Seward, February 21, 1879, General Records of the Department of State, Record Group 59, M108, roll 12, National Archives and Records Service, Washington, D.C.

5.   Ibid.

6.   Ibid.

7.   *China Mail,* prob. July 1879, General Records, RG 59, M108, roll 12.

8.   David M. Pletcher, *The Awkward Years: American Foreign Relations Under Garfield and Arthur,* p. 20.

9.   Mosby to T. C. H. Smith, March 6, 1879, General Records, RG 59, M108, roll 12.

10.   Ibid.

11.   Ibid., March 9.

12.   Ibid., March 11.

13.   Ibid.

14.   John Pope-Hennessy to Mosby, n.d. (unnamed newspaper, August n.d., 1879, White House Scrapbooks, 62:106).

15.   Ibid.

16.   *China Mail,* prob. July 1879, General Records, RG 59, M108, roll 12.

17.   Mosby to Virginia Stuart Mosby, July 13, 1879, 9836, John S. Mosby Papers, University of Virginia, Charlottesville, Virginia.

18.   Ibid.

19.   Ibid.

20.   Ibid.

21.   Mosby to James D. Blackwell, September 6, 1879, James D. Blackwell Papers, College of William and Mary, Williamsburg, Virginia.

22.   Ibid.

23.   Ibid.

24.   Ibid.

25.   Mosby to Virginia Stuart Mosby, July 13, 1879.

26.   Mosby to unnamed (prob. G. Wiley Wells), August 17, 1879 (*New York Sun,* October 7, 1879).

27.   Ibid.

28.   John M. Forbes to Secretary of State [William M. Evarts], September 19, 1879, "Mosby, John S." Folder, Applications and Recommendations for Public Office, Hayes, Garfield, and Arthur Administrations, 1877–85, RG 59, Legislative and Diplomatic Branch, National Archives.

29.   *National Republican,* prob. September 25, 1879, White House Scrapbooks, 63:30.

30.   Ibid.

31.   *Milwaukee Sentinel,* September 27, 1879.

32.   *Hartford Evening Post,* September 29, 1879.

33.   *National Republican,* prob. September 1879, White House Scrapbooks, 63:31–32.

34.   *Philadelphia Times,* September 26, 1879.

35.   Ibid.

36.   Mosby to Seward, October 18, 1879, RG 59, Consulate of the U.S., C8.1, vol. 1, Despatches to the Department of State, August 1, 1873, to August 4, 1881, National Archives.

37.   Ibid.

38.   Mosby to Alexander K. McClure, October 18, 1879, John S. Mosby Collection, Tracy W. McGregor Library, University of Virginia.

39.   Ibid.

40. Ibid.

41. *Cincinnati Gazette,* November 25, 1879.

42. Mosby to E. M. Spilman, January 13, 1880, 7872, John S. Mosby Papers, University of Virginia.

43. Ibid.

44. Mosby to John W. Daniel, May 9, 1902, John Warwick Daniel Papers, Duke University, Durham, North Carolina.

45. Mosby to James A. Garfield, December 24, 1879, James A. Garfield Papers, Library of Congress, Washington, D.C.

46. Ibid.

47. Mosby to John Hay, January 3, 1880, RG 59, C8.1, vol. 1, Despatches, August 1, 1873, to August 4, 1881, National Archives.

48. Mosby to unnamed, prob. February 1880 (*San Francisco Chronicle,* February 22, 1880).

49. Ibid.

50. Mosby to Garfield, March 18, 1880, James A. Garfield Papers.

51. Ibid.

52. Ibid.

53. *Washington Post,* prob. March 1880, White House Scrapbooks, 71:39.

54. *San Francisco Chronicle,* prob. April 1880, White House Scrapbooks, 107:25.

55. Ibid.

56. Mosby to Garfield, October 28, 1880, James A. Garfield Papers.

57. Mosby to Garfield, May 12, 1880, James A. Garfield Papers.

58. Mosby to Garfield, October 28, 1880.

59. Mosby to Garfield, November 11, 1880, James A. Garfield Papers.

60. Ibid.

61. Ibid.

62. Ibid.

63. Mosby to Garfield, November 24, 1880, James A. Garfield Papers.

64. Ibid.

65. Ibid.

66. Mosby to Francis H. Smith, June 7, 1880, Box 20, Tucker-Harrison-Smith Collection, University of Virginia.

67. Mosby to Francis H. Smith, October 7, 1880, Box 20, Tucker-Harrison-Smith Collection.

68. Mosby to John S. Mosby, Jr., January 12, 1881, 9836, John S. Mosby Papers.

69. Ibid.

70. Mosby to John A. Halderman, February 16, 1881, John A. Halderman Papers, Virginia Historical Society, Richmond, Virginia.

71. Mosby to Walker Blaine, September 28, 1881, no. 148, General Records, RG 59, M108, roll 13.

72. Ulysses S. Grant to unnamed (prob. Charles W. Russell), January 12, 1882 (unnamed newspaper, William H. Taft Papers, Library of Congress).

73. Russell to President [Chester A. Arthur], May 23, 1882, "Mosby, John S." Folder, Applications and Recommendations, 1877–85, RG 59, Legislative and Diplomatic Branch, National Archives.

74. Ibid.

75. *Trenton Daily State Gazette,* December (n.d.) 1878, White House Scrapbooks, 52:171–72.

76. *Chicago Tribune,* January (n.d.) 1879, White House Scrapbooks, 52:197.

77. *Cleveland Leader,* prob. January 1879, White House Scrapbooks, 53:45.

78. Ibid.

79. *New York Sun,* February 18, 1879.

80. Unnamed newspaper, December 26, 1878, White House Scrapbooks, 52:171.

81. Mosby to E. S. Sullivan, May 9, 1882, General Records, RG 59, C8.4, vol. 1, Miscellaneous Letters, September 4, 1875, to September 1, 1886, National Archives.

82. Mosby to John C. Bancroft Davis, May 23, 1882, no. 200, General Records, RG 59, M108, roll 14.

83. *China Mail,* February 6, 1882, General Records, RG 59, M108, roll 14.

84. *Philadelphia Evening Telegraph,* prob. June 1882, General Records, RG 59, M108, roll 14.

85. Mosby to John Davis, July 21, 1884, no. 325, General Records, RG 59, M108, roll 15.

86. Mosby to John Davis, September 12, 1883, no. 278, General Records, RG 59, M108, roll 14.

87. Mosby to John Davis, July 21, 1884, no. 326, General Records, RG 59, M108, roll 15.

88. *Hong Kong Telegraph,* July 8, 1884, General Records, RG 59, M108, roll 15.

89. Mosby to John Davis, July 9, 1884, no. 320, General Records, RG 59, M108, roll 15.

90. Mosby to John Davis, November 3, 1884, no. 356, General Records, RG 59, M108, roll 15.

91. *See* Pletcher, *Awkward Years,* p. 207.

92. Mosby to John Davis, August 4, 1884, no. 331, General Records, RG 59, M108, roll 15.

93. *Brooklyn Eagle,* April 11, 1897.

94. Mosby to Alvey A. Adee, April 4, 1885, no. 376, General Records, RG 59, M108, roll 15.

95. Mosby to James D. Porter, July 16, 1885, no. 416, General Records, RG 59, M108, roll 15.

96. John S. Mosby, *The Memoirs of Colonel John S. Mosby,* edited by Charles Wells Russell, p. 399.

10. ON THE SHOALS

1. Ladislas Farago, *Patton: Ordeal and Triumph* (New York: Dell Publishing Co., 1963), p. 55.

2. John S. Mosby to Benjamin Harrison, November 17, 1888, Benjamin Harrison Papers, Library of Congress, Washington, D.C.

3. Mosby to Benton Chinn, December 1, 1888, John S. Mosby Papers, Fairfax County Public Library, Fairfax, Virginia.

4. *Fairfax Herald,* June 2, 1916.

5. Mosby to Chinn, June 6, 1906, John S. Mosby Papers, Fairfax County Public Library.

6. Mosby to John W. Daniel, January 21, 1896, John Warwick Daniel Papers, Duke University, Durham, North Carolina.

7. John S. Mosby, Political Broadside, August 13, 1896, 516098,

Rare Book Collection, University of Virginia, Charlottesville, Virginia.

8. Mosby to Chinn, October 11, 1896, John S. Mosby Papers, Fairfax County Public Library.

9. Ibid.

10. Mosby to (unnamed) Bryan, March 12, 1897, Bryan Family Papers, Virginia State Library, Richmond, Virginia.

11. George C. Perkins to Mosby, July 19, 1897, 9836, John S. Mosby Papers, University of Virginia.

12. Mosby to Nelson A. Miles, May 4, 1898, 9836, John S. Mosby Papers, University of Virginia.

13. Mosby to Editor, *New York World,* May 6, 1898, 9836, John S. Mosby Papers, University of Virginia.

14. *San Francisco Call,* May 6, 1898.

15. *San Francisco Call,* May 13, June 24, and July 4, 1898.

16. Mosby to Daniel, August 7, 1898, John Warwick Daniel Papers.

17. Ibid.

18. Ibid.

19. Mosby to Daniel, December 22, 1898, John Warwick Daniel Papers.

20. Mosby to Robert S. Walker, January 12, 1899, Mosby-Walker Letters, University of Virginia.

21. Ibid.

22. Mosby to Daniel, January 27, 1899, John Warwick Daniel Papers.

23. Mosby to Daniel, February 12, 1899, John Warwick Daniel Papers.

24. Mosby to Walker, August 4, 1899, Mosby-Walker Letters.

25. Mosby to Walker, June 30, 1900, Mosby-Walker Letters.

26. Mosby to Chinn, February 10, 1896, John S. Mosby Papers, Fairfax County Public Library.

27. Mosby to Walker, June 30, 1900.

28. Mosby to Walker, August 20, 1900, Mosby-Walker Letters.

11. GUTTERING CANDLE

1. Adapted from *Omaha Evening Bee*, November 28, 1902.

2. *Omaha Evening Bee*, November 28, 1902; *New York Times*, November 28, 1902; *Washington Post*, November 27, 1902.

3. *Lincoln Daily Star*, December 9, 1902.

4. Mosby to John W. Daniel, May 9, 1902, John Warwick Daniel Papers, Duke University, Durham, North Carolina.

5. Mosby to Binger Hermann, August 8, 1902, Records of the General Land Office, Record Group 49, Division P, Reports Submitted by Special Agents, 136465, National Archives and Records Service, Washington, D.C.

6. *Alliance Herald*, prob. August 8, 1902 (enclosure, Mosby to Hermann, August 8, 1902, RG 49, Div. P, Reports Submitted by Special Agents, 136465); *Nebraska Farmer*, December 18, 1902.

7. W. R. Lesser to Mosby, prob. August 1902 (enclosure, Mosby to Hermann, August 8, 1902, RG 49, Div. P, Reports Submitted by Special Agents, 136465).

8. Unnamed newspaper, February 19, 1902 (enclosure, Mosby to Hermann, February 20, 1902, RG 49, Div. P, Reports Submitted by Special Agents, 31928).

9. Quoted in Mari Sandoz, *The Cattlemen,* p. 443.

10. Mosby to Hermann, September 16, 1902, RG 49, Div. P, Reports Submitted by Special Agents, 157718.

11. *New York Herald,* November 29, 1902.

12. *Omaha Evening Bee,* November 28, 1902.

13. Mosby to W. S. Summers, November 12, 1902 (unnamed newspaper, November 30, 1902, 9836, John S. Mosby Papers, University of Virginia, Charlottesville, Virginia).

14. Unnamed newspaper, November 28, 1902, Williamson Family Papers, Maryland Historical Society, Baltimore, Md.; *New York Herald,* November 29, 1902; *Lincoln Daily Star,* November 29, 1902; *Omaha Evening Bee,* November 28, 1902.

15. *Lincoln Daily Star,* December 9, 1902.

16. *Rushville Standard,* n.d. (*Lincoln Daily Star,* December 10, 1902).

17. *Omaha Evening Bee,* November 28, 1902.

18. Ibid.

19. *Alliance Times,* December 16, 1902.

20. Ibid.

21. *Lincoln Daily Star,* December 17, 1902.

22. Ibid.

23. Ibid.

24. Mosby to Joseph Bryan, June 30, 1903, Folder 20–46, Joseph Bryan Papers, Virginia Historical Society, Richmond, Virginia.

25. Sandoz, *The Cattlemen,* p. 449.

26. Ibid.; quoted in Nellie Snyder Yost, *The Call of the Range: The Story of the Nebraska Stock Growers Association,* p. 214.

27. Mosby to Daniel, December 8, 1902 (unnamed newspaper, January 11, 1903, 9836, John S. Mosby Papers).

28. Hermann to Mosby, December 26, 1903, Folder 129–36, Joseph Bryan Papers.

29. Mosby to Bryan, June 3, 1903, Folder 20–46, Joseph Bryan Papers.

30. Bryan to Mosby, June 5, 1903, Folder 25, Bryan Family Papers, Virginia Historical Society.

31. Bryan to Joseph Wilmer, June (n.d.) 1903, Folder 25, Bryan Family Papers.

32. George R. Sheldon to Philander C. Knox, July 2, 1903, Folder 145–48, Joseph Bryan papers.

33. Bryan to Mosby, July 7, 1903, Folder 25, Bryan Family Papers.

34. Mosby to Bryan, October 7, 1903, Folder 20–46, Joseph Bryan Papers.

35. Mosby to Bryan, February 9, 1904, Folder 47–106, Joseph Bryan Papers.

36. Henry Cabot Lodge to Charles Francis Adams, February 24, 1904, Folder 145–48, Joseph Bryan Papers.

37. Mosby to Bryan, prob. May 1904, Folder 47–106, Joseph Bryan Papers.

38. Mosby to Bryan, May 15, 1904, Folder 47–106, Joseph Bryan Papers.

39. Mosby to John Mosby Campbell, May 11, 1903, John S. Mosby Collection, Tracy W. McGregor Library, University of Virginia.

40. Bryan to Mosby, October 9, 1903, Folder 25, Bryan Family Papers.

41. Mosby to Bryan, November (n.d.) 1904, Folder 47–106, Joseph Bryan Papers.

42. Mosby to Bryan, December 27, 1904, Folder 47–106, Joseph Bryan Papers.

43. Mosby to Charles W. Russell, June 24, 1905, Folder 137–43, Joseph Bryan Papers.

44. Unnamed newspaper, August 5, 1905 (Scrapbook, 15:24, Fred Barde Collection, Oklahoma Historical Society, Oklahoma City, Oklahoma).

45. Russell to Mosby, August 14, 1905, Records of the Department of Justice, RG 60, Bureau of Insular and Territorial Affairs, Letterbook, vol. 7, National Archives.

12. THE DEFENSE RESTS

1. John S. Mosby to E. Leroy Sweetser, July 13, 1910, Mosby-Cocke Letters, University of Virginia, Charlottesville, Virginia.

2. James Keith to George W. Wickersham, June 13, 1910, William H. Taft Papers, Library of Congress, Washington, D.C.

3. Mosby to Betty Cocke, prob. June 1910, Mosby-Cocke Letters.

4. Mosby to Joseph Bryan, May 3, 1906, Folder 1338–48, Section 19, Albert G. Nalle Papers, Virginia Historical Society, Richmond, Virginia.

5. Mosby to Beverly C. Mosby, May 9, 1906, Item 1340, Section 19, Albert G. Nalle Papers.

6. Ibid.

7. Mosby to Louise Cocke, January 16, 1911, Mosby-Cocke Letters.

8. Mosby to Betty Cocke, January 27, 1911, Mosby-Cocke Letters.

9. Ibid.

10. Mosby to W. Ben Palmer, May 25, 1906, Folder 1338–48, Section 19, Albert G. Nalle Papers.

11. Mosby to H. C. Jordan, August 23, 1909, Bryan Family Papers, Virginia State Library, Richmond, Virginia.

12. Ibid.

13. Mosby to unnamed (prob. Willie Mosby), prob. 1907, 9836, John S. Mosby Papers, University of Virginia, Charlottesville, Virginia.

14. Mosby to Alexander Spottswood Campbell, February 25, 1909, Special Collections, University of California, Santa Barbara, California.

15. Ibid.

16. Ibid.

17. Ibid.

18. Mosby to Keith, January 27, 1906, John S. Mosby Papers, Fairfax County Public Library, Fairfax, Virginia; Mosby to Spottswood Campbell, February 25, 1909.

19. Mosby to Spottswood Campbell, February 25, 1909.

20. Ibid.

21. Mosby to Sam Chapman, September 30, 1909, John Singleton Mosby Papers, Duke University, Durham, North Carolina.

22. Ibid.

23. Mosby to Mrs. Robert S. Walker, October 24, 1914, Mosby-Walker Letters, University of Virginia.

24. Mosby to John Mosby Campbell, January 14, 1915, John S. Mosby Collection, Tracy W. McGregor Library, University of Virginia.

25. Mosby to Eppa Hunton, November 18, 1909, Box 2, Hunton Family Papers, University of Virginia.

26. Ibid.

27. Ibid.

28. Ibid.

29. Ibid.

30. Mosby to Thomas P. Bryan, December 7, 1909, Mosby-Cocke Letters.

31. *Philadelphia Post,* prob. 1867 (John S. Mosby, *The Memoirs of Colonel John S. Mosby,* edited by Charles Wells Russell, p. xxv).

32. Mosby to Spottswood Campbell, September 9, 1915, John S. Mosby Collection, Tracy W. McGregor Library.

33. Mosby to Mosby Campbell, September 1, 1915, John S. Mosby Collection, Tracy W. McGregor Library.

34. Mosby to Mosby Campbell, June 12, 1912, John S. Mosby Collection, Tracy W. McGregor Library.

35. Woodrow Wilson to Mosby, August 27, 1913, Woodrow Wilson Papers, Library of Congress.

36. *Fairfax Herald,* November 6, 1914.

37. *Norfolk Ledger-Dispatch,* March 14, 1916 (Mosby-Parrish Papers, University of Virginia).

38. Ibid.

39. Ibid.

40. Mosby to Spottswood Campbell, January 27, 1915, John S. Mosby Collection, Tracy W. McGregor Library.

41. Mosby to Mosby Campbell, February 16, 1915, John S. Mosby Collection, Tracy W. McGregor Library.

42. *Fairfax Herald,* February 19, 1915.

43. Mosby to Chapman, January 12, 1907, Thomas Nelson Page Papers, Duke University.

44. Mosby to Spottswood Campbell, May 30, 1915, John S. Mosby Collection, Tracy W. McGregor Library; Mosby to Mrs. Charles W. Kent, May 9, 1915, Box 41, Tucker-Harrison-Smith Collection, University of Virginia.

45. Mosby to Mrs. Kent, May 10, 1915, 11:00 A.M., Box 41, Tucker-Harrison-Smith Collection.

46. Mosby to Mosby Campbell, March 2, 1916, John S. Mosby Collection, Tracy W. McGregor Library; March 9, 1916, John S. Mosby Collection, Tracy W. McGregor Library; March 18, 1916, John S. Mosby Collection, Tracy W. McGregor Library.

47. Virginia Stuart Mosby Coleman to Lena N. Haxall, May 11, 1916, Mosby-Parrish Papers.

SELECTED BIBLIOGRAPHY

BOOKS AND ARTICLES

"A Horror of the War," *Southern Historical Society Papers,* 25: 239–44.

Adams, Henry. *The Education of Henry Adams,* 1918. New York: Modern Library, Random House, 1931.

Alexander, John H. *Mosby's Men.* New York: Neale Publishing Co., 1907.

Baker, L. C. *History of the United States Secret Service.* Philadelphia: L. C. Baker, 1867.

Blackford, Susan Leigh, comp. *Letters from Lee's Army.* Edited and abridged by Charles Minor Blackford III. New York: Charles Scribner's Sons, 1947.

Blackford, William Willis. *War Years with Jeb Stuart.* New York: Charles Scribner's Sons, 1945.

Cooke, John Esten. *Wearing of the Grey,* 1867. Edited by Philip van Doren Stern. Bloomington: Indiana University Press, 1959.

Cooling, B. Franklin. *Symbol, Sword, and Shield: Defending Washington During the Civil War.* Hamden, Conn.: Archon Books, 1975.

Crawford, J. Marshall. *Mosby and His Men.* New York: G. W. Carleton and Co., 1867.

Dennett, Tyler. *Americans in Eastern Asia,* 1922. 3d ed. New York: Barnes & Noble, 1963.

Dictionary of American Biography, edited by Allen Johnson and Dumas Malone. 20 vols. New York: Charles Scribner's Sons, 1928–36.

Dowdey, Clifford, and Manarin, Louis H., eds. *The Wartime Papers of R. E. Lee.* New York: Clarkson N. Potter, Bramhall House, 1961.

Franklin, John Hope. *Reconstruction: After the Civil War.* Chicago History of American Civilization Series, edited by Daniel J. Boorstin. Chicago: University of Chicago Press, 1973.

Freeman, Douglas Southall. *Lee's Lieutenants: A Study in Command.* 3 vols. New York: Charles Scribner's Sons, 1942.

———. *R. E. Lee.* Abridged by Richard Harwell. New York: Charles Scribner's Sons, 1961.

Garland, Hamlin. *Ulysses S. Grant: His Life and Character,* 1898. New York: The Macmillan Company, 1920.

Grant, U. S. *Personal Memoirs,* 2 vols., 1885. 2 vols. in 1, edited by E. B. Long. Cleveland: World Publishing Co., 1952.

Hofstadter, Richard; Miller, William; and Aaron, Daniel. *The United States.* 3d ed. Englewood Cliffs, N.J.: Prentice-Hall, 1972.

Jones, Virgil Carrington. *Gray Ghosts and Rebel Raiders.* 2 vols. New York: Ballantine Books, 1956.

———. *Ranger Mosby.* Chapel Hill: University of North Carolina Press, 1944.

Monteiro, A. *War Reminiscences by the Surgeon of Mosby's Command.* Richmond, 1890.

Moore, Frank, ed. *The Rebellion Record: A Diary of American Events,* 11 vols., 1861–68. New York: Arno Press, 1977.

Mosby, John S. "The Dawn of the Real South," *Leslie's Weekly,* April 6, 1901, p. 328.

———. *The Memoirs of Colonel John S. Mosby,* edited by Charles

Wells Russell, 1917. Bloomington: Indiana University Press, 1959.

———. *Mosby's War Reminiscences and Stuart's Cavalry Campaigns,* 1887. New York: Pageant Book Co., 1958.

———. "Retaliation," *Southern Historical Society Papers,* 27: 314–22.

———. *Stuart's Cavalry in the Gettysburg Campaign.* New York: Moffat, Yard, & Co., 1908.

———. "Stuart in the Gettysburg Campaign," *Southern Historical Society Papers,* 38: 184–96.

Pletcher, David M. *The Awkward Years: American Foreign Relations Under Garfield and Arthur.* Columbia: University of Missouri Press, 1962.

Sandburg, Carl. *Abraham Lincoln: The War Years.* 4 vols. New York: Harcourt, Brace, & Co., 1939.

Sandoz, Mari. *The Cattlemen: From the Rio Grande Across the Far Marias.* American Procession Series, edited by Henry G. Alsberg. New York: Hastings House, 1958.

Scott, John. *Partisan Life with Col. John S. Mosby.* New York: Harper & Bros., 1867.

Sheridan, Philip H. *Personal Memoirs.* 2 vols., 1888. St. Clair Shores, Mich.: Scholarly Press, 1977.

Terrell, John Upton. *Land Grab: The Truth about the "Winning of the West."* New York: Dial Press, 1972.

Williamson, James J. *Mosby's Rangers.* 2d ed. New York: The Macmillan Company, 1909.

Yost, Nellie Snyder. *The Call of the Range: The Story of the Nebraska Stock Growers Association.* Denver: Sage Books, 1966.

MANUSCRIPT COLLECTIONS

BALTIMORE, MD.
  Maryland Historical Society
  Williamson Family Papers

CHARLOTTESVILLE, VA.
  University of Virginia
  Burnley Family Papers
  Cabell Family Papers
  Douglas Southall Freeman Papers
  Hunton Family Papers
  Robert G. Kean Commonplace Book
  Mosby-Cocke Letters
  Mosby-Parrish Papers
  Mosby-Walker Letters
  John S. Mosby Collection, Tracy W. McGregor Library
  John S. Mosby Papers (7872)
  John S. Mosby Papers (9836)
  John S. Patton Papers
  Tucker-Harrison-Smith Collection

DURHAM, N.C.
  Duke University
  John Warwick Daniel Papers
  John Singleton Mosby Papers
  Thomas Nelson Page Papers
  Edward C. Turner Papers

FAIRFAX, VA.
  Fairfax County Public Library
  John S. Mosby Papers

FREMONT, OHIO
  Rutherford B. Hayes Library
  Rutherford B. Hayes Papers

RICHMOND, VA.
  Museum of the Confederacy
  John S. Mosby Papers

Virginia Historical Society
  Wyndham Bolling Blanton Papers
  Bryan Family Papers
  Joseph Bryan Papers
  John A. Halderman Papers
  Lyons Family Papers
  John Singleton Mosby Papers
  Albert G. Nalle Papers
Virginia State Library
  Bryan Family Papers
  Mosby Pardon Material
  William H. Payne Papers

SAN MARINO, CAL.
  Huntington Library
  Brock Collection

SANTA BARBARA, CAL.
  University of California
  Special Collections

WASHINGTON, D.C.
  Library of Congress
    Benjamin H. Bristow Papers
    Jubal A. Early Papers
    James A. Garfield Papers
    Benjamin Harrison Papers
    John S. Mosby Papers
    Theodore Roosevelt Papers
    J. Henley Smith Papers
    Alexander H. Stephens Papers
    William H. Taft Papers
    Woodrow Wilson Papers
  National Archives and Records Service
    General Records of the Department of State, Record Group 59
    Records of the Department of Justice, Record Group 60
    Records of the General Land Office, Record Group 49

WILLIAMSBURG, VA.
  College of William and Mary
  James D. Blackwell Papers

GOVERNMENT DOCUMENTS

U.S. War Department. *The War of the Rebellion: A Compilation of the Official Records of the Union and Confederate Armies.* 70 vols. Washington, D.C.: Government Printing Office, 1880–1901.

INDEX